Magnificent Women
and their Revolutionary Machines

With special thanks to
the Women's Engineering Society
in their centenary year

By the same author

William Armstrong: Magician of the North
La Vie est Belle
Coastal Living
Amazing and Extraordinary Facts about Jane Austen
Cragside, Northumberland: a National Trust guide

Magnificent Women
and their Revolutionary Machines

Henrietta Heald

unbound

This edition first published in 2019

Unbound

6th Floor Mutual House, 70 Conduit Street, London W1S 2GF

www.unbound.com

All rights reserved

© Henrietta Heald, 2019

The right of Henrietta Heald to be identified as the author of this work has been asserted in accordance with Section 77 of the Copyright, Designs and Patents Act, 1988. No part of this publication may be copied, reproduced, stored in a retrieval system, or transmitted, in any form or by any means without the prior permission of the publisher, nor be otherwise circulated in any form of binding or cover other than that in which it is published and without a similar condition being imposed on the subsequent purchaser.

While every effort has been made to trace the copyright owners of material reproduced herein, the publisher would like to apologise for any omissions and will be pleased to incorporate missing acknowledgements in any further editions.

Text design by Ellipsis, Glasgow

A CIP record for this book is available from the British Library

ISBN 978-1-78352-660-4 (hardback)
ISBN 978-1-78352-679-6 (ebook)

Printed in Great Britain by CPI Group (UK) Ltd, Croydon

1 3 5 7 9 8 6 4 2

For my granddaughter, Isobel Seren Orr – the future

Contents

With thanks to
Institution of Engineering and Technology (IET)
and Loughborough University
for their support

Introduction

This book began as the story of one intriguing, enigmatic and inspirational character: Rachel Parsons – daughter of a volcanic genius, scion of an Irish earl who in the 1840s built the largest telescope ever seen. Rachel was the founding president of the Women's Engineering Society. It was during her presidency of the society, immediately after the First World War, that Rachel met Caroline Haslett, an equally extraordinary woman of a very different kind. From a lower-middle-class background of Victorian strictness, Caroline would go on to become the pre-eminent female professional of her age and mistress of the great new power of the twentieth century: electricity.

The idea of exploring the parallel lives of these two largely forgotten women – looking at how their paths converged and diverged, and comparing their challenges and successes – was irresistible. What I hadn't anticipated was the number of other amazing individuals who, along the way, would clamour to get into the book. For the Women's Engineering Society was a magnet for many of the ambitious and intellectual women of the 1920s and 1930s who sought to express themselves and earn a living outside writing or the arts. As well as securing the vote and the right to stand for Parliament, women were making some progress in law, medicine and other areas, but those with technical, mathematical or scientific interests had a harder struggle. The Women's Engineering Society and, later, the Electrical Association for Women, drew them together in a common purpose, opened up new opportunities, and encouraged them to make alliances across boundaries of wealth, politics and class.

It wasn't all plain sailing, of course. While showing the effectiveness of a strong body of women working together, the Women's Engineering Society also exposed the weaknesses of such an organisation, as illustrated by the rift that occurred in the mid-1920s, and by the estrangement of Rachel Parsons from her former colleagues. In a forerunner of today's familiar assassination by social media, women who stepped outside the boundaries of 'normal' female behaviour were often subjected to ridicule and suspicion; they reacted by ignoring such treatment or asserting their independence in diverse ways, with many remaining single or having same-sex relationships.

Engineering covered a broad range of disciplines at the time – as remains the case now, more than ever – but in 1919, when the society was founded, it brought together those women who had contributed to industrial production and related activities during the war and felt angry and disappointed at being, as some put it, 'thrown on the scrapheap' afterwards. Some were trained in particular skills, others absorbed skills along the way, or became brilliant managers, but all had had their eyes opened to the advantages of social and economic liberation. They felt motivated to act not only for their own sakes but also to avoid the waste of human talent that the ejection of women from industry implied.

Achieving equal pay with men was an important goal of the Women's Engineering Society from the start, but it was not only financial security and public recognition of their achievements that mattered to these women. In the wartime munitions factories, the positive effects of supporting female workers in all aspects of life had become clear. To sustain a strong and resilient workforce, high priority had been given to healthcare and good nutrition, including the introduction of canteens; special provision had been made for pregnant women and mothers of young children, including subsidised childcare schemes. Effort had gone into providing good-quality accommodation for women working far from home, along with sporting and leisure facilities, which offered the workers plenty of opportunity to meet people from outside their usual social sphere. Training and education had been implemented on an unprecedented scale for female workers, who had shown that they could excel in many areas; this was particularly significant at a time when only a tiny proportion of university students in all subjects were female, and the number taking mathematics and engineering subjects was vanishingly small. Taken together, these elements might have been seen to prefigure a feminist utopia – until, when the war ended, it all started to go badly wrong.

The magnificent women who populate this book called themselves engineers, but their revolutionary machines were more than simply mechanical objects such as cars and boats and planes. Through their achievements at work and their campaigns to promote women's liberation – born of the fight for the franchise and their own wartime experiences – they prepared the ground for a social revolution that would put fair and equitable treatment of the sexes firmly on the political agenda. It amounted to a vibrant 'wave' of feminism that, until now, has largely eluded the attention of historians.

ONE

—•—

Leading Ladies

On 23 June 1919, seven exceptional women gathered at 46 Dover Street in London's Mayfair to do something that had never been done before – to create a professional organisation dedicated to campaigning for women's rights. It was the official birth of the Women's Engineering Society, the fruit of an idea conceived several months earlier, as the guns of the Great War fell silent.

Each of the seven women was required to sign a document giving her name, address and marital status. Outside the inner circle, but keeping a eagle eye on its every move, was Caroline Haslett, a young electrical engineer and former suffragette, who earlier that year had been appointed the society's first administrator.

At the head of the table was Katharine, Lady Parsons, a commanding and charismatic figure, who gave her address as 6 Windsor Terrace, Newcastle upon Tyne. Katharine was the wife of the revered engineer Sir Charles Parsons, whose development of the steam turbine had changed history by revolutionising the propulsion of ships and providing the means for the cheap and widespread generation of electricity. In 1927 Charles Parsons would be admitted to the Order of Merit, an honour in the personal gift of the sovereign.

From the early days of their marriage, Katharine had been immersed in her husband's work, supporting the creation of his engineering works at Heaton and Wallsend, east of Newcastle, in the 1880s and 1890s. She had championed the employment of women in engineering and shipbuilding during the war, and delivered an influential speech in 1919 highlighting this phenomenon.[1]

The first signatory in the group was Eleanor, Lady Shelley-Rolls, a keen balloonist, the sister of the late Charles Rolls, with whom she shared a passion for speed and danger. Charles had partnered Henry Royce in a fabulously successful automobile production business, set up in 1906, until he was killed in a flying accident four years later, at the age of thirty-two. After the death of her two remaining brothers during the war, Lady Shelley-Rolls became heir to a large fortune and the Hendre, the family mansion and estate in Monmouthshire. On her marriage in 1898 to Sir John Shelley, a great-nephew of the poet Shelley, the couple changed their name to Shelley-Rolls.

The youngest founder, and one of only two in the group identified as 'spinsters', was thirty-four-year-old Rachel Parsons, the sole surviving child of Charles and Katharine Parsons, who was living at her parents' London address, 1 Upper Brook Street, near Hyde Park – having left behind early in the war her familiar haunts in northeast England. In 1910 Rachel had become the first woman to study Mechanical Sciences at Cambridge University. During the war she had served briefly as a director of her father's firm at Heaton before joining the training department of the Ministry of Munitions. Her brother Algernon, her only sibling, had died just over a year earlier in action on the Western Front.

Janetta Mary Ornsby was the wife of Robert Embleton Ornsby, a mining engineer at Seaton Delaval colliery in Northumberland, where he became resident agent and later qualified as a manager of mines.

The Ornsbys lived at 7 Osborne Terrace, Jesmond, a short distance from Windsor Terrace, the Newcastle home of the Parsons family.

The second spinster in the group was Margaret Rowbotham, who gave her address as: c/o The Galloway Engrs. Co. Ltd, Kirkcudbright. Margaret had studied mathematics at Cambridge before training and working as a maths teacher. But her real passion was motor engineering, and she spent several months training at the British School of Motoring in workshop practice and driving, at the end of which she was the proud possessor of a Royal Automobile Club Driver's Certificate. In 1917 Margaret had become works superintendent at the Galloway Engineering Company at Tongland in the southwest corner of Scotland, where the workforce was largely female.

The woman with the grandest address was Margaret, Lady Moir, of 54 Hans Place, Knightsbridge – but, in spite of her position of apparent privilege, Margaret Moir had worked during the war as a lathe operator in a munitions factory. As the wife of the prominent Scottish civil engineer Sir Ernest Moir, in whose bridge-building, tunnelling and harbour projects she took a keen interest, she liked to describe herself as 'an engineer by marriage'.

By contrast with the others in the group, Laura Annie Willson had grown up in poverty. Having started work in a textile factory in Halifax, west Yorkshire, at the age of ten she became a campaigner for workers' rights and a suffragette, and was twice imprisoned for her political activities.[2] After her marriage in 1899 to George Willson, she and her husband jointly ran a machine-tool factory in Halifax, which favoured the employment and training of women. Laura Annie had received an MBE for her wartime munitions work, and she would go on to design and build hundreds of houses for working people, some of them equipped with electricity, in Halifax and in two towns in Surrey.

In the normal course of events, the paths of these seven women would have been unlikely to cross, but they had been drawn together by their wartime experiences and by trenchant opposition to a parliamentary bill that sought to outlaw the employment of women in engineering. They relished the strides towards gender equality that had been made during the war – especially the opportunities that had opened up for female technical education – and were determined to preserve those hard-won advantages.

Although Katharine Parsons took the senior role at the Dover Street meeting, there was little doubt that her daughter, Rachel, was the dynamic force behind the new movement. At the annual meeting of the National Union of Women Workers at Harrogate in October 1918, Rachel had spoken in support of female munitions workers who 'wish to study, and learn from a scientific point of view'.[3] A few weeks later, as the secretary of the Engineering Committee of the National Council of Women, she had led a campaign to promote female entry to 'all suitable institutes of engineers' and to secure equal opportunities for men and women in technical schools and colleges. Her vision was to create an alliance of women with technical and mechanical skills, with the aim of bringing those skills to bear in the huge amount of reconstruction work that was needed after the war.

The time for such a bold initiative might have seemed propitious, in that many doors previously closed to women were being forced ajar. On 14 December 1918, a month after the signing of the Armistice, there was a general election in the UK. For the first time, women over thirty with property qualifications were allowed to vote and, unexpectedly, a bill allowing women to stand for Parliament had been enacted three weeks earlier. The former Liberal Home Secretary, Herbert Samuel, a convert to the cause of women's suffrage, had proposed a motion on 23 October to allow women to be eligible as

Members of Parliament. The vote was passed overwhelmingly and the government rushed through a bill to make it law in time for the 1918 election. The Parliament (Qualification of Women) Act 1918, which allowed any woman over twenty-one to stand, received royal assent on 21 November. In the event, seventeen women stood for election in 1918, but only one, Constance Markievicz, was elected; as a member of Sinn Féin, she never took her seat at Westminster.

Women were making progress in medicine, the civil service and the law – but the door was slammed shut against female engineers. Although Prime Minister Lloyd George had acknowledged that it would have been 'utterly impossible' for the country to have waged a successful war without the 'skill and ardour, enthusiasm and industry' of British women, he had been persuaded to honour a pact with the engineering unions, led by the Associated Society of Engineers, that clearly discriminated against women.

The infamous Treasury Agreement, as it was known, originated in the Shell Crisis of May 1915, which had triggered a political earthquake in Britain, leading to the fall of the Asquith government. At its heart was the revelation that heavy British losses on the Western Front had been caused by a catastrophic shortage of artillery shells.[4] Immediate measures to deal with the crisis included the creation of a Ministry of Munitions and a massive recruitment drive for industrial workers of both sexes.

By the first spring of the war, more than 2 million men had joined the armed forces and the military authorities were pressing for more, while the government simultaneously needed a huge increase in the supply of war materials. When Lloyd George, previously Chancellor of the Exchequer, was appointed Minister of Munitions in a new coalition government, he characterised the conflict as 'an engineers' war',[5] insisting that its outcome would ultimately depend on the achievements of engineers: 'We need men, but we need arms more than men.'

The Women's War Register had been set up in March 1915 to enrol women for war work regardless of their previous experience.[6] Meanwhile, Lloyd George set about coaxing the engineering unions to accept 'dilution' – the entry of unskilled workers of both sexes into jobs traditionally held by skilled men – on condition that wage levels would be maintained and dilution would last only as long as the war itself. The all-male unions feared not only losing their jobs to women, but also that women would accept lower wages than men for the same work, leading to a general cut in pay rates.

The suffragette leader Emmeline Pankhurst seized the opportunity of the War Register to champion women's paid employment, joining forces with Lloyd George, a former adversary, to organise a march demanding women's 'right to serve'. Held in London on 17 July 1915, the march attracted an estimated 60,000 supporters, in spite of torrential rain. The sense of triumph experienced by the participants was reflected in some parts of the press. 'To call it historic – this procession of wives and mothers, matrons and girls, all demanding the right to serve – is not enough,' remarked the *Daily Chronicle*. 'It is the first time in history that the womanhood of England or, indeed, of any country, has made so simple, so spontaneous, so overwhelming a manifestation of its dauntless and undivided spirit.'[7]

Other observers adopted a more sober approach. After noting the leading role played by the Women's Social and Political Union, founded in 1903 by the Pankhursts, the *Newcastle Journal* highlighted the 'essentially democratic' nature of the procession: 'An Indian princess, peeresses, the wives of men high in the state, women distinguished in arts and letters, walked shoulder to shoulder with school teachers, typists, shop girls, factory lasses, and British matrons whose sons and brothers are already in the fighting line.'[8]

In addition to Emmeline Pankhurst, the prominent women deputed to speak in person to Lloyd George on this occasion included Katharine, Lady Parsons, as well as Edith Mansell-Moulin and Annie Kenney, both leading suffrage campaigners. As the petitioners already knew, they were pushing at an open door – since the minister was well aware that he could not provide the vast quantity of munitions required without female labour.

The July 1915 march and the campaign that followed did much to lure women into the factories, and by the end of the war more than a million had been recruited. As it turned out, the women who answered the call not only provided the vital production capacity to conquer the munitions shortage, but also made great strides towards economic emancipation.[9]

Work in the factories would prove to be hard, exhausting and sometimes dangerous, but many recruits found it highly rewarding. 'Though we munition workers sacrifice our ease, we gain a life worth living,' said Naomi Loughnan, one of the 25,000 women employed at the Royal Arsenal in Woolwich.[10] Naomi vividly evoked the trials of labouring in the machine shops. 'The day is long, the atmosphere is breathed and re-breathed, and the oil smells. Our hands are black with warm, thick oozings from the machines,' she wrote, going on to describe 'the great wall of noise – the crashing, tearing, rattling whirr of machinery – that seems to rise and confront one like a tangible substance'.

Even more daunting was the experience of the 'Danger Buildings', where high explosives were packed into shells. 'There is the same rush and excitement [as in other munitions work], the same weariness and thrill, only it is intensified by the knowledge that we hold our lives in our hands,' wrote Naomi. 'Loaded fuses, explosive powders, detonators, bombs, and mines become objects of familiarity, to be handled with more speed than fear.'

In fact, accidents in ordnance factories were more frequent than the public ever knew, and some had horrific consequences. The worst event occurred on 19 January 1917 at Silvertown in east London, when an explosion at the Mond munitions factory killed sixty-nine people and injured more than 1,000, many of them women.

Workers at the National Filling Factories – the specially created shell-filling facilities, of which there were more than fifty across the country – were vulnerable to poisoning from many different toxic substances, including TNT. Daily exposure to TNT could not only cause serious illness and death, but also turned workers' skin bright yellow or orange, which earned them the nickname of 'the canaries'.

One of the influential figures to recognise the extraordinary strain placed on women in the shell shops, where production never ceased, was Margaret, Lady Moir, who organised a weekend respite scheme for full-time female workers. Launched at the Vickers factories at Erith in Kent, the scheme was the subject of a contemporary report in *The Times*, which described the middle- and upper-class relief workers making shells and shrapnel: 'They do rough turning, boring and the preliminary processes, and Messrs. Vickers have set aside a special foreman to train them, the training to take three weeks.'[11] During the first week anyone who found the work too hard had the right to leave and be replaced, but all longer-term recruits had to work for six months of weekend shifts, which ran from 2.30 p.m. on Saturday to 6.30 a.m. on Monday. Among several titled women to take on relief work at Vickers was Lady Scott, the widow of the Antarctic explorer Captain Scott, who joined the electrical department. 'Her deftness, acquired in her art as a sculptor, allows her to do work requiring great delicacy of touch,' remarked *The Times*. The women wore a distinctive uniform: 'butcher-blue overall, caps to match, leather gloves, and strong boots – a necessary item, as there is much standing'. Lady Moir herself worked the weekend shift as a lathe operator for more than eighteen months. She also secured accommodation for the relief workers by, among other things, making a tour of the Erith neighbourhood and, according to *The Times*, 'suggesting to people with large houses that they might like to take a holiday'.

Margaret Moir later became treasurer and secretary of the Women's Advisory Committee of the National War Savings Committee, and she organised a sale of war savings certificates and war bonds in London department stores and at Victoria station, which reputedly raised several hundred thousand pounds for the war effort. In recognition of the value of her fund-raising initiatives, she was awarded an OBE.

A government initiative to enable the swift education of engineers, both male and female, was supported by the National Union of Women's Suffrage Societies, which also financed a scheme to train female oxyacetylene welders. By the autumn of 1915, state-financed training centres were opening up all over Britain, from Aberdeen to Plymouth, including eleven in London, offering courses lasting six to eight weeks. 'These technical schools proved that an intelligent girl can learn almost any mechanical process in a few weeks, a prolonged apprenticeship not being necessary,' remarked Katharine Parsons.[12]

There was a great deal more to 'munitions' than the guns, bombs, shells and other items required on the battlefield. Any tool, machine or activity deemed vital to supporting the work of the armed forces came under the umbrella of the ministry, including the generation of electricity.[13] Indeed, there was massive demand for new turbine manufacture during the war, with hospitals, factories and transport systems all operating at full tilt – and fulfilling this demand was the main challenge for the Parsons works at Heaton. Heaton also produced mirrors for searchlights, first used to light the Suez Canal, and during the war period the factory's mirror department became the largest in the world.[14] Meanwhile, at nearby Wallsend, the Parsons Marine Steam Turbine Company was building steam turbines for the ships of the Royal Navy.

Searchlights and other optical instruments – including telescopes, periscopes, range-finders, compasses, binoculars and gun-sights – were a well-established Parsons interest, inspired by the work of Rachel Parsons's astronomer grandparents, William and Mary Rosse, who had built the world's largest telescope on their estate in the middle of Ireland. In this highly demanding area of precision engineering, which required intensive training as well as the utmost skill, women were judged to excel. 'The glass must be cut, ground and curved exactly to the requisite design, which in itself takes many days of high mathematical computation,' wrote L. K. Yates, a female welfare supervisor who conducted a survey of women's work on behalf of the ministry.[15] 'It must be smoothed and polished, cleaned with meticulous care, and adjusted to a nicety in the particular instrument for which it is fashioned.' The difficulties and pitfalls were incalculable. 'From start to finish the glass obeys no fixed laws, but answers only the skilled handling of the scientist and craftsman.'

In her victory speech delivered in Newcastle after the war, Katharine Parsons lavished praise on women's achievements in the field of optical munitions. 'We are all familiar with the beautiful beams of light travelling over the sky in the search for Zeppelin and aircraft,' she said. 'Here on the Tyne we may feel a great pride in the mirrors and searchlights, as most of us know that Tyneside girls polished the mirrors and so added to the brilliancy of the searchlights.'[16]

Government propaganda designed to entice women into the engineering shops had proved more successful than the Minister of Munitions might have dared hope. As soon as they knew that their services were needed, women had come forward in their hundreds of thousands. 'They have come from the office and the shop, from domestic service and the dressmaker's room, from the high schools and the colleges, and from the stately homes of the leisured rich,' wrote Yates in her survey.[17] The recruits hailed not only from all over the British Isles but also from far-flung parts of the Empire, including Australia, New Zealand, Canada and South Africa. Yates also noticed the breakdown of the traditional social hierarchy. 'I have seen working together side by side the daughter of an earl, a shopkeeper's widow, a graduate from Girton, a domestic servant and a young woman from a lonely farm in Rhodesia.'

The first female recruits learned simple, repetitive processes such as how to make and fill shells. Those who showed dexterity were taught tool-making and gauge-making, where the work had to be finished to a fraction of the width of a human hair. More surprisingly, women also undertook many operations dependent on physical strength and stamina. During her travels around Britain, Yates saw women in the shipyards 'chipping and cleaning the ships' decks, repairing hulls, or laying electric wire on board battleships'. Other women were 'working hydraulic presses, guiding huge overhead cranes, lifting the molten billets, setting, or fitting the tools in the machines'.[18]

To many women, the most appealing and glamorous activity was aircraft production. Before the war, women had been allowed to perform tasks such as the sewing of fabric aeroplane wings by hand or by machine, or the painting of the woodwork. 'Today they undertake almost every other process both at the carpenter's bench and in the engineering shop,' wrote Yates, who watched in awe as the women worked on the metal parts of the aeroplane, 'drilling, grinding, boring, milling on the machine, or soldering tiny aluminium parts for the fuselage, and in each process gauging and regauging, measuring and remeasuring'.[19] Women also worked on aeroplane engines and helped in the manufacture of the magneto, 'the very heart of the machine'.

In 1916, exhibitions of women's work were held in several large industrial centres. The extraordinary variety of exhibits 'proved conclusively that women were able to work on almost every known operation in engineering, from the most highly skilled precision work to the rougher sort of labouring jobs', said Katharine Parsons.[20] Ridiculing the myth that they were capable of no more than repetitive work on foolproof machines, Katharine observed that many women developed great mechanical skill and a real love of their work.

The official history of the Ministry of Munitions listed 374 distinct processes, many with their own subdivisions, on which women were employed on 1 June 1916.[21] These ranged from various aspects of steam-turbine manufacture to many of the tasks involved in ship-building.

The women workers in the munitions factories forged a path for all the women who came after them by proving that they could hold down difficult and demanding jobs, often in the face of great danger. All of them had to endure fear, heartache and discomfort, and many had to acquire complex skills in a short time. Some had been radicalised by perceived injustices, leading them to embrace socialist or feminist causes. On the whole, they were well trained and relatively well paid – and they gained a taste of freedom that would never be forgotten. Lured into the workplace in large numbers, they experienced the pleasure and camaraderie of independent communal living. Their horizons were broadened by meeting people from all walks of life. Then – with the signing of the Armistice – it all came to a juddering halt.

Within a few weeks of the end of the war, the Restoration of Pre-War Practices Bill threatened to make it illegal for a woman to be employed in any engineering trade where female workers had not been employed before the war – with the result that hundreds of thousands would lose their jobs and livelihoods, though some accepted this more willingly than others.

Katharine and Rachel Parsons, mother and daughter, articulated the widespread anger at the cruel turn of events and resolved on a campaign to oppose the bill and to fight for women's rights. 'Great hopes [had been] entertained by many women that a new profession was open to them, where they could earn good wages and where they would have some scope for their skill and intelligence,' said Katharine.[22] Training women for munitions work was reckoned to have cost more than £30 million (perhaps £1.5 billion in today's money), but the services of some 1.5 million prospective wealth producers had now been dispensed with. 'It has a been a strange perversion of women's sphere,' said Katharine, 'to make them work at producing the implements of war and destruction and to deny them the privilege of fashioning the munitions of peace.'

In January 1919, Rachel Parsons became the first president of the Women's Engineering Society. Writing later that year in *National Review* magazine, she exposed the 'extraordinary' fact that, although women could now become MPs, doctors, lawyers and scientists, in the ranks of industry they were in a worse position than before the war.[23] Contrary to the fears of the male trade unions, women did not wish to undercut men's pay, she wrote. Rather, they were demanding 'equal pay for equal output'.

Rachel argued that the only way in which women could make headway in the industrial world was by organising themselves into a fighting force. It was useless for them to wait patiently for the closed doors of the skilled trade unions to swing open, she said. Instead, they should form a strong alliance, which, bolstered by the parliamentary vote, should become as powerful an influence in safe-guarding the interests of women engineers as the men's unions had been in improving the lot of their members. 'Women have won their political independence. Now is the time for them to achieve their economic freedom too.'

This was the great rallying cry for the founders of the Women's Engineering Society and the common belief that drove them forward. Bringing at least some of their aims to fruition would depend on the tenacity and practical wisdom of an individual who, for the moment, stood outside the central group as a sympathetic observer – Caroline Haslett.

The daughter of a railway signal engineer from Sussex, Caroline had developed an early interest in women's rights, joining the Women's Social and Political Union at the age of eighteen – to the dismay of her narrowly conventional parents.[24] During the war she had acquired a basic training in electrical engineering at the Cochran Boiler workshops in Annan, Dumfriesshire, where, as a woman, she struggled to be taken seriously. By Caroline's own account, her great opportunity arrived early in 1919, when, at Lady Parsons' instigation, she was installed as secretary of the Women's Engineering Society[25] – a role that, through her own actions, grew gradually more influential in the early years of the society's existence.

In 1924 Caroline Haslett was appointed the first director of the Electrical Association for Women, and she would go on to become the leading professional woman of her age. Among many other roles, she was made vice president and, later, president of the International Federation of Business and Professional Women. Caroline's crowning achievement occurred in 1947, when she became the first female member of the British Electricity Authority, a body set up to run the electricity industry under state ownership. In that same year, she was made a Dame Commander of the Order of the British Empire.

Indeed, soon after her first encounter with the Women's Engineering Society, Caroline Haslett – who had set out with relatively few advantages – saw her career go from strength to strength. For Rachel Parsons, however, it was a very different story. As the gifted daughter of an engineering genius and the granddaughter of a peer of the realm who became president of the Royal Society, this energetic campaigner for women's rights seemed set to make a lasting mark on the world. Her confidence in her own destiny was symbolised by her decision, in 1918, to become a member of the Royal Institution, one of Britain's leading scientific bodies, based in Albemarle Street, Mayfair. It was an early demonstration of her keenness to emulate her father, an active member of the institution, who had given a number of lectures at Albemarle Street on the steam turbine. Three years later, she joined the Royal Institute of International Affairs, of which she remained a member until her death.

In the event, however, Rachel was thwarted in most of her ambitions and, as time passed, she became increasingly disillusioned, with the result that she retreated into solitude and loneliness. The young woman who had so impressed the magnificent gathering at Dover Street in June 1919 with her verve, articulacy and freedom of spirit would end her life in dramatic tragedy.

TWO

—•—

A Brilliant Inheritance

The Parsons family's immersion in engineering and invention had its roots in an ancient settlement in the geographical centre of Ireland. So closely was Parsons history woven into Birr and its romantic medieval castle that, by 1885, when Rachel was born, the place had been known for 365 years as Parsonstown. Its name came from the activities and influences of two Parsons brothers who had migrated from East Anglia to Ireland in late Tudor times, acquiring land and titles, which they passed on to generations of descendants.[1] From this inheritance would eventually derive the earldom of Rosse.

Parsonstown's prominent status in King's County (now County Offaly) indicated a longstanding allegiance to the English Crown, but Rachel's great-grandfather Laurence, a politician, had broken with tradition by his trenchant opposition to the proposed union between Great Britain and Ireland. Described by the Irish republican leader Wolfe Tone as 'one of the very, very few honest men in the Irish House of Commons',[2] Laurence, who favoured complete independence for Ireland, had resigned from politics in protest when the Acts of Union became law in 1800. That year also saw the birth of his

17

son William, the future engineer and astronomer who would one day bring worldwide fame to the name of Parsons.

By the time William Parsons inherited Birr and the earldom of Rosse from his father in 1841, he was already well on the way to transforming human understanding of the stars.[3] Two years earlier, Thomas Romney Robinson, the director of the Armagh Observatory, had visited Birr to inspect an extraordinary telescope that had been erected in the castle grounds. Called a Newtonian reflector, and based on a design by John Herschel, the instrument included a three-foot-diameter speculum, or mirror, and had been built to observe objects farther out into space and more clearly than had ever been possible before.

Robinson stayed at Birr for more than a week, trying out the new telescope with the help of another prominent astronomer, the Englishman James South. The two men were amazed by what they saw. Star clusters, nebulae, double stars – all stood out magnificently, and a host of new objects were identified on the surface of the moon. 'It is scarcely possible to preserve the necessary sobriety of language in speaking of the moon's appearance with this instrument,' wrote Robinson.[4] Indeed, the Earl of Rosse would later draw on these observations in his contribution to the development of lunar mapping. But, as far as the noble inventor was concerned, the three-footer was only the start. He had already conceived of the idea to build at Birr a telescope far surpassing any of its predecessors – an instrument with a six-foot-diameter speculum that would acquire notoriety as the Leviathan of Parsonstown.

Construction of the Leviathan, which took almost two years and entailed many setbacks, was an astonishing feat.[5] Casting the speculum required a huge foundry – created in the dry moat surrounding the castle – in which peat-fired furnaces were used to heat three iron crucibles, each twenty-four inches in diameter and containing

1.5 tons of a tin and copper alloy. The molten metal was transferred by means of cranes into an enormous mould, where it was carefully cooled over a period of sixteen weeks.

Thomas Romney Robinson was present on one occasion when the crucibles were lowered into the furnaces. 'The sublime beauty can never be forgotten by those who were present,' he wrote. 'Above, the sky, crowded with stars and illuminated by a most brilliant moon, seemed to look down auspiciously on the work. Below, the furnaces poured out huge columns of nearly monochromatic yellow flame, and the ignited crucibles during their passage through the air were fountains of red light.'[6]

The next stage was the laborious and time-consuming process of grinding and polishing. 'The speculum was successfully cast, but the surface was covered with minute fissures, about the breadth of a horse hair,' explained William Rosse later in a paper to the Royal Society. 'These we resolved to grind out.' The grinding continued for nearly two months, the machinery working for part of the time at night. The speculum was then polished, and its performance equalled expectations.

The telescope's fifty-six-foot-long wooden tube and hoist were fixed between two castellated brick walls fifty feet high and seventy feet long.[7] Movement of the tube was controlled by chains, pulleys and counterweights. A platform for observing objects at low altitude was built at the southern end of the walls. For high altitudes, a long gallery mounted on the west wall moved across the central space to follow the tube's lateral motion. At least three assistants were needed to help the observer by moving the winch and shifting the galley.

It had long been recognised by astronomers that the larger a telescope's mirror, the more light could be 'grasped', or collected, allowing fainter and more distant objects to be studied – and what made the Leviathan so powerful was its tremendous light-grasp.[8] At

the time of its creation in the 1840s, it was by far the most substantial telescope ever built, and it would remain the largest telescope
in the world for almost three-quarters of a century, until it was over-
taken in 1917 by the one-hundred-inch Hooker telescope on Mount
Wilson in California.

One issue that obsessed early nineteenth-century astronomers was
the true nature of nebulae – objects resembling luminous clouds of
gas among the stars, many of which are now known to be galaxies
outside the Milky Way. William Rosse used his Leviathan to deter-
mine that some of these nebulae had a spiral structure, and he and
his assistants recorded their observations in meticulous notes and
drawings – at a time when photography was not a practical option.
(The remarkable accuracy of the drawings, dating from early 1845,
was later confirmed by photographic techniques.) News of Rosse's
discoveries spread like wildfire, and visitors flocked to Birr, eager to
see and use the wondrous instrument for themselves, while guide-
books and newspaper articles helped to establish the earl's astronomical and technological reputation. Some reports distinguished between
the world BR and AR – before Rosse and after Rosse.

Among the most ardent admirers of the Leviathan was David
Brewster, a leading physicist and mathematician of the day and a
frequent visitor to Birr. 'We have in the mornings walked again and
again, and ever with new delight, along its mystic tube, and at mid-
night, with its distinguished architect, pondered over the marvellous
sights which it discloses,' wrote Brewster in 1855.[9] 'The satellites and
belts and rings of Saturn . . . the rocks, the mountains and valleys,
and extinct volcanoes of the moon . . . the crescent of Venus, with
its mountainous outline . . . the nebulae and starry clusters of every
variety of shape – and those spiral nebular formations which baffle
human comprehension, and constitute the greatest achievement in
modern discovery.'

Scientific experiments at Birr were interrupted by the devastating famine that gripped Ireland in the mid-1840s, a catastrophe that would eventually claim the lives of more than a million people and cause the emigration of 2 million more. The Rosse family made strenuous efforts to relieve unemployment during this period – a move that tightened their bond with the people of King's County. As the famine gradually receded, the Leviathan was brought back to life and celestial investigations resumed.

Three years after revealing his monster telescope to an incredulous world, William Parsons, 3rd Earl of Rosse, was appointed president of the Royal Society, Britain's oldest and most august scientific body. He was later appointed a special adviser to the Prince Consort for the Great Exhibition of 1851, and more honours followed. In 1862 he became chancellor of the University of Dublin. When he died in 1867, Queen Victoria wrote warmly to his widow, expressing sorrow at the loss of an 'excellent and distinguished husband', but remarking how gratifying it must be to Lady Rosse to feel that 'his name will for ever be known and gratefully remembered for the great benefits he conferred on science'.[10]

William Rosse's inventive genius and the significance of his contribution to the advance of human knowledge are beyond doubt. Less widely recognised is the fact that Rosse's achievements would not have reached fruition without the active involvement of two remarkable women. He owed a supreme debt to his wife, Mary (née Field), who provided intellectual, practical and, above all, financial assistance. Since there was no public money available to pay for the expensive instruments, materials and machinery that the inventor required at Birr, he had to fund his experiments and the purchase of his equipment from his own pocket – but he was far short of possessing the huge sums required. In the event, the cost of building the Leviathan, reckoned to be about £12,000 (more than £500,000 in today's money), was met largely from the income of his wife's Yorkshire estates.[11]

Mary Field was Rachel Parsons' paternal grandmother – one of the three outstanding female relatives who, directly or indirectly, had a powerful effect on Rachel's intellectual aspirations. The daughter and co-heir of a rich landowner, Mary was born at Heaton Hall, the family home in Bradford, in 1813. She and her sister Delia were educated at home by a governess, Susan Lawson, who encouraged Mary's creative talents and wide-ranging interests, which included astronomy.[12] By the time the Leviathan came to be built, Mary knew enough about astronomy to help her husband with his calculations. Even more unusually for a woman of her class, she was a skilled blacksmith, and much of the ironwork that supported the telescope was made by her.

William and Mary were married in Yorkshire in April 1836 in circumstances that seemed less than auspicious. Just a year earlier, in the family's absence, a disastrous fire had broken out at Birr, started by the flame of a candle left burning in an attic. The central section of the castle had been completely destroyed, so that when the newly married couple came home, they had to live in the two wings on either side, which had survived because of the extraordinary thickness of their walls.

In the years that followed, the castle was restored and – under Mary Rosse's direction – many alterations and additions were made to the demesne, as the estate was known. In the dry moat between the castle and the town, a forge and workshops were constructed, and furnaces for melting brass were installed in a corner tower. A storehouse for peat or turf – used to fuel the forge – was created in another tower, and an engine house with grinding and polishing machinery for making the telescope mirrors was set up in the keep.

When the Irish famine took hold in 1845, Mary Rosse initiated bold schemes at Birr to provide jobs for local people. In collaboration with her uncle Richard Wharton-Myddleton, a former army officer, she redesigned part of the castle grounds, employing more than 500 men in building works that would continue for several years. Later she added a new wing to the castle to accommodate her growing family of children and their tutors. She also built a stable block and a gatehouse, which would be used by her sons as a laboratory.

Mary Rosse's many skills included modelling in wax, and she made all the moulds for the ornamental bronzework on the front gates of the castle. She was also responsible for the design and manufacture of cast-iron and bronze gates for the keep, and she used her knowledge of heraldry to embellish them with heraldic devices. When the designs for the various gates were complete, she used the peat-fired forge, originally constructed to cast the mirrors for the Leviathan, to cast them herself, with the assistance of the estate workers.[13]

Mary not only made detailed architectural models, using visiting cards, of the various new buildings to be created, but also embarked on an experimental venture to record in images the groundbreaking developments that were taking place at Birr – for she was a pioneer in the art of photography.

'At the time when photography was invented, [my mother] had a photographic room fitted up adjoining the workroom and spent much time there,' recalled her son Randal.[14] 'The process of printing on wax paper was her special delight and many were the beautiful photographs that she took. She joined the London amateur society, and obtained a prize for a photograph of the large telescope.' The countess also tried stereoscopic photography, which gave the illusion of three-dimensional depth. Her darkroom was closed up after her death, only to be rediscovered intact a hundred years later, with all its original equipment and shelves of bottled chemicals – representing a treasure trove for historians of the art.

Ambitiously, Mary Rosse sought to record the development of the monster telescope, often including human figures in her compositions to emphasise the instrument's giant proportions. Writing in the 1850s to the inventor and photography expert William Fox Talbot, her husband enclosed a few examples of Mary's early attempts to capture the Leviathan.[15] Fox Talbot commented that the images were 'all that [could] be desired' and recommended them for exhibition at the first show of the Photographic Society in London.

By the end of 1854, the year in which she took up photography, Mary Rosse had given birth to eleven children. Her first child, Alice, was born in 1839 but died of rheumatic fever at the age of thirteen. Other children died in infancy, leaving six brothers, only four of whom – Laurence, Randal, Clere and Charles – survived to adulthood. Randal, who entered the church, becoming rector of Sandhurst military college and an honorary canon of Christ Church, Oxford, wrote a brief memoir of his childhood, which vividly evokes the routine of life at Birr, where the family spent eight months of the year.

From late spring the Parsons children resided in London, where their father had professional and political duties to attend to. Apart from his seminal role in various scientific institutions, William Rosse was an Irish representative peer who sat in the House of Lords in the Conservative interest. In summer the boys went to Brighton to stay with their grandmother or joined their parents aboard the yacht *Titania*, which had once belonged to the engineer Robert Stephenson. As well as making regular trips through Irish waters, *Titania* took the family to Spain and the Mediterranean, or along the English Channel for visits to Belgium and Germany – instigating in the Parsons children a lifelong love of boats and the sea. Mary Rosse's independence of spirit was reflected not only in her enthusiasm for travel but also in her passion for yacht racing, while the long voyages aboard *Titania* gave her plenty of opportunity to try out different styles of photography.

In early autumn the family returned to Birr. 'There were no school days, for we were educated at home, as my father wished,' wrote Randal. The alternative would have been one of the English public schools – none of which at the time offered any scientific instruction. The children were taught by tutors and governesses, and from an early age those who showed an interest were encouraged to study science and engineering. 'Clere and Charles spent most of their time in the workshop, and my father was generally with them. There were lathes for turning woodwork, and every kind of repair was done. They were brought up to use their brains and fingers practically, which was so useful to them in after-life as engineers.'[16]

Although he showed a warm affection for his children, William Rosse was totally absorbed in his work. 'He was constantly out at night at the telescopes and the observatory, in which he was assisted by the tutors, who were in succession scientific men,' recalled Randal. The allure of the Leviathan meant that the Rosses had no problem attracting the leading mathematicians and scientists of the day to Birr to educate their sons. The tutors lived as members of the family, and sometimes accompanied the boys on their summer holidays aboard *Titania*. Among them was Robert Ball, who later became Royal Astronomer of Ireland.

Ball was struck by the extraordinary ability of the youngest son, Charles, who even as a young boy seemed always to be busy making machines. Charles – Rachel's father – would one day take his place among the first rank of engineers as the inventor of the compound steam turbine. 'It would seem that he inherited his father's brilliant mechanical genius, with an enormous increase in its effect on the world,' said Ball later, admitting how honoured he felt to have been responsible for 'instilling the elements of algebra and Euclid into the famous inventor who has revolutionised the use of steam'.[17]

Three of the four surviving Parsons boys grew up to become distinguished engineers. The eldest, Laurence, who succeeded his father to the earldom in 1867, inherited his parents' love of astronomy and was involved in observations of the Orion nebula made at Birr over a twenty-year period, of which he made drawings. Laurence is best remembered for measuring the heat of the moon with astonishing accuracy – an achievement that was recognised only long after his death.[18] Like his youngest brother, Charles, Laurence was a gifted inventor who was never happier than when busy in his workshop. Among his creations were clock-drives designed to improve the efficiency of his father's telescopes. Clere's destiny, meanwhile, directed him to the railways and water engineering systems, in Britain and South America. He became a partner in Kitson & Company, a locomotive factory in Leeds, and in J. F. La Trobe Bateman, a company started by his father-in-law, the pioneering water engineer Frederick Bateman.

The Parsons family may have represented a phenomenal combination of talents, but they often displayed a reckless attitude to danger. As a child, Charles, in particular, was notorious for getting into scrapes. His brother Randal remembered an occasion when he '[ran] into my mother with a splinter of steel hanging in the white of an eye from the lock of an air-gun he had made himself'. Mary had the courage to draw out the splinter and no permanent harm was done. 'Another time he had the whole of his eyebrows taken off by an explosion of gunpowder. The family motto was never "Safety First".'[19]

Brilliance, ingenuity, innovation, recklessness – all came together to provoke one horrific incident that occurred at Birr when the Parsons quartet were still children. At its centre was the second exceptional woman to whom William Rosse and his Leviathan owed so much: his first cousin and neighbour, Mary Ward.

Born in 1827 and brought up at Ballylin in King's County, Mary Ward (née King) was a constant visitor to Birr, where she formed a close friendship with the Countess of Rosse. Despite a fourteen-year difference in their ages, the two women were kindred spirits and together they embarked on ambitious projects such as a spectacular show of homemade fireworks to mark the Great Exhibition of 1851. 'Fireworks were then the fashion, made on the spot,' noted Randal Parsons, 'and a great display was once given in front of the castle to which all the neighbourhood was invited.'

Although she became well known as an artist, naturalist, astronomer and microscopist, Mary Ward never received any formal marks of distinction, reflecting the virtual impossibility at the time for women to achieve recognition in the scientific field. Educated at home like the Parsons children, but deriving huge intellectual benefit from her association with Birr, Mary was the first woman to write a book about microscopes.[20] Published in London in 1858, with colour illustrations by the author, *A World of Wonders Revealed by the Microscope* was reprinted several times and became a bestseller. Mary went on to write more books and numerous articles on scientific subjects, which she illustrated herself with exquisitely executed drawings and paintings – a torrent of creativity that she somehow managed to reconcile with performing the duties of a wife and mother of eight children.

More importantly, from William Rosse's point of view, Mary Ward used her artistic talents to sketch each stage of the construction of the Leviathan, providing an invaluable record for contemporary and future astronomers. One of her books was a popular guide to astronomy, in which she explained from her own experience how to get the most from a small telescope, what to look for and where.[21] When working with microscopes, she made her own slides from slivers of ivory, prepared her own specimens and drew what she saw in near-photographic detail. Among Mary's many admirers was the physicist and mathematician David Brewster, who asked her to make microscope specimens for him and used her drawings to illustrate his books and articles.

William Rosse held his cousin in the highest regard and kept in close touch with her throughout his life. During his presidency of the Royal Society (1848–54), he would regularly invite her to dinner parties at his London home, where she would meet all the leading scientists of the day – but sometimes it was his young cousin who emerged as the expert. On one occasion when he was unable to answer the query of an eminent guest, Rosse replied, 'My cousin Mary knows rather more than I do on that subject. I recommend that you address your question to her.'[22]

Birr Castle retained a magnetic attraction for Mary Ward after her marriage in 1854, and she continued to visit whenever she could, sometimes accompanied by her husband, Henry. She took a lively interest in the activities of the Parsons children, especially when they showed themselves to be true sons of their father by experimenting with mechanical devices of their own design – and the children reciprocated her affection.

In the mid-1860s, Clere and Charles Parsons, aged fourteen and eleven respectively, decided to build a steam-driven car. Such an idea was controversial at the time, since earlier attempts to produce vehicles propelled by steam had ended in failure – there were frequent breakdowns and occasional boiler explosions, and it was difficult to make progress along the deeply rutted roads. A further constraint arrived in 1865 in the shape of the Red Flag Act, which imposed a vehicle speed limit of 4 mph in the country and 2 mph in towns – as well as requiring someone to walk ahead of each vehicle with a red flag. Despite these hurdles, the Parsons boys forged ahead with building a four-wheeled carriage, with boiler and engine mounted on a flat base at the rear and a bench seat for the driver and passengers at the front. As long as the steam pressure was kept up by the coal-stokers at the rear, the car could travel up to 7 mph.

After their father's death in 1867, the boys still took out the carriage from time to time. On the evening of 31 August 1869, Mary and Henry Ward joined Clere and Charles and one of their tutors for a ride through the streets of Parsonstown. The car was negotiating a corner 'at an easy pace', according to one onlooker, when there was a sudden jolt and Mary fell from her seat and under one of the rear wheels.[23] She died a few moments later, aged forty-two, from what a doctor described as a broken neck. At the inquest, one witness said he saw 'the wheel hit the lady and [push] her to one side'. The cause of death was recorded as 'Accidental death from a steam engine. Sudden.' Mary Ward's death is believed to be the first fatal automobile accident in history.

'The deceased lady was the sister of J. G. King Esq., Ballylin, and the untoward occurrence will plunge several noble families into grief,' noted the *King's County Chronicle*. 'The Hon. Mrs Ward was a lady of great talent and accomplished in literary and scientific pursuits. A very interesting book of hers, *Sketches with a Microscope*, was published by Shields of Parsonstown some years ago.'

No picture or drawing of the steam carriage survives. It is believed that the eldest brother, Laurence, by then 4th Earl of Rosse, decreed that it be broken up and destroyed on the evening of the accident – harking back to an ancient Irish tradition whereby inanimate objects involved in human deaths were destroyed.

All sorts of stories circulated about the exact cause of Mary Ward's death, which the Rosse family did what they could to silence. But there was one rumour that refused to die down. Some people said –

including those who had been close enough to see for themselves –
that, when Mary Ward had fallen out of the carriage, its heavy iron
wheel had run over her neck and decapitated her.

The horrifying and tragic death of Mary Ward apparently did little
to deter Charles Parsons from his pursuit of scientific discovery. At
the time of his wedding in January 1883 to Katharine Bethell, he was
so absorbed in the development of an early torpedo that his bride
was obliged to spend the first days of their marriage shivering on the
bank of Roundhay Lake in Leeds while her husband carried out
endless tests on the new underwater device.[24] Perhaps as a result of
her wifely devotion, Katharine contracted rheumatic fever, a serious
and painful illness lasting several months.

During this period, Charles was employed at Kitson's, the locomotive manufacturer in Leeds in which his brother Clere was a partner,
and Charles's obsession with experimentation was already clear. 'He
had the character of being an extraordinary and weird young man
socially,' said Katharine later, 'but it was understood that he was a
genius.'[25] The ambitious Yorkshirewoman was irresistibly attracted to
the enigmatic Irish aristocrat, perhaps sensing that he was on the
brink of a world-changing career. Following the example of her
mother-in-law, Mary Rosse, Katharine would always take a fervent
interest in Charles's work, as well as teaching herself about the intri-
cacies of engineering and involving herself in various aspects of the
Parsons business. The couple had two children – Rachel, born in
January 1885, and Algernon George, known as Tommy, born in
October 1886.

Charles Parsons was one of the first people in Northumberland
to drive a car, and his wife's individuality and independence was
epitomised by her insistence on following his example – at a time
when private-car ownership was a rarity and women drivers even

rarer. She would drive alone for long distances, with sometimes disastrous results; she once had a serious accident outside Ripon in North Yorkshire, which left her unconscious by the side of the road. 'She had, in some ways, a very masculine brain – and a love of business organisation and leadership,' wrote an obituarist, 'and yet she was full of womanly thought, insight and kindliness.'[26]

Katharine was the twelfth child and sixth daughter of William Froggatt Bethell and Elizabeth (née Beckett) of Rise Park, not far from Hull, in the East Riding of Yorkshire. The Bethells were a long-established family of Yorkshire landowners with interests in politics, farming, horse riding and horse racing. As the youngest of such a large brood, Katharine learned to assert herself and take responsibility from a young age, especially after the death of her mother in 1870, when she was only eleven. Katharine was described after her death as 'a woman of great force of character with tremendous determination' and these traits were evident from childhood. Like most girls of her class and generation, she was educated at home, but developed a youthful interest in all things mechanical. Perhaps this had something to do with her relationship on her mother's side to Edmund Beckett, a lawyer, engineer and horologist, who designed the mechanism for Big Ben.

During the early months of their married life, Charles and Katharine made regular visits to Mary Rosse's London home in Connaught Place, Bayswater, where the dowager countess had moved permanently in 1870 following the marriage of her eldest son, Laurence. The new châtelaine at Birr was Cassandra Harvey-Hawke, another Yorkshire heiress, with whom Mary Rosse did not see eye to eye. Over afternoon tea at Connaught Place, Mary amused Katharine with stories about how, as a boy, Charles could not be persuaded to eat any meals unless he had his bricks or his mechanical toys to play with, and how, while still in the nursery, he made a machine that could walk.

It was at Connaught Place that Rachel Mary Parsons was born on 25 January 1885. Mary Rosse rejoiced in the arrival of her eighth grandchild, but the seventy-two-year-old dowager was in poor health, and within six months she died, bequeathing part of her extraordinary talent and indomitable spirit to the new girl in the family.

Rachel's brother, Tommy, made his appearance eighteen months later – by which time his parents were well established in northeast England, where they had set up home at Elvaston Hall, Ryton, County Durham. After graduating in mathematics from St John's College, Cambridge, Charles had been lured to the Tyne in 1877 to take up a premium apprenticeship at the Elswick Works of Sir William Armstrong, who would soon add shipbuilding to his hugely successful hydraulics and armaments business. Since no English university offered a course in Mechanical Sciences at that time, an apprenticeship was the only option for an educated young man who wished to become an engineer. After completion of his four-year term, Charles was put in charge of the electrical department at Clarke Chapman engineers in Gateshead, where he was allowed to try out his new inventions, and it was not long before he decided to establish his own engineering works in the Newcastle suburb of Heaton.

Charles and Katharine Parsons showed an enlightened attitude towards their children's upbringing, nurturing a spirit of confidence and ambition that gave Rachel and Tommy no reason to doubt their own ability to achieve. Sister and brother shared an idyllic childhood that – unusually for people of their class at the time – was closely entwined with their parents' lives. From the early days, the family was constantly on the move, making regular visits to London, as well as to Bethell relatives in Yorkshire and the Rosse family in Ireland.

Charles would often take his wife and children to sea, reliving his youthful holidays aboard *Titania*.

Elvaston was the first of three houses in northeast England where Rachel and Tommy lived – and ran wild – during their formative years. By late 1893, when Rachel was eight, they had moved to the village of Wylam, the birthplace of the railway engineer George Stephenson. Their new home was Holeyn Hall, a squat but elegant nineteenth-century brick building with balustraded parapets and a wide grassy terrace on its southern side overlooking the valley of the upper Tyne. In an echo of his mother's bold interventions at Birr Castle, Charles erected workshops at Holeyn, behind the stable block. He also created a private laboratory inside the house and other test sites around the estate, including an experimental propeller tank, which was used in the development of his revolutionary little ship, *Turbinia*.

There was never a dull moment at a Parsons family home. Although reticent and somewhat awkward with strangers, Charles had a generosity of spirit, love of life and mischievous sense of humour that made him many close friends. His children felt deprived by his long and frequent absences, but when at home he was a constant source of entertainment. In the early days, he produced a succession of toys never before seen in a nursery – not even in his own childhood nursery at Birr – and he encouraged his children to take part in designing and refining them.[27] Prominent among these was the Spider, a low-slung, three-wheeled driverless vehicle with an engine that ran on methylated spirits. 'It careered at a great pace round our lawn,' said Katharine, 'with the two children, Charles and three dogs rushing and shouting after it.' Even earlier, Charles had made a steam pram for moving the children about without the need for muscle power – a contraption that did not find favour with their mother. Perhaps most astonishing of all, he built a small flying machine with a methylated-spirit boiler, which was photographed both in full flight and after apparently hitting the ground, with six-year-old Tommy standing anxiously beside it. It was a sign of Charles's prescient faith in the possibilities of aviation.

When Charles was at home, he spent most of his time in his workshop, where he lingered until late into the evening, developing, testing and modifying his many inventions. Particular problems emanated from his work on a sound amplifier nicknamed the 'bellowphone', which resembled a gigantic trumpet.[28] To the dismay of his family, Charles would start work on perfecting the valves of this instrument immediately after dinner each evening and continue for many hours. 'Strange and weird were the noises through the nights,' said Katharine, who admitted that at least the sound produced by the finished instrument was 'sweet and beautiful'. To rapturous acclaim, Charles demonstrated the auxetophone, as it was officially known, at a meeting of the Royal Society on 13 May 1904. Cellos and double basses fitted with auxetophones were used by Henry Wood in the Queen's Hall Orchestra in London during the 1906 season of Promenade concerts – until his musicians rebelled against what they saw as a threat to their livelihoods.

From a very young age, Rachel was Charles's constant companion during daylight hours while he was busy in his workshop or testing his inventions in the open air. Many years later, when unveiling a memorial to her father at his factory at Heaton, Rachel revealed her deep admiration for his achievements and her desire to have played a more prominent role in his life.[29] She pointed out that he had spent most of the hours of every day working on the scientific and engineering ventures 'which appealed to him above everything else'. He had a complete grasp of modern scientific thought, she said, and a remarkable gift of intuition, which enabled him to judge the soundness of any scientific proposition very quickly. He also had the power of intense concentration. One of her earliest memories was of her father hurrying to his workshop as soon as he returned home in the evenings, depriving his wife and children of a full family life. He would often remain there for many hours, she said, 'unconscious of the passage of time and oblivious of any interruption'.

It was perhaps unsurprising that in later years, as Rachel forged her own path in the professional world, she felt a growing disquiet at the perceived exclusion from her father's realm, which would eventually lead to an estrangement from both parents. Her close involvement in his work and the many opportunities she had had to share in the thrill of his inventions had sown the seeds of her ambition and instilled in her a profound fascination with engineering, which she was determined to put to good use in her own career.

THREE

---·---

Fires of Ambition

The morning of 26 June 1897 dawned dull and hazy on the south coast of England, and it was not until after midday that the sun burst through to illuminate a scene of feverish activity at the great naval base of Portsmouth – the prelude to a spectacular review of the fleet in the Spithead channel. Victoria, who was then Britain's longest-serving monarch, had been on the throne for sixty years and Empress of India since 1876, and the extravaganza was just one of myriad celebrations across the globe to mark her diamond jubilee.

More than 150 vessels ablaze with bunting, including twenty-two battleships, stood to attention in four rows that stretched for a total of twenty-five miles. As the appointed hour approached, the lines were cleared of passing ships and the remaining clouds dissolved. 'That moment of anticipation, when nothing but warships could be seen throughout the length and breadth of the anchorage, was one of the most impressive of the day,' remarked a reporter for *The Times*.[1]

At 2 p.m. precisely, the guns of a royal salute on shore announced that the royal yacht was under way, and shortly afterwards *Victoria and Albert* was seen steaming slowly towards the fleet. On board was the Prince of Wales, deputising for his eighty-year-old mother, sur-rounded by an animated group of staff and guests, with more royal hangers-on following in the P&O liner *Carthage* and a second royal yacht, *Alberta*. Behind them came *Enchantress*, carrying the Lords of the Admiralty; *Danube*, with members of the House of Lords; and *Wildfire*, with the colonial premiers. Members of the House of Commons were crowded aboard the vast Cunard liner *Campania*; in their wake came a clutch of foreign ambassadors aboard *Eldorado*.

As the royal procession moved up and down the lines in stately fashion, allowing the dignitaries to cast a critical eye over the ranks of naval ships, a team of patrol boats tried with limited success to fend off intruders. Then, in a moment of high drama, the diminutive *Turbinia*, powered by Charles Parsons' steam turbines – and hailed by *The Times* as 'the fastest vessel in the world' – burst onto the scene. Resembling one of the newfangled torpedo boats, *Turbinia* was just a hundred feet long and nine feet in the beam. Taking virtually everyone by surprise, she raced along between the lines of the fleet, at times reaching a speed of thirty-four knots. This was a higher speed than any torpedo boat could achieve – and, indeed, faster than any other ship in service at that time. Christopher Leyland, *Turbinia*'s captain, later described the Spithead review as 'almost too exciting' and insisted that his antics at the helm amounted to much more than an attention-seeking stunt.[2] 'The *Turbinia* was some ten knots faster than any other craft,' he explained. 'People were not quick enough in giving us right of way, whilst some lost their heads completely.'

Although those aboard *Turbinia* were repeatedly drenched as she tore through the waves, and temporarily deafened by the roar of rushing water, for some it was the most exciting moment of their lives. For Charles Parsons, it marked his entry onto the world stage – as the designer of an entirely new form of marine propulsion – and friends and family were on board to share his triumph. Among the younger daredevils were Rachel Parsons and Joan Leyland, daughters of, respectively, the inventor and the skipper. Dashing about at high speed was a familiar experience for both girls, who had taken part in some of *Turbinia*'s many trials off the mouth of the River Tyne.[3]

Observers could hardly fail to be impressed by the vessel's astonishing performance, but there were some who disparaged the 'brilliant but unauthorised' exhibition orchestrated by Parsons and Leyland as 'a deliberate disregard of authority'.[4] The politician George Baden-Powell, who was among *Turbinia*'s passengers, sprang to his friends' defence, explaining that the amazing runs made by the little ship between the lines had been requested by the Admiral of the Fleet, who wanted her to show off her prowess to, among others, Prince Henry of Prussia, the Kaiser's brother, who was watching from a German man-of-war.[5] 'The exhibition of speed, so far from being unauthorised, was specially invited by the authorities,' wrote Baden-Powell, who added that the most notable feature of travelling aboard *Turbinia* was 'the entire absence of vibration'.

The diamond jubilee review at Spithead was a matchless opportunity for the Royal Navy to display its formidable strength and, at a time of mounting rivalry between the Great Powers – Britain, France, Germany, Austria-Hungary and Russia – there was little doubt that Parsons had received unofficial encouragement from the Admiralty to stage a demonstration of British supremacy.[6] As it turned out, there were important military and commercial consequences of the incident. By the end of the following year, 1898, construction of the first turbine-driven destroyer, HMS *Viper*, was well advanced – with the Parsons Marine Steam Turbine Company of Wallsend-on-Tyne as main contractor.[7] *Viper* was soon joined by *Cobra*, another destroyer, which was already under construction but would now be equipped with turbines instead of reciprocating engines. By common consent, both vessels performed admirably. The launch in 1906 of HMS

Dreadnought – the first battleship to be fitted with steam turbines – opened a new era in the naval arms race, with Britain, Germany and the United States as the main players. Such was the superiority of the dreadnought and super-dreadnought class that, within a few years, it was recognised around the world that all pre-dreadnought battleships had been rendered obsolete. Before long, in another revolutionary development, steam turbines would be used to power record-breaking ocean liners such as *Lusitania* and *Titanic*.

By the time of Queen Victoria's diamond jubilee celebrations, Rachel Parsons was twelve years old and already a collaborator in her father's long crusade to give material form to his dream of speed. She had experienced many excitements in her young life, but the adventure aboard *Turbinia* showed what could be done against the odds through ingenuity, self-belief and restless determination – and it left an indelible impression.

Rachel's month of birth, January, indicates that she had been conceived during her parents' long-delayed honeymoon in the United States – a five-month-long expedition that had taken them as far south and west as New Mexico and California. Charles and Katharine had put off their travels for more than a year after the wedding on account of Charles's obsessive absorption in his work – and because he was developing an invention that, as he probably knew, would change the course of history.[8] 'About the year 1884,' he wrote later, 'I determined to attack the problem of the steam turbine and of a very high-speed dynamo and alternator to be directly driven by it.' While working for Clarke Chapman in Gateshead, he constructed a small turbo-generator, which worked well from the start. Its first commercial application would be to light the interior of steamships, where the use of electricity was still in its infancy, but that was some months in the future.

His delight in invention meant that, in some respects, Charles Parsons remained a child throughout his life, which must have strengthened his bond with Rachel and Tommy. According to his friend Robert Strutt, an eminent physicist who became Lord Rayleigh in 1919, Charles showed a boyish pleasure in any experiment that ended in a big bang.[9] Rayleigh described the multitude of mechanical models in evidence at Holeyn Hall, made of 'cardboard or paper with corks, cotton reels, knitting needles, wire, sealing wax and string'. As his thoughts about the turbine evolved, Charles built some small generating machines in his home workshops to enable the use of electric lighting, first by arc lamps and later by Joseph Swan's incandescent light bulbs. If a machine broke down during dinner, Charles would get up from the table in his evening clothes and go out to deal with it himself. Nothing would absorb his attention more completely than a machine that failed to work.

Charles and Katharine remained owners of Holeyn Hall until their deaths, but in the early years of the twentieth century they bought the much larger estate of Ray at Kirkwhelpington, twenty miles northwest of Wylam, and began to build a house for themselves on a plateau amid the rugged heather moorland, extending what had been a small shooting lodge into a comfortable modern home. Katharine had discovered the site for the house while exploring the area on horseback, and was keenly aware that the Ray estate would give her unlimited opportunities to indulge her love of riding. Drawing on her childhood experiences as the daughter of a Yorkshire squire, she took a great interest in the farming practices at Ray, in addition to planning and planting a spectacular terraced garden.

Covering more than 10,000 acres, Ray Demesne offered excellent grouse shooting, as well as trout fishing in a pair of loughs called Sweethope. 'Charles was fond of entertaining his friends and neighbours for country sports and their pleasure was his main concern,' according to Lord Rayleigh, a regular visitor to Ray, who noted that Charles himself was a keen fisherman.[10] 'He liked the fishing all the better in that he used a motor boat, which frequently refused to work, and gave him the congenial task of dealing with its deficiencies.' On other occasions, model ships were floated on Sweethope Loughs to test new forms of marine propulsion.

Rachel and Tommy would accompany their mother when she went out walking or riding over the moors and hills – or simply went off exploring on their own from dawn to dusk. They far outstripped their father in the equestrian stakes since, in spite of his Irish upbringing, Charles had rarely sat on a horse. He much preferred to take out groups of children in his boat at Sweethope and teach them to fish before joining a party of guests for a lakeside picnic. Meanwhile, Rachel and Tommy would help their mother to gather fallen branches from the surrounding woodland and build a fire to cook on. Katharine's keen sense of humour and witty tongue made her an amusing host, as did her talent for telling stories. 'She was an ardent student and lover of history and was a fund of information on the local folklore,' according to a friend, Mary Houstoun.[11] 'Her powers of narration were excellent, her cultured quiet voice being one of her great charms.' Mary added that Katharine made Ray a happy place, even in hard times, but she was renowned for her feisty personality. 'She was always a fighter, and dearly loved a fight, and was always at her best when difficulties arose.'

Life was not always sweetness and light in the Parsons household, and Katharine found her resilience tested to the limit. In particular, her husband's obsession with his work, at the expense of outside interests, was hard to endure. Charles was impatient when events did not turn out as planned, or if he felt that he was being obstructed in some way, and would periodically erupt in a rage. On occasion, when he lost his temper in public, Katharine would walk away and disown him.

Never afraid to reveal his contempt for individuals who were unimaginative or dull, Charles put a high value on intellectual curiosity. Katharine told Robert Rayleigh about an incident when Rachel, aged fifteen, brought home from school a mathematical problem that she had solved, but for which she had not been given marks because the solution was regarded as unorthodox. Charles took a close look at her work and endorsed the solution. He went on to complain that school teachers were frequently 'down' on any originality of thought and discouraged their pupils from wasting time on what they called 'useless' experiments.

The Parsons family also owned a town house at 6 Windsor Terrace, Newcastle, not far from the Heaton works, and within walking distance of Rachel's first school, Newcastle High. In an age when educated women were regarded with suspicion – and higher education was generally believed to destroy a woman's hopes of marriage – Katharine Parsons took a untypically enlightened approach to her daughter's schooling. Caught up in the feminist fervour sweeping through late Victorian Britain, Katharine resolved that, unlike most of her female peers, Rachel would be liberated from the straitjacket of home-teaching by governesses. Founded in the mid-1880s, Newcastle High School for Girls aimed to provide a modern education for the daughters of professional men; its gymnasium and chemistry laboratory were regarded as radical innovations in a school for girls.

When Tommy went to Eton in 1899, treading the traditional path of the English upper classes, Rachel had the advantage of a similar opportunity. After a year at Wycombe Abbey school in Buckinghamshire, itself a pioneering institution, she moved to an establishment even more pivotal in the development of women's education in Britain:

Roedean, on the Sussex coast. Founded in 1885 by three remarkable sisters, Penelope, Dorothy and Millicent Lawrence, Roedean had recently expanded into bigger premises to satisfy the growing demand for female boarding schools.[12] Its guiding light was the eldest sister, Penelope, regarded by some as one of the great women of her age. Penelope Lawrence had been among the first students at Newnham College, Cambridge, where she completed the Natural Sciences tripos (as the Cambridge course is known) in 1878, making her a near contemporary of Charles Parsons, who had graduated from St John's the previous year – though it is unlikely that the two of them met, since male and female students at Cambridge were strictly segregated.

Rachel thrived at Roedean, where the Lawrence sisters sought to give girls the kind of intellectual freedom historically available only to boys.[13] For all the students, of whom there were 196 on Rachel's arrival in 1900, it was a mind-broadening and confidence-building experience, although some of them may have found it more of a challenge than they had expected. The girls came from all over Britain, as well as from far-flung parts of the British Empire such as Canada, India and New Zealand. There were some with addresses in Cape Colony, southern Africa, where the Second Anglo-Boer War was raging. The majority came from the professional classes, but there was also a large proportion from merchant or manufacturing families. Most girls entering the school needed a referee, but – perhaps because of her father's national pre-eminence and aristocratic connections – Rachel was among the few exempted from this requirement.

As well as aiming for the highest academic standards, the Lawrence sisters were strong advocates of physical education for girls, seeing it as one of the keys to female emancipation.[14] Penelope valued sports not merely for their own sake, but also because games such as cricket and hockey, both played with distinction by Roedean pupils, fostered loyalty and team spirit, qualities that underpinned the public-school ethos of Britain's ruling class. She herself was a strong swimmer and would often venture into the sea off Brighton to swim from one pier to the other – a distance of nearly a mile.

Cricket and hockey were encouraged as part of a full programme of physical activity that eventually included archery, tennis, fencing, swimming, water polo, life-saving, diving, running, walking, gymnastics, athletic sports, cycling, golf, rounders, fives, hockey, cricket, lacrosse and netball. The facilities included an eighteen-acre playground, eight tennis courts, a swimming pool and a cricket pavilion.

Drilling, or marching in military-style formation, was also an important part of the curriculum. 'The whole school is drilled for an hour once a week,' explained Penelope in a 1898 report on the school's activities. Each class was divided into sections under a captain and lieutenant, who were responsible for the daily practice of their group, and sections competed against each other for prizes.

Penelope Lawrence was a powerful role model for Rachel Parsons. According to another Lawrence sister, Theresa, who established a branch of Roedean in Johannesburg, 'Penelope had a breadth of view and character that is generally associated with a man. She was moreover a born teacher. Science of all sorts was, naturally, Penelope's paramount interest, an interest which she communicated to us all and to her pupils, and to her direct influence is due the fact that Roedean was in this way one of the first of a modern type of school.'[15]

Penelope's scientific passions included a love of astronomy – giving her a strong link with the granddaughter of William Parsons, 3rd Earl of Rosse, creator of the world's largest telescope. She also anticipated a revolution in women's role in society. 'Early in her life [Penelope] saw the responsibilities which would come to women in the political arena and other powers which they now enjoy,' wrote one of her students, 'and her life was spent in endeavouring to show girls that they must discipline and educate themselves so that they might be of service to others, and worthy of the vocation to which they would be called.'[16]

In their energy and force of character, the Lawrence sisters also had much in common with Rachel's mother, Katharine. Millicent Lawrence, for example, organised a system of 'scouts' at Roedean, helping to inaugurate the nationwide Girl Guide movement – a cause later taken up by Katharine in the north of England. And Millicent, like Katharine, was involved in the campaign for women's suffrage and calmly optimistic about its outcome. 'Her faith in the ultimate triumph of the cause was unshaken by constant disappointment,' wrote one of her students, 'and she inspired us all with a burning wish to do our utmost to hasten the day of that triumph.'[17]

Rachel's personality and motivations chimed harmoniously with the spirit of Roedean. Apart from academic work, she was keen on drama and various types of sport, particularly hockey and lacrosse.[18] Another activity in which she did well was gymnastics, and in spring 1903 she was awarded her school colours for drilling, helping her house to win the Drilling Cup. Girls who played for the first teams were regarded as heroes by the rest of the school, and Rachel's success – and her family connections – acted as a source of inspiration to others. Eily Keary, who attended Roedean soon after Rachel, and went on eventually to become a distinguished aeronautical and naval engineer, said later that getting to know Rachel at school was an event that changed her life. Eily's elder sister, Elsie, a contemporary of Rachel at Roedean, was also destined for a career in engineering.[19]

Perhaps unsurprisingly for a son of Mary Rosse, Charles Parsons shared his wife's confidence in the talents and capabilities of the female sex. Indeed – long before the exigencies of the 1914–18 war transformed choice into necessity – he had pioneered the employment of women in his engineering shops in Newcastle. Prominent among the women who worked in the technical department was Edith Stoney, the sister of Gerald Stoney, his right-hand man at Heaton.

Edith Stoney made some of the early calculations for the original steam turbine and for optical instruments such as telescopes and searchlights. Her father, George Johnstone Stoney, was one of the brilliant men who had been hired to educate the Parsons boys at Birr – the physicist who coined the word 'electron' to describe the fundamental unit quantity of electricity. In a letter of 1903 to his former tutor, Charles wrote, 'The problems [Edith] has attacked and solved have been in relation to the special curvature of mirrors for obtaining beams of light of particular shapes. These investigations involved difficult and intricate original calculations . . . Your daughter also made calculations in regard to the gyrostatic forces brought on to the bearings of marine steam turbines through the pitching of the vessel.'[20]

Edith Stoney had attended Newnham in the early 1890s, gaining an excellent result in mathematics, but her gender excluded her from recognition as a wrangler, the title traditionally given to first-class maths graduates at Cambridge. (Female students had been admitted to Cambridge since 1869, following the foundation of Girton College, but the university did not grant degrees to women until 1948.) Edith was the first woman to be awarded an MA at Dublin University, later becoming a physics teacher at the London School of Medicine for Women and setting up an X-ray service at London's Royal Free Hospital. During the 1914–18 war, she worked in field hospitals in France, Serbia and Greece, and her pioneering work with X-rays – which made it possible to diagnose gas gangrene and to identify the exact location in the body of bullets and shrapnel – would help to save the lives of many wounded soldiers and civilians. She also helped to build the giant searchlights used during the war to combat the Zeppelin raids on London.[21]

Spurred on by role models such as the Lawrences, Edith Stoney and her own mother – who was increasingly prominent among the suffragettes of northeast England – Rachel Parsons set her sights on a university education. Before she took on such a challenge, however, there was in 1909 another naval adventure in store – a thrilling journey aboard the luxury Cunard liner *Mauretania*, driven by her father's steam turbines, which two years earlier, with an average speed of 23.69 knots, had captured the Blue Riband for the fastest eastbound crossing of the Atlantic Ocean.

In April 1910, Rachel followed the example of her mentor Penelope Lawrence by going up to Newnham, where she read Mechanical Sciences, becoming England's first female student of the subject – an achievement that doubtless owed something to her father's growing pre-eminence in the engineering world, which was recognised in 1911 by a knighthood. Rachel was soon followed at Cambridge by Elsie Keary and, two years later, by Elsie's sister, Eily. Katharine Parsons enjoyed recounting the reaction of the engineering professor, Bertram Hopkinson, when the women first appeared in a lecture hall full of men. Ostentatiously throwing open the door to let them in, Hopkinson declared, presumably tongue-in-cheek: 'It has come!'[22]

During the war Elsie Keary worked in a technical role at one of the handful of government aircraft factories, while Eily became an assistant at the National Tank, the 549-foot-long tank at the National Physical Laboratory in Teddington, Middlesex, where model ships were tested. Her work was partly on the hydrodynamic properties of seaplane hulls.[23] In November 1917, Eily was elected the first female member of the Aeronautical Society, and two years later she, Rachel Parsons and Blanche Thornycroft (daughter of the naval architect Sir John Thornycroft) were the first women to join the Royal Institute of Naval Architects.

Rachel's course at Cambridge consisted of papers in mathematics, mechanics, strength of materials and theory of structures, heat and heat engines, and electricity and magnetism.[24] She left the university in the winter of 1912, after eight terms, during which she took the preliminary exam for the first part of the tripos and a qualifying exam in mechanical sciences in 1911. The fact that she did not complete the entire course was not unusual at the time. Indeed, before the war, it was common for men to take few, if any, of the tripos exams while at Cambridge. Women more often did so, but, in the words of a former principal of Newnham, 'It may have been her decision that in her position, and with the very unusual opportunities she had, it was not necessary to proceed to the full tripos.'[25] The first woman to complete the Mechanical Sciences tripos was Eily Keary in 1915.

According to Christina Keith, a Classics student who attended Newnham at the same time as Rachel, the unequal status of men and women at Cambridge created an atmosphere very different from that of Edinburgh, where Christina had studied earlier.[26] For example, at both Cambridge and Oxford the awarding of degrees to women was aggressively resisted, and was a topic of controversy at the time. 'Female students knew that any apparent failure on their part, be it academic or moral, could damage their cause,' wrote Christina. Strict rules governed the conduct of women students, and chaperones were often required to accompany them to lectures. 'Walking in the street with a man was forbidden – which was sometimes awkward when moving together from one class to another.' No man could be entertained by a woman in her room – unless he happened to be her father or brother, in which case the woman's friends were not allowed to be present.

Another woman who studied at Newnham at the same time as Rachel was Eliza Butler, who complained that the female students were kept firmly apart from the rest of the university, so that, in retrospect, she got to know Cambridge as an institution 'only dimly', and that breaking the chaperone rules on a few occasions did nothing to make it seem more familiar.[27] 'I was of course susceptible to its atmosphere,' wrote Eliza. 'I felt the civilising influence of its buildings; leaning over some ancient bridge and watching the Cam flow quietly along with its flotilla of punts and canoes containing studious or larking undergraduates, I felt that medieval and modern had harmoniously coalesced.'

While at Cambridge, Rachel consolidated the engineering skills she had absorbed in her father's workshop and added theoretical knowledge to practical experience, but she doubtless found the rarefied existence of the university too restrictive for her liking and longed to get back to the revitalising energy of life on the Tyne, where her father's firm, C. A. Parsons & Company, continued to lead the way in technological innovation and business success.

There was also the pull of London – the epicentre of a political and social revolution that could not fail to attract the attention of the educated younger generation. 'It was partly the feeling of relief and release as we broke out of the fog of Victorianism,' wrote the author and publisher Leonard Woolf.[28] 'The forces of reaction and barbarism were still there, but they were in retreat.' Such optimism would prove misguided, with the horrors of the Great War to come, but, in Woolf's words, this could not alter the fact that it was exciting to be alive in London in 1911 and that there was reason for exhilaration. 'Profound changes were taking place in every direction, not merely politically and socially. The revolution of the motor car and the aeroplane had begun; Freud and Rutherford and Einstein were at work beginning to revolutionise our knowledge of our own minds and of the universe.' Equally thrilling events were happening in the arts, including theatre and literature, while in painting 'the profound revolution' of Cézanne, Matisse and Picasso was under way. 'And to crown it all, night after night we flocked to Covent Garden, entranced by a new art, a revelation to us benighted British, the Russian Ballet in the greatest days of Diaghilev and Nijinsky.'

Soon after the outbreak of war in 1914, Tommy Parsons, Rachel's brother, joined the Royal Field Artillery, resuming an earlier military career that he had given up in 1909 to work at his father's firm, and Rachel took his place as a director, becoming one of the first women in Britain to sit on the board of a major industrial concern. When the need for 'dilution' of labour became an accepted fact and female workers were allowed into the engineering shops in large numbers, Rachel took on the supervision of the women at Heaton – who, according to another director, proved themselves to be 'very competent' at many jobs.[29] It seems that Rachel appeared at only two board meetings before she joined the training department of the Ministry of Munitions and moved to London. Based at the Parsons family home in Upper Brook Street, she travelled to factories and educational institutions in London and other parts of Britain teaching women workers how to do everything from assembling aircraft parts to installing electrical wiring on battleships.

Although no clear record has survived of Rachel's romantic entanglements at the time, it is possible that a love interest may have influenced her decision to leave Cambridge early and return to Tyneside. After her death in 1956, stories in the press alluded to a relationship with another director of C. A. Parsons – an affair that ultimately came to nothing, when the man in question married someone else, leaving Rachel, in the words of the *Daily Express*, 'a woman scorned'.[30]

The most likely candidate for the role of Rachel's lover is Alexander Henry Law, known as Alex, a Dublin-born engineer who was held in high regard by Charles Parsons. Born in Dublin in 1878, Alex Law was a talented engineer who had joined the Parsons firm in 1899 after graduating from Trinity College with distinction in all subjects.[31] After completing his apprenticeship in 1902, he began work in the electrical design office, and within a year had been appointed chief draughtsman and designer in the electrical department.

Another young recruit to Parsons at that time was Gordon Bedford, who had been attracted to the firm after hearing about the exploits of *Turbinia* and was hoping to work on marine turbines.[32] Only after joining the Heaton works did he discover that Heaton made turbines for land power stations only, the exclusive rights to build marine turbines having been granted to the Parsons Marine Company at Wallsend. Gordon Bedford, who wrote an unpublished memoir about his time with the firm, was proud to have worked on Neptune Bank, the first power station in which Charles Merz, as consulting engineer to the Newcastle Electric Supply Company, installed a Parsons turbine, opening a new era in the electricity supply industry. Gordon at first shared lodgings with Alex Law and found him a congenial and sociable companion. A friendship developed between the two of them, and they later moved together to a house in Benton, on the northeast side of Newcastle, from where they travelled to the Heaton works on their motorbikes.

There was one serious incident involving Alex Law that marred this happy state of affairs. He shared with the Parsons family a love of fast-moving vehicles and, like them, was among the first people to own a car in Newcastle. On 13 January 1910, while driving through the centre of the city, he knocked down and fatally injured a forty-five-year-old barmaid, Margaret Ann Maynes, and was charged with her manslaughter.[33] At the trial, Alex said that, at the time of the accident, the car had been travelling at fifteen or sixteen miles an hour; he first saw the woman when she was about three yards away, and had found it impossible to avoid her, although he put on the brakes. He was found not guilty and discharged, but, while the known details of the case are less shocking, it carried disturbing echoes of the accident of 1869 in Parsonstown that had caused the death of Mary Ward.

The 1911 census record for Ray Demesne shows that Alex Law was staying at the Parsons home on the night of the census, with the only other occupants, apart from servants, being Charles, Katharine and Rachel. When C. A. Parsons became a private limited company on 31 March 1913, with Charles as chairman, Alex was appointed joint managing director with W. M. Johnston. Rachel's brother Tommy, another of Alex's close friends, was also made a director.

Like Tommy Parsons, Alex served with the Royal Field Artillery in France, until he was wounded in the eye in 1916 and forced to return home for treatment and convalescence. Later that year, he started work at the Ministry of Munitions, following in the footsteps of both Charles and Rachel Parsons. Before the end of the war he returned to Parsons as sole managing director, where he stayed until the end of 1919. In June 1920 he married Isabel Norton Marshall, a former nurse at 10 Northumberland Voluntary Aid Detachment (VAD) hospital based in Pendower Hall, Newcastle.

In his memoir, Gordon Bedford made no bones about the fact that Charles Parsons was a difficult man to work for.[34] His employer had strong ideas about how things should be done and, if crossed, was apt to explode in anger, sowing fear in his workforce. One such incident in late 1919 was so serious that it resulted in Alex Law's abrupt departure from the company after a twenty-year association. It is not clear what part Alex's relationship with Rachel and his decision to marry Isabel Marshall played in his decision to sever ties with the Parsons firm. However, Rachel's erratic behaviour around this time and her apparent failure to form another close relationship with a man indicates the possibility of a deep emotional wound.

FOUR

A New Dawn

In contrast with Rachel Parsons' carefree childhood in the wilds of Northumberland, Caroline Haslett – who would one day spearhead the creation of the Electrical Association for Women – was brought up in a strict Victorian household in which Christian teaching was rigorously applied, and from which, as she grew older, she longed to escape.[1] The family had few luxuries. Her father, Robert, was a railway signal engineer, a pioneer of the co-operative movement, and distinctly conservative by nature. He practised as a lay preacher at the mission chapels near the family home at Worth (now part of Crawley) in Sussex, and Caroline was occasionally asked to deliver a sermon on his behalf. As a practical manifestation of her strong religious belief at that time, it was a task she undertook with gusto.

Caroline also had to cope intermittently with a chronic but unspecified illness. 'I regularly spent five hours a day lying on my back to strengthen my spine,' she wrote later.[2] She won a scholarship to Haywards Heath High School, which she attended from 1906 to 1913, but she took no pleasure from her lessons, finding the 'usual ladylike subjects', such as needlework and drawing, uncongenial, and failing to shine academically. Caroline had something in common with the young Rachel Parsons, however, in that she spent a lot of time with her father in his home workshop, where, under his instruction, she learned to use tools with skill and confidence.

Caroline's illness obliged her to endure long periods of enforced idleness, during which she became a voracious reader. She would also watch her mother, Caroline Sarah, and other members of the household carrying out their daily chores, and she became preoccupied by the waste of human energy these entailed, as she revealed later in a radio broadcast: 'The stove burnt coal which had to be brought in buckets from the outhouse, and the flues had to be cleaned and the stove itself polished with blacklead by hand. On washing days the scullery copper was lit and it took all day to get the piles of dirty linen washed . . . and so the work of the house went on, sweeping, scrubbing, polishing and dusting, all done by hand.'[3]

These observations laid the foundation for Caroline's lifelong mission to relieve women from domestic drudgery by replacing manual labour with mechanical devices. She came to believe that a limit should be put on a woman's working day and that society should be transformed to make life as exciting and fulfilling for women as it was for men. The growth of her political consciousness coincided with the campaign for the female franchise.[4] 'I grew up at a time when women in England were demanding that they should have a full part in everything that was going on in the country,' she wrote in an essay of 1938, 'that they should be regarded as full citizens, and therefore be given the parliamentary vote, that they should be allowed to share in the education and career of their brothers.'

After a love affair at seventeen, which ended in acrimony – 'I became a suffragette and fell out with the young man over that' – Caroline was expelled from school and soon afterwards moved to London. Her mother and father were both distressed by their daughter's decision to join the suffragettes, prompting Caroline to tell

Emmeline Pankhurst that, since she was still dependent on her parents, she would respect their wishes until she was twenty-one, but felt free to make her own decisions after that. There was no turning back: 'In my dreams I was confined by no limits, my energies admitted no restrictions, my mind roved over many fields of women's activities. I saw my mother and all the other mothers in the country released from household cares, I saw women engaging in the professions for which their talents and temperaments fitted them.'

As Caroline described it, the immediate pre-war period was a thrilling time for feminists. 'The joy of marching and carrying a banner, the frenzy of great speeches, the defiance of unjust laws, the opposition to anything that prevented the coming of the great new world – no thrill of soldierly music could equal their appeal,' she admitted. Like many other young people of her generation, she believed that a stifling, restrictive period in history was ending and that an exciting future beckoned, especially for women. However, when war broke out in August 1914, many suffrage campaigners turned their energies to what they saw as their patriotic duties, and Caroline's life took a different direction.

Although a disappointment to her teachers as well as her parents, Caroline owed a debt of gratitude to her mother's friend Moya Llewelyn Davies, who – having taken the young woman's ambitions seriously – encouraged her to pursue a business career, and then introduced her to her brother-in-law, Harry Llewelyn Davies, the managing director of Cochran Boiler Company.[5] After secretarial training in London, Caroline was taken on in 1914 as a junior clerk at Cochran's London office on a wage of ten shillings a week. She was also appointed superintendent of a Wesleyan Sunday school, where, still only nineteen, she was in put in charge of twenty teachers and several hundred young children. (Caroline remained close friends for many years with Moya Llewelyn Davies, who was later imprisoned in Ireland for her involvement with the Irish republican organisation Sinn Féin.)

Caroline's work at Cochran's was largely administrative, consisting of compiling quotations and specifications for the ships' boilers that the company made and sold. Although some clients were sceptical about her grasp of technical matters, she received encouragement from colleagues, and by early 1918 she was managing the London office. This role lasted only briefly, however, because she was soon transferred to the Cochran works at Annan in Dumfriesshire, on the shores of the Solway Firth. As soon as she arrived at the works, Caroline knew that it was the place for her. 'In this new and exciting atmosphere of men and machines, she found her spiritual home,' wrote her sister Rosalind Messenger.[6] Caroline's engineering knowledge and skills now developed rapidly, and she was inordinately proud of the first blueprint for a boiler that appeared with her initials, together with the boiler's specification and shipping instructions for its journey to New York. Caroline Haslett had become what she herself described as 'a real live engineer'.

At Annan, Caroline picked up the rudiments of mechanics, although she never received any formal training. Early in the war, when many of Cochran's men joined up, she had learned how the company operated. 'They knew I was intelligent and reliable, and they began to leave things to me,' she said. She was asked to look after some important contracts, and she persuaded her manager to give her four months on the shop floor to get practical experience. However, when the men came back from the war, they wanted their old jobs back and work was gradually taken away from her. If she protested, they would laugh dismissively and tell her not to worry because she would soon be getting married. Infuriated by this patronising attitude, she decided to look elsewhere for more fulfilling employment.

'My great chance came in 1919, when the newly formed Women's Engineering Society advertised for its first secretary,' Caroline wrote almost twenty years later, adding that, after an interview with Lady Parsons, she was taken on.[7] 'Imagine the horror of my dear, good, practical parents who saw their daughter leave a safe job with a good salary for such a change.' It was her belief in Katharine Parsons' foresight that had given her the confidence to take on this new challenge. '[Lady Parsons] was the person of vision who saw the chance coming for the woman engineer.'

Another individual destined to become a leading light in the Women's Engineering Society was Gertrude Entwisle, who was employed during the war at British Westinghouse (later Metropolitan-Vickers) in Manchester. Gertrude had been studying physics at Manchester University when the Engineering faculty was first opened to women. Her decision to take electrical engineering as a subsidiary subject gave her the qualification she needed to be hired by Westinghouse in 1915, when the firm needed to fill the vacancies left by the men who had joined up.

'My first job was to write up test results, but after three months another girl came to do that and I went on to design, and together she and I struggled to establish our position,' recalled Gertrude later in a lecture about engineering as a career for girls.[8] Their evenings were spent at the local technical college but they soon realised that, to get anywhere as engineers, they needed practical experience. The idea of an office worker transferring to the engineering shops was revolutionary but Gertrude jumped at the chance when it was suggested to her by the chief engineer. Her department at Westinghouse was devoted to the design of DC motors – rotary electrical machines that convert direct current electrical energy into mechanical energy. Women then began to be employed in other areas of the company and before the end of the war there were quite a few of them doing proper engineering jobs. After the war, Metropolitan-Vickers, as it had become, took on female apprentices and was the first (and for a long time the only) firm to do so.

Gertrude recalled that, in the early days of her life in the engineering shops, she had had to endure a string of embarrassments. Women had never been allowed to walk round the works, and everywhere she went the men drew attention to her presence by hammering loudly with any implement they could find. Being very shy at the time, she found this experience upsetting. The proposal that women should work as engineers had had to be ratified by the firm's directors. '[They] said that I might do so but that I must wear trousers,' she said. 'The enormity of that, however, struck them later and they sent word that I could only go if I did *not* wear trousers.'

Gertrude Entwisle was the first woman to join the Institution of Electrical Engineers (IEE) in each of three grades: student member (1916), graduate member (1919) and associate member (1920). When she heard about plans to form the Women's Engineering Society, she swiftly offered to set up a branch in Manchester, where she became the first secretary. She was an energetic member of the society's council for many years and served as its president from 1941 to 1943.

While Gertrude Entwisle was forging her individual path to engineering glory in Manchester, a revolution on a much larger scale was taking place in the Scottish borders, at Gretna, where – in response to the Shell Crisis of 1915 – the Ministry of Munitions was building a vast cordite-producing factory, which would be staffed predominantly by women. At its height, HMS Factory Gretna would stretch for nine miles across former farmland and employ 30,000 workers to manufacture RDB cordite, a new type of propellant.[9] By 1917 the factory was making 1,100 tons of cordite per week, more than all other munitions plants in Britain combined. The cordite was produced at Gretna and then sent to other factories for packing into bullets and shells.

In the first year of Gretna's operation, more than 11,000 girls and women from all over Scotland and northern England answered the call for recruits. They were attracted by the good wages – far higher than those paid to domestic servants and farm workers – and keen to contribute to the war effort, even though the dangers of the work were clear, especially the constant threat of explosions. The most hated job was mixing nitric acid and waste cotton in huge vats to make nitro-cotton, one of the first stages in producing cordite. This was known as 'the devil's porridge' and its fumes turned the workers' skin bright yellow. Much of the work was physically demanding. 'We made the cordite, cut it in lengths, packed it in trays and then carried it to small trucks at the doorway, and two girls pushed the trucks a mile or so to the large stoves where it was dried out,' recalled one employee. Sophisticated medical facilities were provided to treat those who became ill in the course of their work.

The huge influx of women into the munitions factories all over the country set off a social revolution that had its roots in the realisation by government and employers that, to be fully productive, the female workforce had to be fit, healthy and alert.[10] New recruits were given a medical examination and workers' health was regularly monitored. Expectant mothers received special treatment – they were exempt from doing night shifts, for example, and from handling TNT. The Ministry of Munitions set up a Welfare and Health department, which appointed welfare supervisors in the factories. As part of the supervisory regime, protective clothing was universally adopted, first-aid rooms were opened, and canteens were established. Organised recreation included swimming, tennis, dancing, piano playing, bowls, cricket, concerts, dramatic entertainments and art classes.

Providing housing for the new army of female workers, especially in already overcrowded industrial districts, was an enormous challenge, and the rigid restrictions on building during the war made the situation more difficult. Lists of suitable lodgings were drawn up by special committees in munitions areas, leading to the creation of a Billeting Board, which collaborated with local authorities and individuals to find thousands of temporary homes. Schools and workhouses were converted into living spaces, and large numbers of temporary cottages and hostels were erected. The cottages – one-storey wooden or concrete structures with three to five rooms – were allocated to married couples, while unmarried women lived in hostels fitted out with kitchens, dining rooms and common rooms. Several hostels might be grouped into a 'colony' with cubicled dormitories for between 100 and 130 people in each unit and a separate communal dining room. This popular arrangement offered good opportunities for socialising.

A female factory employee who gave birth was expected to resume work two months after the delivery. Mothers could have their babies or infants looked after in one of the state-sponsored nurseries that sprang up in industrial areas. Under a scheme of 1917, the Ministry of Munitions agreed to pay 75 per cent of the initial cost of the day (or night) nurseries for munition workers' children. Good diet and hygiene were high priorities in the nurseries. An unexpected consequence of the war was that the health and wellbeing of ordinary individuals, especially young people, was taken much more seriously than it had been earlier.

The quality and quantity of workers' food was another important issue. As director of her machine-tool factory in Halifax, Laura Annie

Willson noticed that many of the mothers were going without proper nourishment in order to feed their children, prompting her to set up a works canteen, one of the first of its kind. Canteens – virtually unheard of before the war – were made obligatory in certain filling factories, as well as in establishments where women were employed on night shifts, and they soon spread to other workshops and factories. Often state-aided, the canteens were run by voluntary staff, some from aristocratic families with no experience of domestic work. Larger canteens were well supplied with labour-saving appliances, including electric washing-up machines, electric bread-cutters and tea-measuring machines.

Another woman who influenced workers' conditions for the better during the war and went on to become a founder member of the Women's Engineering Society was Margaret, Lady Moir, the wife of the celebrated civil engineer Sir Ernest Moir. She had travelled all over the world with her husband, and – describing herself as 'an engineer by marriage' – entered fully into the development of all his great enterprises, among which were the Forth Bridge across the Firth of Forth and docks, harbours, tunnels, bridges and railways in many different countries. According to her friend Caroline Haslett, 'She would descend the workings [of bridges and tunnels] to inspect the construction closely, ignoring the very real dangers of compressed air.'[11] Margaret Moir was the first woman to walk under the Thames from Kent to Middlesex, via the Blackwall Tunnel, another of Ernest's major projects. Appalled by the high death and injury toll among construction workers at the time, she supported her husband in his endeavours to promote safer working conditions. These culminated in the invention of a 'medical airlock' to treat potentially fatal decompression sickness, which saved many lives.[12] As women entered the factories in large numbers during the early part of the First World

War, Lady Moir trained as a lathe operator and was employed in this role for more than eighteen months. Her empathy with working people prompted her to organise a scheme to provide weekend respite to full-time workers; their places were taken by Lady Moir herself and other educated and privileged women.

Margaret Moir had got to know the Parsons family through her husband Ernest, who joined the Ministry of Munitions in 1915 and was soon appointed head of the Inventions branch. In this role, he worked closely with other leading engineers, including Charles Parsons, who chaired the ministry's Tyne & Wear board of management.[13] In 1916 Ernest was made a baronet in recognition of his work in America on behalf of the ministry. Meanwhile, his wife forged an alliance with Katharine and Rachel Parsons, based on their shared belief that women's talents and abilities must be put to good use in industry during the war, and that formal training was needed to give female workers the necessary skills.

Fifty miles west of Gretna, at the southwest tip of Scotland, a very different enterprise involving women engineers was under way. At Tongland, a small village outside Kirkcudbright, the Galloway Engineering Company had been set up to manufacture aircraft engines and components with the financial backing of William Beardmore, the prominent Clydeside industrialist and major shareholder of Arrol-Johnston. Arrol-Johnston already had a larger factory at Heathhall in Dumfries, opened in 1913, under the management of Thomas Charles (T. C.) Pullinger, but they needed more capacity to respond to government pressure for a greatly increased number of aircraft. Before the war, Arrol-Johnston had been better known for making cars – indeed, it was credited with producing, in 1896, the first automobile to be manufactured in Britain.

One of the impressive characters at the heart of the Tongland venture was Margaret Rowbotham, a former mathematics student at Girton College, Cambridge, who had pursued a career in teaching – first at Roedean, Rachel Parsons' old school, and then at Havergal College in Winnipeg, Canada. But Margaret's real love was motor engineering, which, before going to Canada, she had studied at the British School of Motoring for six months, gaining the Royal Automobile Club Driver's Certificate.[14]

After her return to Britain, in 1916 Margaret Rowbotham, known as Madge, was taken on by Arrol-Johnston at Heathhall, where she trained for several months in the machine workshops and drawing office. She made such a good impression that, when the Galloway Engineering Company opened at Tongland the following year – after a small hydroelectric plant had been built on the River Dee to power the factory – she was appointed machine-shop and works superintendent. This meant that she was personally responsible, under the direction of a works manager, for the organisation and running of the workshops, as well as the continuing development of the site – which included rooms for relaxation and tennis courts on the roof. In her leisure time, Madge caused a stir by riding her motorbike around the sparsely populated rural area, and in November 1917 a photograph of her on the motorbike appeared in various magazines, including *The Gentlewoman* and *The Autocar*, to illustrate articles about women in engineering.

The indirect influence of another female engineer, Dorothée Pullinger (the daughter of T. C., as he was known), meant that the Tongland works was conceived from the start as much more than just a factory.[15] Aware of the need to recruit more well-educated women into industry, especially in view of the wartime dearth of skilled workers, T. C. had had the idea of creating at Tongland an engineering university for women in parallel with the production of munitions for the war effort and, to that end, he planned to introduce apprenticeships and training courses. For T. C. this represented a complete change of heart, since he had previously been trenchantly opposed to his daughter's desire to follow in his engineering footsteps.

Dorothée Pullinger was born in France in 1894 to a French mother and her English father, T. C.[16] In 1904 the family moved to Britain and T. C. later secured a job with Arrol-Johnston in Paisley, owned by William Beardmore, and turned around the ailing automobile company, before going on to run the firm's new factory at Heathhall. Brought up in a world where engineering was everything, Dorothée was fascinated by mechanics from a young age – and she had a particular wish to design cars. But when she left school at seventeen, her father insisted that it would be much more sensible for her to confine herself to a traditional female role.

Dorothée persisted, however, and at last got her father's permission to enter Arrol-Johnston's drawing office, which was considered a more appropriate place for a woman than the engineering shops. It was her linguistic abilities – she could speak German as well as French and English – that helped to advance Dorothée's career.[17] One of her tasks was to translate into English the German plans for the Austro-Daimler aero-engine, for which T. C. had secured the manufacturing rights. This proved particularly valuable when war came and Britain was desperate for planes.

Dorothée remained frustrated in her ambitions, however, and left Dumfries for London in 1914. She applied to join the Institution of Automobile Engineers, but was refused on the grounds that 'the word person means a man and not a woman'. Undaunted, she wrote to Vickers in Barrow-in-Furness after reading an article in *The Times* about the firm's employment of French women. Vickers were so impressed by her application that they provided a first-class train fare from London to Barrow – and Dorothée never looked back.[18] Two years later she became a superintendent at the Barrow factory, and by the end of the war she was in charge of a workforce of 7,000 women building everything from submarines and airships to shells and grenades. She was responsible for hiring and dismissing the workers, discipline, employee accommodation and upgrading staff canteens, which before her arrival had supplied only hot water. She bought ingredients and cooking equipment and made soup, sold at a penny a bowl; cooked meals were later provided at four-pence each.

After the war Dorothée Pullinger returned to the Arrol-Johnston factory at Heathhall, where business was booming as a result of the growing demand for cars. When the company was reorganised, Dorothée, by then on the board of directors, took over the running of Galloway Motors, with its mainly female workforce, at Tongland. The factory would achieve national prominence as the producer of the pioneering Galloway car, designed specifically for women drivers (see page 95).[19] Dorothée was awarded an MBE for her wartime work at Vickers and was finally admitted to the Institution of Automobile Engineers as its first female member.

Meanwhile, doubtless influenced by his daughter's success, and by observing the efficiency of other women workers, T. C. Pullinger had altered his views. According to an article in *The Lady* entitled 'A New Profession for Women', the man who had been so vehemently opposed to his daughter's aspirations 'not only became a convert but saw the immense future this profession would open to women of the right type'.[20]

Anticipating an increased demand for automobiles after the war, Galloway Engineering Company had decided to offer apprenticeships for 'educated and refined' women with a taste for mathematics and mechanics. Commenting on the female apprentices who had recently started work at Tongland, T. C. said, 'They are born mechanics who work with their brains as well as their hands, and they work with astonishing rapidity,' which made it possible to reduce their period of training to three years, compared with five or seven years for young men.

In the same month, *The Autocar* magazine revealed that the Tongland works had been built with the intention of permanent operation by women.[21] 'The factory, producing high-powered aeroplane engine components, is now run [in this way], and after the war, when producing automobile work of one kind or another, it will continue to be so run.' It was not the intention, said *The Autocar*, to employ 'female labour of the usual factory class'. By contrast, educated women who were keen on mechanical work were being offered the opportunity, not only to use their skills to produce war materials, but also 'in surroundings, congenial both physically and socially' to study and prepare for a permanent career in engineering.

When it came to attracting educated middle-class women from other parts of the country, however, the isolated location of Tongland was a difficult hurdle to overcome, and in the event the works evolved into a more typical munitions factory, employing mainly local women along with any available men. By the end of the war, Madge Rowbotham, as works superintendent, had come to regard the experiment as a failure, since only about a quarter of the women employed there had taken the courses provided alongside the ordinary factory work.

Even though Tongland continued to prosper for a few years as an automobile plant, there was a sense of disappointment in the air, combined with frustration at the widespread loss of jobs for women in industry, that prompted Madge and Dorothée to join the Women's

Engineering Society soon after its formation in early 1919. With Caroline Haslett's encouragement, both women were signatories of the society's deeds of covenant and would remain lifelong members and supporters of the cause of women's work in professional engineering.

FIVE

Seeds of Revolution

'The war revolutionised the industrial position of women. It found them serfs and left them free,' said Millicent Fawcett in 1920, in a moment of heady optimism, celebrating the opportunities that had opened up for women in skilled employment.[1] Even more important, proclaimed the suffragist leader, women's achievements during the war had 'revolutionised men's minds and their conception of the sort of work of which the ordinary everyday woman was capable'.

A similarly positive view infused the first committee meetings of the Women's Engineering Society in April and May 1919, though such hopefulness could not quell the deep anger that many felt at the poor treatment of female engineers who had served their country so effectively during four years of hostilities. It was a cause of celebration, however, that Katharine Parsons had been admitted to membership of the North East Coast Institution of Engineers and Shipbuilders, and that Rachel Parsons, Eily Keary and Blanche Thornycroft had become associate members of the Institution of Naval Architects, since these 'firsts' for women were seen as crucial steps on the road to equal treatment of the sexes. During this period, Rachel Parsons was confirmed as president of the Women's Engineering Society, with Mary Selby as honorary secretary and Lady Parsons as honorary treasurer. Among an array of other influential women in regular attendance were Lady Moir, Lady Eustace Percy, Lady Shelley-Rolls, Margaret Rowbotham and Dorothée Pullinger. Janetta Ornsby, one of the founding signatories, remained very active in the society, especially following the death of her husband Robert, manager of the Seaton Delaval colliery, who had become one of the best known mining engineers in Northumberland.

Public protest was mounting at families' loss of income following the dismissal of hundreds of thousands of women from munitions factories, and in March 1919 a huge meeting was held at the Albert Hall to demand that – if they were to be deprived of jobs – women should receive unemployment benefit on the same terms as men. '[Women] do not ask their country to maintain them in idleness. They ask to be set to productive work,' insisted *Woman Worker*, the newspaper of the National Federation of Women Workers. 'They merely plead for a minimum of security, comfort and leisure; not for any distant utopia, but for a means of escaping from the grinding poverty, the overwork and the desperate uncertainty of their prewar lives.'[2] Anger had been stoked by government proposals that women should receive lower rates of unemployment benefit than men, and that those who were unwilling to take jobs in domestic service should be denied benefit altogether. In the event, the Unemployment Insurance Act 1920 provided fifteen weeks of unemployment benefit to more than 11 million workers – almost the entire civilian working population, excluding domestic servants, farm workers, railway workers and civil servants. Unemployed men received a weekly payment of fifteen shillings and unemployed women received twelve shillings.

Rachel Parsons suggested that one way to address the unemployment problem was to train women in the kind of activities they had already proved they were good at. 'They have shown that they can make parts of aeroplanes and motor-cars, that they are expert tool makers, tool setters and welders, and that many are capital inspectors and examiners in workshops,' she told the *Daily Mail*. 'Motor-car and bicycle repairing would suit the abilities of many women, and a number are already engaged in this work.'[3] She explained that the main aims of the Women's Engineering Society were to obtain proper recognition for women in the engineering profession and provide them with opportunities and facilities for training.

The overriding concern of the society's leaders was the inexorable progress through Parliament of the Restoration of Pre-War Practices Bill, which would make it illegal for engineering firms to employ women on the shop floor if they had had no female employees before the war. The problem was illustrated by Olivia Forbes, the female superintendent of Ferranti Ltd, electrical engineers of Hollinwood, Lancashire in a letter of 2 February to Caroline Haslett: 'The present position of women in engineering shops requires immediate backing and assistance. The attitude of the men's unions here is to clear them all out.'[4] Caroline responded to Olivia on 10 April asking for her support for the Women's Engineering Society's campaign. 'There is an enormous amount of prejudice to overcome,' admitted Caroline, 'but we believe that with a strong organisation behind us we shall succeed in our endeavour.'

The new legislation would compel all engineering firms to return to pre-war industrial practices within two months of the passing of the Act and to maintain such practices for a year following the Act. Any employer not complying with these requirements – particularly by continuing to employ 'unskilled' workers, mostly women – would be liable to appear before a special tribunal and to pay a substantial fine.

The role of the trade unions in opposing equal treatment of women was starkly illustrated by the response of the Amalgamated Society of Engineers (ASE) to Rachel Parsons' request for a meeting. The engineering unions operated a closed shop, and their fear was that admitting women members would not only deprive men of jobs but also serve to depress wages – in the belief that women would be prepared to accept lower pay than men. On 19 March 1919, the ASE representative wrote a letter addressed to 'Miss Rachel M. Parsons' that began with the words 'Dear Sir and Brother'. The correspondent said he could see no good reason to receive a deputation 'having regard to the fact that our percentage of unemployment is on the increase'. Whether women who had worked in industry during the war could be permitted to 'return' would need to be considered by all the engineering unions, he said, 'having regard to all the circumstances under which the Trade Unions relaxed their trade rights and customs in the interests of the nation'. This was a reference to the Treasury Agreement concluded with Lloyd George in 1916, following the Shell Crisis.

Not all the ASE leaders were hostile to women, however. A supporter of the Women's Engineering Society from the start was Frederick Stephen (F. S.) Button, a Labour Party activist and member of the ASE executive, who joined the society's council in the early days. Button also worked with Mary Macarthur, the general secretary of the Women's Trade Union League, and, later, with Margaret Bondfield and Susan Lawrence, two of the first women MPs. 'Few men could speak from greater knowledge of labour problems,' wrote

Rosalind Messenger in her biography of Caroline Haslett,[5] pointing to Button's leading role in the Industrial Welfare Society, which was dedicated to improving working conditions and human relationships in industry. F. S., as he was known, provided Caroline with help and advice throughout her career and, although he was twenty-two years her senior, an intimate friendship developed between them.

Caroline had begun her work at the Women's Engineering Society on 5 February 1919 at a salary of £200 a year. Her accommodation at the Dover Street office consisted of one small room with a filing cabinet, a table, two chairs and a typewriter. In spite of a large injection of funds by Katharine Parsons, the society was always short of money in the early years, and there was sometimes not enough to pay Caroline her salary, but she threw herself wholeheartedly into achieving its ambitions. With the backing of the society's council, she launched a quarterly illustrated magazine, *Woman Engineer*, whose first edition appeared in December 1919, with Caroline as editor – a role she held until 1932. The journal's stated aim was to record the progress made by women in all branches of engineering, and to publish a wide range of articles by both female and male engineers. While acknowledging that 'the outlook for women in the engineering world [had] become increasingly gloomy', the first edition proclaimed the society's philosophy that no individual should be prevented from doing certain types of work on grounds of sex. It noted that, in addition to the London headquarters, four branches of the society had already been formed – in Newcastle, Kirkcudbright, Manchester and Aberdeen.

Caroline would often find herself having to defend in public the work of the society, which was accused, among other things, of fuelling a sex war – a charge she emphatically refuted. 'More than ever today women are realising that it is only the closest co-operation with men that will bring them the success in business and industry at which they are aiming,' she wrote in the *Daily Mail*. 'The Sex Antagonism which existed during the old suffrage days, when women were fighting for the vote, is fast dying down, and there is more true comradeship between men and women than there has been before.'

In the early days of the society, Katharine Parsons continued to spend much of her time at Ray Demesne, her home in Northumberland, or at Windsor Terrace in Newcastle, from where she conducted a lively and frank correspondence with Caroline in London. The initial concern was to build up membership, through giving talks, holding meetings for potential recruits and getting publicity in the press, as well as spreading the word through personal contacts. Katharine often included in her letters titbits of information about her life, which hinted at the development of a friendship between the two women. 'I am independent with my car and drive the 25 miles to Newcastle in about an hour,' she wrote on one occasion. 'The intervening days I ride over the moors.'

In March 1919, Katharine wrote to Caroline to congratulate her on attracting new members and to offer advice: 'Miss Whitty ought to be followed [up], perhaps you would get Miss Parsons to try and see her. I hope you are getting a little help!' While Katharine apparently remained on good terms with Rachel at this stage, she clearly thought her daughter could be giving more practical help. She complained to Caroline that the advertisements in local papers had brought no replies at all. 'I am going to be "at home" on Wednesday afternoons and see if anyone turns up,' she continued. 'Also am trying the *Yorkshire Post* for an article ... Miss Parsons was thinking of getting her article from *The Queen* reprinted as a leaflet ... I am expecting some girls from the aerodrome next Wednesday.'

The Queen magazine had recently published a piece by Rachel attacking the Restoration of Pre-War Practices Bill.[6] Rachel found it particularly galling that the new law was being introduced at a time of supposed liberation for women, just a few months after some of them had won the right to vote. She described the situation as 'a startling revelation of the powerlessness of a mere vote' and expressed her anger that 'Thousands of newly "enfranchised citizens" [were] spending weary and useless days waiting in long lines to sign their names and draw their unemployment pay.' It was not a question of class, or a disagreement between capital and labour, she wrote, 'for in the ranks of the demobilised women every class is included'. The government had not done enough to encourage the development of industries in which women could work and earn adequate pay, but the lion's share of the blame had to go to the intransigent trade unions. 'Let us hasten to turn our manufacture of war into industries of peace, our "Berlin bombers" into passenger aeroplanes, our shops where guns were made into factories for sewing machines – only let this be done speedily.'

Meanwhile, on 4 April, Caroline wrote to Katharine in northeast England about her recruitment work for the society: 'One girl who had been driving Lord Leverhulme for some time came to the office on Wednesday and asked whether we could help her to get into the Rolls-Royce Works at Derby, as she wanted to thoroughly understand the cars in order to eventually take entire charge of one.'

On the same day, Katharine reported her progress to Caroline: 'I had quite a busy afternoon on Wednesday at Windsor Terrace. About 20 people and all the press reps. They were a mixed lot of people and most of them poor types wanting jobs; but two or three better educated who will most likely join.' In an early reference to the involvement in the campaign of the irrepressible Viscountess Rhondda, Katharine wrote, 'A Miss Pym has arrived in Newcastle for Lady Rhonddha's Health Consultation Council and I expect she is doing the Industrial League too. I believe she is coming to see me.'

A week later Caroline was writing to Katharine about a visit from Laura Annie Willson, who wanted to retain the women workers she had employed at her firm in Halifax during the war, which would contravene the terms of the new parliamentary bill: 'Mrs Willson called here yesterday morning and told me of the trouble they are having with the men at Halifax. She seemed to think we might do something in the matter. She went on from here to see Miss Parsons and I have not seen her since.' Meanwhile, Lady Moir was asking members of the committee '[to] use their influence with Members of Parliament to vote for any amendment [to the bill] which it would be considered advisable to lay down in the interests of women engineers'.

Although Rachel had initially been rebuffed in her approach to the ASE, a letter from Katharine to Caroline on 14 May indicates that the union officials had been persuaded to agree to a meeting with the women – but it came to nothing. 'I am glad you went with the deputation to the Associated Society of Engineers,' wrote Katharine. She suggested emphasising at any later meeting that, as pointed out by the training schools, 'a short intensive training will turn out very useful women workers', and that a long apprenticeship was not necessary 'as their working years are generally much shorter than those of men'.

Another major preoccupation during this period was to identify job vacancies in engineering firms and to find suitable candidates from among the society's members to fill them, as revealed in further extracts from letters between the two women.[7]

Caroline to Katharine, 16 May 1919
I am very glad that you will go to Aberdeen [to interview job

candidates] if possible. I have received another letter from Miss Forbes [at Ferranti] . . . Mrs Willson called at the offices before the meeting yesterday and I think she will engage one of our members in the Manchester district.

Caroline, 19 May

I have today received a reply to the advertisement in *Engineering*. It is for a 'Lady who, in addition to doing tracing, must also be able to prepare arrangements of propelling machinery from dimensioned drawings of the various parts'. The salary offered is 35/– to 45/– [shillings] per week according to experience, and the name of the firm is the British Ljungström Marine Turbine Co. Ltd. I have written to several suitable members asking them to come to the office tomorrow.

Katharine, 21 May

I had a visit last week from Mr John Murray MP, who was in Newcastle making enquiries about women's employment for the Ministry of Labour . . . I enclose two adverts from *The Times*. It might be worth while for you to answer them. The Capable Lady ought to join us . . . I think if you are in a fix any time Lady Moir would come to the rescue.

Caroline, 23 May

It seems a great difficulty to get new members. Most of the people who come to the office now say they feel that engineering for women is practically hopeless and have in most cases decided to take up some other sort of work . . . Miss Edwards, who worked at the Gun Carriage department at Woolwich called this morning and left a short description of her work there . . . Would you please let me know how I should answer the letter from Miss Green of the National Council of Women.

Katharine, 24 May
I send you letters from Mrs O. Strachey [the feminist campaigner Ray Strachey]. I think the NEC [North East Coast Institution of Engineers and Shipbuilders] summer meeting will help our society. They are asking lots of women. Would you like to come? I will pay your ex. but cannot put you up . . . You could write to the Station Hotel for a room. I too cannot get members at present! but feel convinced there is a future.

Caroline, 26 May
The Women Welders certainly seem to have done wonderful work . . . Newspaper cuttings arrive here almost every day announcing the fact that you are reading a paper [at the NEC summer meeting] . . . I, too, believe there is a great future for the women engineers, but unfortunately many of the women who come here now seem to be lacking in imagination and incapable of looking ahead. There is one new member this morning . . . Also I called to see Miss Borthwick on Friday and she will probably join us this week. She took me over her workshops and told me some of her plans for the future. I think perhaps I shall be able to arrange for one of our members to go to her as Car Demonstrator.

Caroline, 28 May
You no doubt saw in yesterday's *Times* the text of the Restoration of Pre-War Practices (No. 3) Bill . . . I hear from Miss Scott (one of our members) today that she has obtained the post at the British Ljungström Marine Turbine Co. Ltd. This is, so far, the only result of the advertisement in *Engineering*.

Caroline, 29 May
Enclosed is a copy of the new Restoration of Pre-War Practices Bill. It has been very considerably modified. Mrs Willson wrote me this morning suggesting that I should consult with Miss Parsons and Lady Moir about it at once . . . Miss Parsons had an interview with Miss Key-Jones (of the Industrial League) yesterday at Upper Brook Street. There was some suggestion made at this interview that there should be a joint meeting of the WES, the Industrial League and Mrs Strachey's society, to consider an amendment to the Bill.

Katharine, 30 May
The Bill, no. 3, is worse than 2 as it spreads its tentacles over firms that have not been subject to these rules . . . In *The Times* of Thursday, 29th, Sir R. Horne [Minister of Labour] mentions in his speech a factory owned by a lady who would not dismiss her female employees and so gave great trouble. I wish we could find out who the lady is.

Caroline, 4 June
I thank you for yours . . . enclosing cheque value £25. I have taken my salary from this and have placed the balance of £8.6.8 [8 pounds 6 shillings and 8 pence] in the petty cash. The correspondence with [Lady Rhondda's] Industrial League is very interesting . . . Lady Moir is working very hard to get members interested in the Bill from our point of view.

Caroline, 11 June
In the *Daily Chronicle* of 5 June it mentioned that Lady Rhondda was telegraphing to the Prime Minister pressing for an amendment to the Bill to the effect that 'Whatever may be the regulations for the

employment of workers in the engineering trade, sex shall not disqualify a woman from employment.' It is evident from newspaper reports that Mrs Strachey's Society and Lady Rhondda's League are working together in this matter.

Caroline, 17 June

As I am a member of the London Society for Women's Service, I called at their offices last Friday and was fortunate in meeting Mrs Strachey [the society's head]. She introduced me to Miss Kelly, who is head of their Engineering Dept. This lady said that they had had an enquiry for a woman engineer who would be capable of organising the machinery and the labour in a factory which was making domestic utensils . . . Miss Parsons thinks that Miss Pullinger would be suitable for the post.

Katharine, 18 June

I had an adventure today. My car was going very badly for some days lately, however I risked going to address a Guide Meeting at Morpeth 20 miles. Had to leave my car in a ditch, got myself taken on by a passing car and arrived in time.

Caroline, 20 June

At the committee meeting yesterday morning, there was a good deal of discussion about the Restoration Bill, and it was decided to send a letter to each member of the House of Commons.

Caroline, 26 June

Mrs Willson called at the office yesterday and I discovered that she was the lady employer to whom Sir R. Horne referred in his speech as being the only employer who refused to dismiss her female employees. I have received quite a number of sympathetic replies from Members of Parliament this morning. There certainly seem to be quite a fair number of members who are capable of seeing our point of view.

Caroline, 27 June
I have received ten more acknowledgements from Members of Parliament this morning, including one from the Prime Minister, one from Sir Robert Horne, and one from Mr Winston Churchill.

A central figure in the campaign against the bill was Margaret Mackworth (née Haig Thomas), second Viscountess Rhondda, who had inherited the title in 1918 from her father, D. A. (David Alfred) Thomas, Viscount Rhondda of Llanwern. A former Liberal MP who had made a fortune from business, chiefly in coal, D. A. Thomas had served as food controller in Lloyd George's wartime coalition. He and Margaret, his only child, had achieved unwanted fame in 1915 as survivors of the German torpedo attack on the Cunard liner *Lusitania*, in which 1,198 people lost their lives.

Margaret had briefly studied history at Somerville College, Oxford, but left the university in 1905 after only two terms. Her subsequent marriage to Humphrey Mackworth, a Monmouthshire landowner, was not a success, and the couple were eventually divorced. Following the example of her mother, Sybil Haig, an active suffragist, Margaret found her true métier in politics and the fight for the female franchise. She took a leading role in the suffragette movement and, with Annie Kenney, helped to found the Newport branch of the Women's Social and Political Union.

Margaret, Sybil and Annie were among more than a quarter of a million women who took part in a pro-suffrage demonstration in

Hyde Park on 21 June 1908. Dubbed 'Women's Sunday', it brought together suffragettes from across Britain, and it was enlivened by the display of some 700 banners in purple, white and green – the first time that the distinctive trio of suffragette colours had been used in such a way. In her autobiography *This Was My World* Margaret described the effect of the day on her and her colleagues, echoing the sentiments that had been expressed on a different occasion by Caroline Haslett: 'It gave us a release of energy, it gave us that sense of being of some use in the scheme of things, without which no human being can live at peace. It made us feel that we were part of life, not just outside watching it.'[8] In November the same year, with Annie Kenney, Margaret spoke on behalf of the Women's Social and Political Union at Aberdare Liberal Club in her father's Merthyr Boroughs constituency.[9] The two women were shouted down by young men in the audience and pelted with herrings, tomatoes, cabbages and dead mice. When the protesters began to break chairs and smash windows, the women were forced to leave. It was the first of several such incidents.

In June 1913 Margaret was arrested for setting fire to a letterbox. She was tried, found guilty and fined. When she refused to pay the fine, she was sentenced to a month's imprisonment in Usk, where she went on hunger strike, later describing the experience as 'sheer taut misery'. Freed on licence after six days because of worries about her health, she did not have to return to prison because her fine was paid by an unknown person.

During the war – following the *Lusitania* catastrophe – Margaret Rhondda was appointed commissioner of Women's National Service in Wales and recruited a host of female volunteers to work in agriculture, where more labour was desperately needed to overcome food shortages – part of a nationwide initiative that led to the establishment in 1917 of the Women's Land Army. At a war service

Both images: Birr Castle Archives

Mary Parsons, Countess of Rosse (seated), was a pioneer of photography and used her knowledge of engineering and astronomy to help construct the Leviathan of Parsonstown.

Below: Katharine and Charles Parsons with their two children outside the family's first home, Elvaston Hall, County Durham, c.1890.

Birr Castle Archives

Built in the 1840s, the Leviathan still stands in the grounds of Birr Castle, County Offaly. Its six-foot-diameter speculum is displayed at London's Science Museum.

As a child, Rachel Parsons spent many hours with her father, Charles, in his workshop at Holeyn Hall, Wylam, Northumberland.

Tyne & Wear Archives & Museums

On 26 June 1897, a Review of the Fleet was held at Spithead, off Portsmouth on England's south coast, to celebrate the diamond jubilee of Queen Victoria. Charles Parsons' *Turbinia* astonished onlookers by arriving uninvited and far outpacing all other ships afloat.

Katharine Parsons championed the employment of women in engineering and shipbuilding during the Great War.

Rachel Parsons was the first president of the Women's Engineering Society; in 1923, when this photograph was taken, she stood for Parliament in the Lancashire seat of Ince.

© Illustrated London News Ltd / Mary Evans

Courtesy of Joanna Stoddart

IET Archives

Top: Laura Annie Willson (pictured with husband and children) ran a munitions factory in Halifax, Yorkshire, which was staffed largely by women.

Above: Margaret Moir, who liked to call herself 'an engineer by marriage'.

Right: Eleanor Shelley-Rolls (centre) was the sister of car magnate Charles Rolls (right) and joined him in many balloon flights.

IET Archives

Left: Caroline Haslett set up the Electrical Association for Women and supported the creation of Atalanta Ltd, a women-only engineering business.

Bottom: Margaret Partridge (third from left) employed only women at her electrical supply firm in Devon. They included Margaret Rowbotham (far left) and Beatrice Shilling (second from left). On the right of the picture is Caroline Haslett.

IET Archives

Women's Engineering Society and IET Archives

Above: Viscountess Rhondda, founder of the Women's Political and Industrial League.

Below: Verena Holmes (left) and Claudia Parsons, two of the early 'lady engineers' at Loughborough Technical Institute.

Women's Engineering Society and IET Archives

Women's Engineering Society and IET Archives

POWER STATION
· EQUIPMENT ·

Reaction Steam Turbines·Alternators
Condensing Plant · Reduction Gear
Turbo-Blowers and Compressors

GIRLS BUILDING UP MICANITE INSULATING SHEETS.

C.A.Parsons & C⁰., Lᵀᴰ..
Heaton Works
NEWCASTLE-ON-TYNE
LONDON OFFICE: 56, VICTORIA ST, S.W.

During the 1914–18 war, women made up a large proportion of the workforce at the Heaton Works of C. A. Parsons and Company in Newcastle.

exhibition in Cardiff in April 1918, she gave a speech during 'the greatest crisis in our country's history' that included a rousing call for volunteers to join the Women's Army Auxiliary Corps (WAAC), the Women's Royal Naval Service (WRNS) and the Women's Royal Air Force (WRAF).

This and other bold interventions had led to Margaret's appointment as chief controller of women's recruitment at the Ministry of National Service in London.[10] Her assistant in this role was Helen Archdale, with whom she would embark on a long-term love affair. Margaret also helped to guide government policy on female employment, arguing that the war had given women the confidence to undertake the most difficult and challenging tasks. She sat on the Women's Advisory Committee at the Ministry of Reconstruction from its formation in 1917 and set up the Women's Political and Industrial League in 1919 to lobby for equal employment opportunities. From the very beginning, she was a stalwart and influential advocate for the Women's Engineering Society.

Advantages of birth, resolute determination and an indomitable and engaging personality combined to put Margaret Mackworth in a unique position.[11] On the death of her father, Viscount Rhondda, on 3 July 1918, she gained not only his title (as he himself had insisted should happen when he accepted the honour earlier that year), but also his coalmining, shipping, newspaper and other interests, making her a very rich woman. Having inherited twenty-eight directorships from her father, she sat on thirty-three company boards throughout her life and chaired seven of them. In 1926 she became the first female president of the Institute of Directors, and the following year she was described in the *New York Tribune* as 'the foremost woman of business in the British Empire'.[12]

Lady Rhondda had her own battle to fight, however. When she

tried to take her father's seat in the House of Lords, citing the Sex Disqualification (Removal) Act of 1919, which enabled women to exercise 'any public office', her application was ultimately rejected by the Committee of Privileges.[13] She spent the rest of her life trying to put right this injustice, but it was not until August 1958, less than a month after her death, that women were allowed to sit in the House of Lords for the first time, following the passage of the Life Peerages Act.

In spite of the best efforts of sympathetic MPs and other influential supporters of the women engineers, including Lady Rhondda and Ray Strachey, the Restoration of Pre-War Practices Bill passed through all its parliamentary stages on 23 July 1919. 'There were quite a number of women present at the debate,' reported Caroline to Katharine. 'Our society was represented by Miss Parsons, Mrs Willson, Miss Selby and myself.' It was not long before Smith, Barker and Willson, Laura Annie Willson's firm, were successfully prosecuted under the Act, and their subsequent appeal was rejected at a tribunal hearing, with the result that they were obliged to dismiss all their female workers and pay a large fine.

Although the passing of the Act represented a serious setback for the society, the campaign to oppose it had brought together a group of disparate women and united them behind a common purpose, making them more determined than ever to secure jobs for women in engineering. Their position was encapsulated in a resolution by Lady Parsons at the society's first annual general meeting,[14] which was carried unanimously: 'This society deprecates the continued exclusion of women from training and employment in many productive industries, and calls upon all leaders of industry and trade unions to act in the best interests of the nation by uniting with women in overcoming all artificial barriers to progress and development in production.'

The attempt to break down the doors of the engineering institutions had more success. At the start, none of the institutions except the Electrical Engineers was open to women, so Caroline Haslett wrote to ask if they would change their admissions policy. At first they all refused. However, when invited to send a representative to sit on the council of the Women's Engineering Society, the institutions gradually fell into line and, once the precedent had been established, continued to send someone every year. 'I've always tried to get the co-operation of men engineers because I thought by advising and helping us they would get interested in us and want us to succeed,' Caroline told the writer Crystal Eastman.[15] The plan worked well. Thanks to Caroline's persistence, within a few years, there were female members of the Institutions of Electrical Engineers, Mechanical Engineers, Automobile Engineers, Marine Engineers and Naval Architects, as well as of the Institute of Metals and the North East Coast Institution of Engineers and Shipbuilders.

Energised by the fight, powerful women such as Margaret Rhondda were determined not to be silenced. In May 1920 Lady Rhondda founded a weekly political and literary review called *Time and Tide*, with an all-women board and Helen Archdale as editor. It championed left-wing and feminist causes and became the mouthpiece of Rhondda's Six Point Group, which sought equality between women and men through changes in the law.[16] The original six aims of the group were superseded by a campaign demanding improvement in six areas of life where greater equality was required: political, occupational, moral, social, economic and legal. Meanwhile, *Time and Tide* published work and articles by many of the leading literary figures of the day, including Vera Brittain, Winifred Holtby, Virginia Woolf, D. H. Lawrence, Robert Graves, Rebecca West and George Bernard Shaw, along with contributions from the first women MPs. Lady Rhondda took over herself as editor in 1926 and remained in post until her death thirty-two years later, having spent an estimated £250,000 of her own money (equivalent to more than £10 million today) in keeping the magazine afloat.[15]

On 1 December 1919, a dynamic, witty and fabulously rich American expatriate by the name of Nancy Astor became the first woman to take her seat in the House of Commons, having won a by-election for the Conservatives in her husband's former constituency of Plymouth Sutton. The inheritance of a viscountcy on the death of his father had obliged Waldorf Astor to give up the parliamentary seat he had occupied for nine years and, reluctantly, to join the House of Lords. Nancy, who had energetically supported her husband throughout his parliamentary career, was soon selected to replace him. Although she had no history of support for female suffrage, Nancy saw her victory as a triumph for women. For those campaigning to improve the prospects of the female sex, its symbolic importance was beyond measure.

Caroline Haslett wrote to Lady Astor on 2 December to congratulate her on behalf of the Women's Engineering Society.[18] 'My committee fully realise and appreciate the great significance of your success, and the consequent effect on the status of women generally,' she said. 'This society has been formed in the interests of women who wish to take up engineering as a trade or profession, and was started nearly a year ago by the Hon. Lady Parsons and Miss Parsons, with the sympathetic support of many prominent engineers.' Lady Astor replied that she was 'much interested' in the society and its members, and issued an invitation – the first of several – to a party at 4 St James's Square, her palatial London home. However, when asked to preside at the opening of a club for women engineers at 46 Dover Street, she politely declined, pleading a prior engagement.

Despite her earlier lack of involvement in feminist activities, Nancy

Astor worked hard to promote the advancement of women, even advocating the establishment of a women-only political party. She tried to bridge the gap between feminists and anti-feminist male politicians by arranging monthly get-togethers at St James's Square – sometimes attended by Rachel Parsons – as an alternative to formal confrontations, but these parties acquired a social cachet that was detrimental to their original purpose. Some feminists complained that the events had become too frivolous because they were swamped by society women. However, the support of Nancy Astor, Margaret Rhondda and other leading figures in the political and business world did much to raise the profile of the Women's Engineering Society and bring its campaign to the attention of a national audience.

SIX

Virgin Huntresses

During the First World War, Loughborough Technical Institute in Leicestershire had been an instructional factory for the Ministry of Munitions, training more than 2,300 people, most of them women, some highly skilled. Set up in 1909 to provide further education for local people, the institute's transformation into a place of national importance was largely due to the entrepreneurial vision and determination of Dr Herbert Schofield, principal of the college for thirty-five years, from 1915 to 1950. Schofield had no doubt about the importance of training women as well as men in engineering skills. After the war he continued his pioneering educational work, as well as encouraging the formation of Atalanta Ltd, the first engineering company run by women for the employment of women.

One of the college's first recruits after the war was Claudia Parsons. Born in 1900, Claudia had been too young to enter a munitions factory but, determined to pursue her early interest in technology, she took a course at a technical college in Guildford, near her home in Surrey, on 'the auto-cyle engine', passing the final exam with flying colours. The diplomat Sir Anthony Parsons, Claudia's cousin, described her as 'obviously a brilliant mechanic and craftswoman from her early teens'.[1] In her autobiography, *Century Story*, Claudia remembers reading an article in *The Times* telling of 'a Woman's Engineering Society that had been inaugurated under the auspices of Lady Parsons, wife of the inventor of the turbine, and Lady Shelley-Rolls'.[2] (Claudia believed that she may have been related to the other Parsons family, but the link is not clear.)

Claudia and her mother went to see Caroline Haslett, who told them about the college at Loughborough, which, as a continuation of the training begun during the war, was offering a few places for women on a three-year diploma course. After a first year of general engineering, students could specialise in either the civil, electrical or automobile field. Practical experience in the workshop, foundry and drawing office would be available throughout the course.

It was a pivotal moment. In an early triumph for the engineering society, Claudia Parsons was invited to join Loughborough later that year. She was accompanied by Dorothea Travers, a friend from Guildford Technical College who turned out to be a brilliant mathematician, and another female student, Patience Erskine. The three girls were accepted to study engineering alongside 300 boys; dubbed 'the lady engineers', they were initially the focus of suspicion and incredulity. For Claudia, however, it was the start of a thrilling voyage of adventure, which would eventually take her to all corners of the earth. For Caroline Haslett, it was an early instance of her effectiveness at persuading colleges and institutes to open their doors to women trainees.

'Our trouser overalls excited much attention,' said Claudia, recalling the young women's time in the Loughborough workshops, 'but we were forced to wear terrible caps in the machine shops on account of the dangerous belting from the overhead drive.'[3] A woman in long trousers had been a rare sight before the war, although a fashion had been imported from the United States for wearing knickerbockers – baggy-kneed short trousers that were ideal for cycling, motorcycling or playing sports such as golf. Women who sought greater political and social freedoms tended also to reject traditional restrictions in their physical activities and, as a reflection of this, female horse riders had taken up wearing breeches and sitting astride their mounts rather than riding side-saddle in skirts. But it was wartime munitions work that brought about the biggest change in female attire. When moving around factories and shipyards full of active machinery, a pair of long, straight-legged trousers was often the only safe option.

While inspecting women workers aboard a battleship, L. K. Yates, author of a survey of female workers for the Ministry of Munitions, was amazed by how quickly they moved up and down steep ladders, while she proceeded cautiously step by step – until she noticed that they were all dressed in trouser suits with tight-fitting caps: 'The suits, of blue drill for the supervisors, and of a similar material in brown for the labourers, were made with a short tunic, and the trousers were buckled securely at the ankle.'[4] It was an outfit that allowed the workers perfect freedom of movement in confined spaces. Some women also took to cutting their hair short for reasons of safety and practicality. Short hair remained fashionable in the 1920s and 1930s, but women in long trousers again became a rarity, until the outbreak of the 1939–45 war.

Claudia Parsons was disappointed to find that there was no direct practical work on car engines at Loughborough; all they had to play with was a large working model of a diesel engine. To keep herself amused, she joined several college societies and spent her spare time acting, dancing and debating, as well as learning to swim, playing tennis and writing for the college magazine, *The Limit*. A favourite diversion for many of the students was taking part in motorcycle rallies. 'Dorothea had bought a motorcyle and sidecar, which much facilitated our transport but failed dismally on test hills,' she said.[5] Dorothea later replaced her motorcycle with a Morgan two-seater 'in which one lay almost prone, not a yard from the ground'. Most unusually for women at the time, the two of them went off in the Morgan on long camping tours around Britain, and discovered that dealing with the various mechanical problems that arose with the vehicle was more instructive than some of their college lectures.

In *Century Story*, Claudia records the arrival at Loughborough in 1920 of Verena Holmes, another 'lady engineer', remarking that, in contrast to her and Dorothea's more light-hearted approach, '[Verena's] career was one of single-minded, indomitable purpose'. The new student had gained a footing in the engineering world through wartime munitions work. Having learned how to build wooden propellers at the Integral Propeller Company in Hendon, and attended evening classes at Shoreditch Technical Institute, Verena had been taken on as a works supervisor by Ruston and Hornsby in Lincoln. The company manufactured aircraft, including the Sopwith Camel, as well as some of the very first military tanks. There she was responsible for the selection, control and welfare of 1,500 female employees. She later managed to secure an apprenticeship at the firm, ending up in the drawing office, which was, in Claudia's words, 'the only safe refuge from the unions intent on ousting all women munitions workers'. Verena had come to Loughborough to get wider technical experience and she graduated in 1922 with a BSc in Engineering, gained extramurally from London University, while Claudia and Dorothea were both awarded second-class diplomas in Auto-engineering.

Claudia and Verena became lifelong friends and both remained active members of the Women's Engineering Society (of which Verena was president in 1930 and 1931), but their careers took very different directions. Having abandoned hope of working in engineering, given the scarcity of jobs in the early 1920s, Claudia indulged her passion for automobiles by becoming a chauffeur-companion, in which role she drove wealthy clients across Europe, the Far East, India and the United States.[6] In 1938 she bought a Studebaker car in Delhi and called it Baker – a name that, in her words, 'was somehow expressive of its plodding advance that never exceeded forty miles an hour'. Accompanied by the American anthropologist Kilton Stewart, she drove Baker through India, Afghanistan, Iran, Iraq, Syria, Palestine, Egypt, Libya and Tunisia, crossing the Mediterranean to Marseilles, from where she continued across France and home to Britain.

Claudia Parsons is recognised as being the first woman to circumnavigate the world in a car. She was described by her sister Betty as '[someone] who had broken the ice of convention that held women down to certain jobs but denied them others, and at a time when to the majority of people the world was unknown'.[7] Loughborough University, as it now is, holds an annual Claudia Parsons Memorial Lecture in honour of its first female student of engineering.

Another pioneer to make her mark in the automobile world was Dorothée Pullinger, who had come to prominence through her exemplary management of the 7,000 women workers at Vickers in Barrow-in-Furness. After the war, Dorothée returned to Arrol-Johnston in Dumfries, the parent company of the Tongland enterprise, and was appointed to the board of directors.[8] She took over the running at Tongland of Galloway Motors Ltd, as it had become, and its predominantly female workforce.

In October 1920 the company started to market a new product – a 10.5 hp two-seater coupé with a collapsible head called the Galloway. According to a contemporary article in *The Motor* magazine, both the gear-change lever and the handbrake lever were mounted centrally – rather than next to the driver's door, which had been a problem for drivers wearing skirts – and the footbrake was applied by depressing the middle of the three pedals, with the accelerator on the left and the clutch on the right. The steering wheel was lower and the driver's seat higher than in earlier cars, all of which had been made for male motorists. 'A wide door is fitted to each side of the body, enabling either driver or passenger to leave the car without disturbing the other,' reported *The Motor*, 'while the body being mounted very low on the chassis renders it easy of access.' Designed by Dorothée herself with female drivers in mind, the relatively light vehicle generated national publicity, becoming known as the 'car made by ladies for their own sex'.

In 1920 Dorothée Pullinger was one of two women admitted to the Institution of Automobile Engineers. The other was the mysterious but powerful Cleone Griff, who played a leading role in the development of the Women's Engineering Society in the 1920s. For unknown reasons, she used a variety of names, including, in her youth, Cleone de Heveningham Benest, under which she was recognised as a pioneering female motorist with her own cars, which she maintained in her home workshop at Ryde in the Isle of Wight.[9]

Before the 1914–18 war, Cleone had gained certificates from the London City and Guilds in motorcar engineering and passed the Royal Automobile Club's examinations in driving and car mechanics. In 1915 she set up a business as a consultant engineer, offering advice on automobiles and electrical installations. Her garage workshop for female motorists at Dover Street in Mayfair, next to the headquarters of the Women's Engineering Society, did mechanical repairs and offered courses in motor mechanics. During the war she was also employed as an aircraft engine inspector, working for, among others, Vickers in Birmingham. She was admitted to membership of the Birmingham Metallurgical Society, the Iron and Steel Institute and the Cast Iron Research Association.

In 1922 Cleone Griff set up in Birmingham the Stainless Steel and Non-Corrosive Metals Company, which made small ornamental items, railway-carriage fittings and tin openers. This enterprise, managed by and employing women, attracted wide press coverage but was not a financial success and closed in 1925. Cleone had joined the Women's Engineering Society in 1920 and became a committee chair, remaining active in the society until 1928. She wrote regularly for *Woman Engineer* on motoring and aviation, and broadcast six talks on BBC Radio, aimed at housewives, on the use of electricity in the home and other aspects of engineering.

To demonstrate the Galloway car's reliability and other attributes, Dorothée Pullinger took up rally driving and won awards in the car around Britain, sometimes breaking lap records, though she had to overcome entrenched opposition to women drivers.[10] When she appeared on the Galloway stand at the Scottish Motor Show, some of the men refused to speak to her. In a letter of 1922 published in *Motor World* magazine, Dorothée pointed out that female owner-drivers were growing fast in number and influence. 'These women will naturally look for a car which they will have no difficulty in handling with the same intimate familiarity as they would their sewing machines,' she wrote. 'A car which a woman can drive throughout the Scottish six-day trials, or for that matter any other event, is likely to prove extremely attractive.'[11]

Regarded as an intrepid and skilful driver, Dorothée won the gold medal in the Birmingham and Sutton Coldfield Vesey Cup and excelled herself at the Scottish Six Days' Trial in 1924. However, like other small car manufacturers, the Galloway company was badly affected by the economic downturn in the early 1920s; in March 1922 the factory closed and production was transferred to Arrol-Johnston's Heathhall works in Dumfries, where it continued until 1928.

In 1924 Dorothée married Edward Martin, a ship's purser, and the couple moved to London. She continued to make good use of her engineering and management skills by setting up the White Service Laundry Company in Croydon, Surrey.[12] The laundry had its own power station and used the latest American equipment, eventually expanding to seventeen shops. During the Second World War, Dorothée advised the Nuffield organisation, founded by the car magnate William Morris, on the employment of women workers, and she was the only woman invited to sit on the Industrial Panel of the Ministry of Production.

Meanwhile, Verena Holmes, an altogether more serious and less flamboyant character than her Loughborough friend Claudia Parsons, went on to become a star of the engineering world. In 1924 she was made an associate member of both the Institution of Mechanical Engineers and the Institution of Marine Engineers.

Throughout her career Verena produced a steady stream of inventions, of which seventeen were patented, including a pneumothorax apparatus, used in the treatment of tuberculosis, a surgeon's headlamp, and a poppet valve for steam locomotives.[13] In the early 1920s she worked with various consultant engineers before setting up her own design consultancy. Through her work with the North British Locomotive Company from 1928 to 1931 she became the first woman admitted to the Institution of Locomotive Engineers. In what she said was the happiest time of her life, Verena was employed from 1932 to 1939 by Research Engineers Ltd, where she became expert on a wide range of engines – marine and locomotive engines, oil, diesel and internal combustion engines – and in 1937 she also gained her private pilot's licence.

It was during the Second World War, however, that Verena would really come into her own. She not only worked on devices for improving the effectiveness of torpedoes and other equipment for the Admiralty, including the complex system used by Lord Mountbatten to ensure that ships kept to prearranged positions during a U-boat attack, but also, with Caroline Haslett, set up a highly successful scheme to train women for the munitions factories. In 1940 she became an adviser to Ernest Bevin, Minister of Labour, on the training of munition workers. After the war, in 1946, she co-founded Holmes and Leather – a company employing only women – to make paper-shearing machines, and other Holmes inventions, in Gillingham, Kent. The Institution of Mechanical Engineers presents an annual Verena Holmes Award in recognition of its first female member.

The idea of an all-women industrial enterprise was not new. Twenty-five years earlier, in February 1921, *The Times* had carried a story about an engineering company set up specifically to employ women and financed mostly by women – of the fifty shareholders, only five were men. Along with Lady Parsons, Lady Shelley-Rolls and Caroline Haslett, the directors included Herbert Schofield, principal of Loughborough Technical College. Also on the board were Annette Ashberry and Dora Turner – both of whom had been employed at the Tongland works during the war – who were appointed, respectively, works manager and secretary. The firm was called Atalanta Ltd, after a character in Greek mythology. Atalanta was a swift-footed huntress who took an oath of virginity and refused to behave in the way women were expected to behave – but eventually, after the intervention of the goddess Aphrodite, she was tricked into marriage.

'The works [is] at Loughborough, where the girls can attend the technical college for further instruction,' reported *The Times*.[14] '[It was] opened at the beginning of the year with a small plant which the girls put in themselves, fixing their own belting and pulley drives. They are . . . engaged on a new invention, a type of atomiser used [in oil-fuelled boilers], and they are also working on bottling machinery.'

Ever since the Restoration of Pre-War Practices Act had made it virtually impossible for women to obtain jobs in traditional engineering shops, the Women's Engineering Society had been talking about the formation of a female-only engineering company. An early supporter was the shipbuilder Sir George Hunter, chairman of Swan Hunter & Wigham Richardson on Tyneside, who wrote to the society in February 1920 to say that 'the capital would doubtless be found [for such a venture] and he would be willing to assist in that direction'.[15] The main difficulty, according to Katherine Parsons, who had led the talks with Hunter, was to know which articles to manufacture. To avoid opposition from the trade unions, the products chosen had to be made from start to finish in the women's factory, and they had to be things that were not already being manufactured in Britain. Typewriters and pianos had been suggested, according to Katharine. As time went on, the suspicion grew that Hunter was simply interested in employing women as cheap labour, and the association with him was dropped.

Among the locations considered for Atalanta Ltd was the Tongland factory in Kirkcudbright, where Madge Rowbotham was works supervisor. When Caroline sought the support of William Beardmore, the Clydeside industrialist who had financed Tongland, he offered to sell the factory to the Women's Engineering Society, but the idea was rejected by Katharine. 'I don't think buying Kirkcudbright would be a business proposition,' she wrote to Caroline in April 1920. 'It is losing money all the time and if it doesn't find its way with the Beardmore firm behind it, how could we make it pay?'

It emerged two months later that Herbert Schofield at Loughborough Technical College was prepared to support a scheme for a women-only factory. The impetus for the Loughborough initiative had come from a small group of Tongland workers, led by Annette Ashberry, who had told Caroline Haslett that the outlook at Kirkcudbright was so discouraging that 'some of the girls feel that unless they can see some prospect ahead they will have to give up engineering altogether'. The plan was to secure a contract from a large firm for the manufacture of machine parts and to create a limited liability company in which each of the women would hold shares.

Woman Engineer reported on the bold venture in an editorial in its September 1920 issue: 'Seeing no scope for their activities, and having the natural road to success barred to them, these women have decided to risk their all and to establish an engineering works where there will be absolute freedom for them to use the ability and skill which they possess.' Publicity for Atalanta was useful in stimulating interest in the engineering society. 'I have been perfectly inundated with letters during the last few days from all sorts of people,' wrote Caroline to Katharine following the announcement.

The premises at Loughborough were primitive and there was no electricity supply, but the eight women who were employed there in 1921 had a successful first year, taking on subcontracts from larger companies as planned. 'We commenced work somewhat ambitiously in Loughborough with a moderate-sized machine shop, a fitting shop and an office,' recalled Caroline later, itemising the limited machinery at the women's disposal: 'two Smith, Barker and Willson lathes, one 8½ inch and one 6½ inch, and three other smaller lathes, one Parkinson milling machine, one drilling machine, one hacksaw, one grinder, a small forge and anvil'.[16]

Although the quality of Atalanta's output was never in doubt, the company faced financial challenges from the start – and it soon became harder to secure contracts. 'During 1922, when the trade depression was at its worst, we struggled to keep the works going,' wrote Katharine Parsons in 1923 in a report to directors. 'While overhead expenses continued as high as before, we could retain the services of only two workers, owing to the small amount of work obtainable.' At the end of 1922, it was decided to move the operation to London, where smaller and cheaper premises were found in Fulham. At first, prospects seemed brighter. 'More work has been done in the last eight months than in any equal period previously,' wrote Katharine in her 1923 report, but Atalanta's future was far from assured. 'The most interesting order taken recently was for a sample Stream Line Filter, for Dr Hele-Shaw, followed by an order for one dozen to be exhibited at the Shipping, Engineering and Machinery Exhibition at Olympia.'

The firm struggled on, and by 1925 it was doing well enough to move to larger and better-equipped accommodation in Brixton. Annette Ashberry gave a talk to the Incorporated Society of Engineers about Atalanta and its products, including the Atalanta Screwdriver, which was advertised as allowing the user 'to reach screws and nuts in difficult corners'.[17] The screwdriver, the Atalanta Hand Chuck and the Atalanta Drilling Jig were exhibited at the British Industries Fair in 1929. At a national Engineering Exhibition in 1931, press interest was aroused by an invention that 'may [save] lives of airmen whose machines have crashed and burst into flames'. The machine resembled a giant pair of tongs and its purpose was, in the words of the *Derby Daily Telegraph*, 'to dismember a burning machine in a matter of moments, so that the passengers may be extricated'. In spite of these innovative products, it was not long afterwards that Atalanta Ltd was wound up, as the depression of the 1930s took hold. 'Women are subject to the same economic laws as men and we were beaten after a most gallant fight,' said Caroline Haslett later.

The disappointment at Tongland, where the engineering university for women envisaged by T. C. Pullinger had failed to materialise,

prompted Madge Rowbotham, its erstwhile supervisor, to look elsewhere for fulfilling employment. In 1920, following the rejection of
her application to join the Institution of Mechanical Engineers, she
was appointed assistant works manager at Swainson Pump Company,
which operated from the site of a well-established foundry in
Newcastle upon Tyne. The company had been set up by Robert
Swainson with financial help from Katharine Parsons on the condition that he employ only women to assemble the pumps and a
woman as an assistant manager, but Madge stayed there for just a
year. After studying laundry management under Ethel Jayne, propri-
etor of the Little Laundries network, followed by a second brief spell
in education, in 1927 she joined an electrical engineering company
in Devon. Like Atalanta, the Swainson Pump Company fell victim to
the economic depression and, having failed to live up to expectations,
went into liquidation in 1928.

In addition to the daily business of running the Women's
Engineering Society and increasing its membership, Caroline Haslett
was preoccupied by the problems facing industry and women's position within it. She attended a conference in Oxford in April 1920
about the need to 'humanise' industry and came away with the opinion that, if women hoped to take a greater share in the industrial
world, they must strive to understand the great changes in processes
and outlook that were under way. 'We, as an industrial organisation,
should attempt to do a little clear thinking with regard to these matters and not merely wait for public opinion to be formed without
our point of view,' she wrote to Katharine, and proposed to Rachel
that the next general meeting of the society should include a debate
on the subject.

Later that year, Caroline and other society members gave evidence
to the parliamentary committee examining the Women, Young

Persons and Children (Employment) Bill about plans to divide the working day into two shifts of up to eight hours (in place of one long shift of twelve hours or more), which would necessitate working up to 10 p.m. There was enthusiasm for the two-shift system, for, in the words of Mary Selby, the honorary secretary, it would give women 'shorter periods of work, and longer and more varied periods of leisure in daylight, to say nothing of the gain to production and the community consequent on the employment of efficient woman labour working under good conditions'.[18]

There was strong opposition, however, to a proposed Labour Party amendment that would prohibit women and young people from being employed after 8 p.m. – which would have made the two-shift system unworkable – and there was also indignation that women should be included in the legislation at all, since it put them in the same class as young persons and children. In Katharine's view, 'Women ought not to be prohibited from night work in industry any more than in domestic service, nursing, etc.' In the event, the society's position prevailed and the Employment Act 1920 made provision for women to work up to 10 p.m., but the controversy over women doing night work continued and came to a head again in the late 1920s.

In more light-hearted mood, and to raise awareness of the frustration and exhaustion caused by the endless domestic routine of cooking and cleaning, in 1921 Caroline Haslett organised a competition to identify items that women considered necessary to the more efficient working of the home. The entries included improvements in saucepans such as a 'quick-boiling lid'; a 'run-about jane', which could be used either as a dinner trolley or as a box for carrying coals; and a floor-cleaning and polishing machine that could be worked from a stooping rather than a kneeling position. Another entry combined the uses of a dustpan and rubbish basket. There was a gas high-pressure boiler that could be used as a cooking stove as well as for heating water. First prize in the engineering and mechanical devices section was won by Annette Ashberry for her dishwashing machine worked by a hand pump. Another prizewinner was an 'ideal' oven that could be used not only to cook food but also as a food warmer and a cool cupboard.

From the start, the Women's Engineering Society was a broad church, as it remains today. In the early 1920s a very different kind of star – as far removed as can be imagined from the designer of the 'run-about jane' – was the first female seagoing engineer, Victoria Drummond. When she made her debut appearance in *Woman Engineer*, in 1921, Victoria had recently completed a five-year apprenticeship at the Caledon Shipbuilding & Engineering Company in Dundee and was described a fully qualified 'journeyman'.

The reason for Victoria Drummond's appearance in the journal was that, to much excitement, she had recently become the first woman admitted to the Institute of Marine Engineers. Victoria acquired her second engineer's certificate in December 1926, having completed five trips on the Blue Funnel liner SS *Anchises* to Australia and China. 'She has been a wonder to us,' said one of her colleagues. 'She has done everything that could be expected of a man engineer.'[19]

In 1927 Victoria joined the British India Company and sailed as fifth engineer to Africa on SS *Mulbera*, followed by four voyages to India, but she left the company in December 1928. During the economic depression of the 1930s there was little demand for marine engineers and Victoria took a back seat, but – like so many other pioneering women of her generation – she came into her own again during the Second World War, displaying brilliant seamanship aboard the Panamanian cargo ship *Bonita* during a terrifying raid by the Luftwaffe in the North Atlantic.[20] Her courage and skill on that occasion earned her the award of MBE and the Lloyd's

War Medal for Bravery at Sea. During the course of her career, Victoria Drummond completed the examination to become a chief engineer thirty-seven times – but each time she was judged to have failed.

SEVEN

———•—

Political Longings

In the very early days of the Women's Engineering Society, Rachel Parsons was constantly at the centre of events. It was her imagination and energy, backed by her mother's more mature wisdom, that had been the catalyst for the society's creation. She had written articles in the press, addressed rallies and lobbied in high places. As president, she had infused the society's meetings with her ideas and boldly championed its aims in the public arena. But, while inspiring admiration and affection in most of those around her, Rachel had an enigmatic and elusive element to her character that sometimes alienated people.

'Rachel was no ordinary woman, blessed with simple feminine tastes and domestic ability,' wrote Anne Parsons, Countess of Rosse, in *The Times* after Rachel's death in 1956.[1] 'The daughter of one of the greatest scientific geniuses that this country has ever produced, she inherited much of her father's brilliant technical brain and volcanic temperament.'

It was this 'volcanic temperament' that got Rachel into trouble, leading to rows and disagreements with family and friends – but it was also at the root of her ambition and her determination to overcome obstacles to success. Given the expectations about women's behaviour at the time, it must also have made it hard for her to form relationships with men. Anne Rosse, the wife of Rachel's cousin Michael, believed that the paradoxical forces at work during Rachel's youth accounted in large part for her rebelliousness and unconventionality. 'Many still remember the lovable, headstrong and attractive girl, brimming over with enthusiasm and with her father's desire to achieve,' wrote Anne Rosse. 'They remember her uncommon ability to grasp mathematics . . . but they also remember her unusual upbringing, in an atmosphere dedicated to and absorbed in science and inventions, mixed with the Victorian restricting decorum that forbade the outlet of a career to such a girl.'[2]

Rachel's unpredictability was evident in her dealings with the engineering society. Having assiduously attended its first deliberations, she was unaccountably absent from two meetings that took place in January 1920, although she did send a message urging members to attend a mass women's rally at the Albert Hall organised by the League of Nations Union. She was absent again from the council meeting in April, having telephoned her apologies at the last minute.[3] Her intermittent attendance meant that her mother, Katharine, often took the chair – and Katharine revealed her impatience with Rachel in some of her letters to Caroline Haslett. After the first four issues of the quarterly *Woman Engineer*, Rachel was no longer described as president, and Katharine formally took over this role in mid-1922.

It may have been pure coincidence that January 1920 was also the month in which forty-one-year-old Alex Law, the Heaton director who had befriended the Parsons family, announced his engagement to twenty-six-year-old Isabel Marshall – but, if Rachel had had an earlier alliance with Alex, she would no doubt have been distracted by this development. Around the same time, a major falling-out with his employer had led to Alex's abrupt departure from the Parsons company. The official version of the story, recounted by Gordon Bedford in his memoir,[4] was that, after the war, the Heaton works became very busy in response to a surge in demand for power station plant, while Parsons Marine Works at Wallsend was quiet, since the need for naval vessels had evaporated. Charles wanted to transfer some of the surplus contracts at Heaton to Wallsend, but Alex, managing director at Heaton, strongly opposed the plan, claiming that Heaton could easily cope with the work. In the event, Alex resigned from C. A. Parsons & Company and moved to Rugby to join the English Electric Company, where he would become general manager in 1926 and chief engineer in 1930.

According to a few letters that have survived from this period, the liaison between Alex and Isabel took place under something of a cloud.[5] There is a suggestion that Isabel's father may not have approved of the match, but a letter of 14 November 1919 from Alex to Isabel hints at something more problematical, referring as it does to 'our rather queer circumstances'. He says in the letter, 'I promise that if – as may happen – I have arranged to do anything else and can't well get out of it, then I will let you know and not feel myself bound to you.' Although there is no documentary evidence to this effect, it is possible that Alex had made a commitment elsewhere, perhaps relating to Rachel, that he feared he could not escape – and that this may have had a bearing on his row with Charles Parsons.

However, the loving couple were not to be thwarted. Two months later, on 13 January, Alex wrote again to Isabel: 'I've been lonely for you all these years even before I knew you.' It was a fortnight before the announcement of their impending marriage, which took place on 10 June at the cathedral church of St Nicholas in Newcastle.

Tensions within the Parsons family itself had been growing since the loss of Rachel's brother during the closing months of the war. On 6 May 1918, six months before the Armistice, Katharine Parsons had sat down in her study at Ray Demesne to perform one of the saddest tasks of her life – composing a death notice to a woman who had done much to nurture her children during their early years. 'Dear Nannie, I know you will be grieved to hear that Major Algy was killed in action on 26 April. The wire came on Sunday. It is a terrible blow to us, though of course we knew it might come any day.'

Algernon George Parsons, usually known as Tommy, had fallen in battle while serving with the Royal Field Artillery near Ypres in Belgium and died soon afterwards, aged thirty-one. He was buried at the nearby Lijssenthoek Military Cemetery. Tommy had returned to the front only a few weeks earlier, having been invalided home the previous autumn. 'I am glad to look back on the time he spent with us lately when he was wounded. He would not have a home job,' wrote Katharine. 'Sir Charles happened to be here, lucky for me. We both feel it terribly.'

The consequence of Tommy's death was felt no less keenly by Rachel, who had assumed her younger brother's mantle during the war as a director at Heaton. With less than two years between their ages, Rachel and Tommy had been inseparable as children, free to roam the fields and woods at Ryton and Wylam, their home villages in the Tyne valley. Together they would conspire in bold adventures, often influenced or led astray by their father's inventions, from the steam-driven pram to the miniature flying machine.

Both fiercely independent by nature, sister and brother had grown apart as they matured, with Tommy keen at first to pursue a military career. Unlike his father, who had been educated by tutors at Birr Castle in Ireland – far from the corrupting influence of the English public school system – Tommy had attended Eton College and the

Royal Military Academy, Woolwich. He received his first commission in 1906, but retired after three years, deciding after all to yield to destiny and join the family firm at Heaton in a junior engineering role. Having acquired a reputation as a 'wild child', Tommy lived a rather solitary life.[6] He became a director of the Heaton firm in his mid-twenties and bought a house with seven bedrooms in nearby Willington Quay, on the north bank of the Tyne, where he reputedly slept in a different room each night. Tommy was being groomed as the heir apparent at Heaton when he decided to join up in September 1914. A high point of his wartime military career was an attachment to the experimental department of the Royal Flying Corps, the predecessor of the Royal Air Force, where he could put his mechanical skills to good use in making improvements to aircraft.

Charles Parsons was devastated by the death of his only son. Since the start of the war, he and Katharine had lived mostly at Ray, while their other home, Holeyn Hall in Wylam, became the 14th Northumberland VAD hospital, where wounded soldiers were sent to convalesce. Although the couple retained ownership of Holeyn Hall throughout their lives, they could never bring themselves to return there, even after the hospital closed, because of its associations with Tommy. While Charles's demanding career offered immediate diversions from grief – in 1919 he was made president of the British Association for the Advancement of Science – Katharine threw herself ever more vigorously into her campaigning activities.

Family turmoil intensified in June 1918 with the arrival of news from Ireland that William (Ocky) Parsons, 5th Earl of Rosse – Rachel and Tommy's first cousin – had died suddenly as an indirect result of war injuries, and his son Michael, Lord Oxmantown, had acceded to the earldom at the age of only twelve. In Katharine's family, the Bethells, the death toll was even worse. Tommy was one of five grandsons of William Froggatt Bethell who lost their lives during the Great War.

There is speculation that, to Rachel's disappointment, her father refused to let her return to the Heaton board to resume the duties she had taken over from Tommy early in the war. In spite of their strong mutual affection, relations between father and daughter had always been fiery, but this episode seems to have caused a serious rift. It is also probable, however, that Rachel had only chosen to remain in London to pursue new interests. Afterwards, she would rarely return to her roots in northeast England.

Charles's reputed intransigence may have been driven by grief and an inability to accept the finality of Tommy's death, but – from Rachel's perspective – his opposition to bringing her back into the corporate fold was a symbolic blow at a time when the tide was turning against female workers in industry. Up until this point in her life, Rachel had had little reason to complain that being female was a barrier to her ambitions. Now, in the same year that women had won the vote after decades of struggle, she felt the walls closing in.

The loss of a brother – and, possibly, a lover too – combined with the apparent rejection by her father meant that the immediate post-war period was an especially difficult time for Rachel. Having turned thirty-five in 1920, she was well established in the realm of spinsterhood – a condition shared by many of her colleagues in the engineering society. None of the women concerned revealed any anxiety about being unmarried but, with the backlash against feminism that took place in the 1920s, they became, as spinsters, objects of suspicion and disdain. The feminist historian Sheila Jeffries identifies a propaganda campaign against the spinster that wrecked the idea of remaining single as a positive choice for women, as it had been seen (by some) before the war.[7] In addition, she writes, 'The promotion of the ideology of motherhood and marriage together with the stigmatising of lesbianism helped to reinforce women's dependence upon men.'

Rachel also faced an insuperable professional challenge in that, having failed to secure a directorship in her father's company, it would have been impossible for her to work at a similar level in any other engineering firm. In any case, her ambitions had moved on. Combined with her personal trials, the war and its aftermath had transformed Rachel into a campaigner and, as soon as an opportunity arose, she immersed herself in politics – believing it to be the most productive way to promote women's rights, especially in employment. This new passion promised to satisfy her intellectual hunger and her idealism and, more than anything else, accounted for her increasingly rare appearances at meetings of the Women's Engineering Society.

Frustration at the anti-women stance of the male trade unions, which were inextricably linked with the Labour Party, and the restraint it imposed on social progress directed Rachel towards the Conservatives. As a first step, she joined the Municipal Reform Party, set up in the early twentieth century in alliance with the parliamentary Conservative Party to wrest control of the London County Council (LCC) from Labour and the Liberal-aligned Progressive Party. By entering local government, she would be taking the only route that had been open to aspiring female politicians before the extension of the franchise in 1918. The first LCC election, in 1889, had returned three women – but, following a successful challenge to their legitimacy, it was not until 1910 that women had again been allowed to sit on the council as full members.[8] Some progress was made in the years that followed; by the end of the war, out of a total of 124 councillors, there were eleven women on the LCC, including the deputy chairman.

Municipal Reform policies included tight public spending controls and the creation of a traffic board to coordinate transport in London. After a successful start, they had lost ground in two LCC elections before the war, and in 1919 they suffered a major reverse at the hands of a resurgent Labour Party. During the next two years, the Reformers fought back, managing to exercise power by forming alliances with the remnants of the Progressive movement. This anti-Labour strategy led to the Reformers regaining control of a number of London boroughs in the 1922 election, after which they continued to hold power until 1934.

More than twenty women stood for election to the LCC in 1922.[9] One of the Municipal Reform candidates was Helen Gwynne Vaughan (North Camberwell), who had had a distinguished career as controller of the Women's Auxiliary Army Corps (WAAC) in France and commandant of the Women's Royal Air Force (WRAF). Another was Rachel Parsons (Finsbury), described by a local newspaper as 'the daughter of Sir Charles Parsons, the famous engineer, and . . . President of the Women's Engineering Society'.[10] Twelve women were successful – and Rachel was one of them.

Woman Engineer soon reported that 'Miss R. M. Parsons AINA, who was recently elected a member of the London County Council, has now been appointed to the Highways Committee and also to the Electricity Supply Committee'.[11] Rachel had wasted no time in finding her way onto the council bodies where she could most usefully exploit her experience in engineering and industry. Over a period of three years, she assiduously attended council meetings and contributed to debates – but, as political turmoil intensified in the country at large, it was not long before she had set her mind on a higher prize: gaining a seat in the House of Commons.

Three general elections – one each year – were held in Britain between 1922 and 1924, giving political leaders plenty of opportunity to assess the voting behaviour of the millions of new electors created by the 1918 Representation of the People Act. According to the historian Martin Pugh, 'It was widely considered that the new electorate was volatile, a characteristic attributed to the women.'[12] This idea gained ground in the 1923 election, which produced a poor result for the Conservatives. The Conservative minister Samuel Hoare, a former member of the Municipal Reform Party on the LCC, attributed the disappointment to 'the ignorant opposition and credulity of women [voters]'.

The poll of November 1922 occurred too soon after Rachel's arrival on the LCC for her to propose herself as a parliamentary candidate, though she spoke at political rallies in favour of the Conservatives, who benefited from a major split in the Liberal Party. Rachel's chance came in December 1923, when Stanley Baldwin, who had taken over from Bonar Law as Conservative leader and Prime Minister earlier that year, took the country by surprise by calling another general election. In response to spiralling unemployment, Baldwin was seeking a mandate for the introduction of trade tariffs, but his policy of protectionism would prove unpopular with the public at large.

Four years after Nancy Astor had taken her seat as the first female MP, it remained very hard for women to get adopted as candidates for Parliament, especially by the Conservative Party, whose central office staff were described by Ray Strachey, who stood as an independent in 1923, as 'violently opposed to women MPs'.[13] Sir George Younger, the party chairman, had reacted to Nancy Astor's adoption in 1919 with the words: 'The worst of it is that the woman is sure to get in.'[14]

By a quirk of fate, the first three women MPs at Westminster were all elected to seats that had been vacated by their husbands.[15] Nancy Astor had been joined in the House of Commons in September 1921 by Margaret Wintringham, a Liberal, who won a by-election in

Louth, Lincolnshire, caused by the death of her husband. And in May 1923, in another by-election, Mabel Hilton Philipson took over as Conservative member for Berwick-upon-Tweed after her husband had been forced to resign because of a financial scandal. It was not until the general election of December 1923 that women with no direct family connections, including three Labour candidates, were elected to Parliament in their own right.

Just two weeks before the December poll, Rachel Parsons was selected as the Conservative candidate for Ince in Lancashire, a solid Labour seat bordering on Wigan. The reputation and influence of her father, Charles, clearly played a part in persuading the local party to adopt Rachel in this traditional industrial and mining constituency, but the activists were also impressed by her presidency of the Women's Engineering Society – and they would be even more impressed by her energetic campaigning and her oratory.

Rachel's only opponent was the Labour incumbent, Steve Walsh, a miners' agent and former vice-chairman of the Labour Party, who had held the seat for seventeen years, having won five previous elections with huge majorities. 'When I arrived, nine days before the poll, I was told that a thousand votes a day had to be wiped off the adverse majority,' she admitted to the *Manchester Evening Chronicle*. 'A mere nothing, of course.'[16] The reporter noted that the candidate had experience of working with trade unions in her father's engineering firm and – unaware of the irony of Rachel's position, given her earlier run-in with the engineers' union – repeated her view that 'Trade unionists themselves are the greatest exponents of protection . . . They allow no one to work without the recognised training and a certain standard of wages and hours must be maintained.' Meanwhile, Steve Walsh was busy reminding voters of the 'sad plight' of the miners, who had suffered large wage reductions as a result of the deregulation of the mining industry – a move that had been masterminded by Stanley Baldwin as financial secretary to the Treasury.

In several rousing speeches during the short campaign, Rachel dwelt on the dire state of the British economy and the fact that unemployment had now reached 2 million. The situation in the country was so serious that it needed women as well as men to solve it. 'In the war the women came forward and helped the men in the factories and workshops,' she said. 'They went to France to drive the motor-cars and take care of the wounded, and why should they not come forward now in this terrible time of unemployment and again lend a helping hand?'[17] In a direct appeal to female voters – who were thought to be particularly anxious that tariffs would lead to a rise in food prices – she recalled Baldwin's pledge not to put a tax on foodstuffs and to reduce the price of food by stimulating agriculture.

Reminding her audience of her roots in Northumberland, 'a county of great industries and a mining county, too', with many similarities to Lancashire, Rachel described her distress on a recent trip along the Tyne at witnessing the silence of the shipyards and the fact that ships were lying idle in the river. The Conservative Party were going to the country entirely on the question of unemployment, she said, because the time had come for a radical change of direction. Large road-building and house-building schemes had been initiated, but these were not enough. A permanent solution would be provided by the imposition of import tariffs, with preferential arrangements to be set up with India, to protect the cotton trade, and Britain's other trading partners in the Empire. Europe had not recovered from the effects of the war, she said, and many foreign nations had a depreciated currency and a reduced standard of living, so they were able to work cheaply and flood the British market with goods, depriving British workers of their livelihood. This had to be brought to an end. What was needed, above all, was a revival of trade in the home market.

It was high time, insisted Rachel, that there were more women in Parliament to tackle the many subjects they knew more about than men. Women were often the 'chancellors of the exchequer' at home, in charge of the family budget, and why shouldn't they look after the national money, too? There were many domestic problems on which women should have a voice in the House of Commons, and she appealed to the Ince electors to send another woman there.

While Rachel's words were warmly applauded by her Conservative audiences in Lancashire, they did not capture the prevailing mood of the nation at large, where there was a great deal of scepticism about tariffs – and Baldwin's stance had allowed the Liberal and Labour parties to present themselves as the champions of free trade. In the event the Conservatives lost eighty-seven seats, although they were still the largest party; Labour and the Liberals gained enough ground to produce a hung parliament. Ramsay MacDonald formed a minority Labour administration – the first ever Labour government – but it lasted only ten months before another election was called. With the tariff issue abandoned, the Conservatives performed much better in 1924 and were returned to power with a large majority.

Thirty-four women had stood in the 1923 poll, and eight were successful: three Conservatives, two Liberals and three Labour. Although the number of women MPs was reduced to four in 1924, five more women won by-elections before the next general election was held in 1929.

Even though Rachel's attempt to enter Parliament could hardly have taken place in more challenging circumstances, her campaign in Ince achieved a creditable outcome. Evoking the atmosphere that built up before the result was announced, the *Wigan Examiner* described a crowd gathering outside the polling station at 8.30 p.m. in thick fog. As it happened, they had almost three hours to wait, but '[they] passed the time in good-natured bantering and singing snatches of popular music-hall songs'. Most were supporters of the Labour candidate, Steve Walsh, whose victory was never in doubt, 'and their only anxiety was to know by how many lengths he had won'. The result, declared at 11.15 p.m., was as follows: Stephen Walsh (Labour) 17,365; Miss Parsons (Conservative) 6,262.

The vote for Walsh had hardly changed since the previous election, but it was remarkable in the circumstances that Rachel had achieved the level of support she had. It would encourage her to try again, though there was inevitable disappointment in the short term. The election officer had to apologise for the 'unavoidable absence of Miss Parsons' from the result. While motoring round the constituency that morning, he said, she had slipped when getting out of her vehicle and had met with 'a rather nasty accident', obliging her to return to her hotel. Rachel's absence on that occasion was part of a pattern that would be repeated in other moments of high drama.

Rachel's experience at Ince reflected a problem faced over many years by numerous other women hoping to enter the House of Commons: how to be selected in a constituency they could win. 'By 1929 the parties were fielding [between them] nearly seventy candidates, a number that remained steady until the 1970s,' wrote the political historian Patricia Hollis.[18] 'The number of women actually elected did not.' From the late 1920s onwards, between twenty and thirty women were elected to each parliament. 'More women stood; no more were elected.' They simply failed, again and again, to be adopted in winnable seats. The fact was that, left to themselves, constituencies almost always choose 'the safe candidate, the middle-aged man from the "articulate" professions'.

Undaunted by the setback in Ince, Rachel continued over many years to seek adoption as a parliamentary candidate and her campaign was reinvigorated in 1928 when the franchise was extended to everyone over the age of twenty-one – which seemed to open up new opportunities for women in politics. In March 1929, two months before a general election, she wrote to Nancy Astor to thank her for a party the previous evening, adding, 'As you so kindly asked me about my constituency could I persuade you to use your great influence to help me to secure one?'[19] Nancy remained MP for Plymouth, a seat she would hold for twenty-five years, from 1919 to 1945. She replied to Rachel the next day: 'I would gladly help you about your constituency but I am afraid I have no influence at all at Headquarters.'

In the event, Rachel put herself forward for selection by the Conservatives in the east London constituency of Romford, but was rejected. A month after the election, she had a letter published in *The Times* urging the adoption of a female candidate in Twickenham, the constituency of the former Home Secretary William Joynson-Hicks, who had been raised to the peerage as Viscount Brentford. Joynson-Hicks had been instrumental in lowering the voting age for women from thirty to twenty-one. 'In view of Sir William's well-known championship of the women's vote,' wrote Rachel, 'surely it would be a fitting recognition of the work done for the party by women all over the country if his constituency were conferred on a women candidate.' Her plea fell on deaf ears.

The next general election was held in November 1935, following the resignation of Ramsay MacDonald as leader of the National Government and his succession by Stanley Baldwin. At the Conservative conference in Bournemouth earlier that year, Rachel had moved a resolution on behalf of the North Newcastle branch of the party calling for an urgent injection of economic help for the depressed areas of northeast England.[20] However, on this and a later occasion, her hopes of being selected in Newcastle, where she and other members of the Parsons family had established such strong connections over many years, would prove futile. In spite of her manifest intelligence, articulacy and spirit of dedication, Rachel was excluded from direct participation in a tumultuous period in British politics, as the abdication crisis loomed – culminating in King Edward VIII's momentous decision to relinquish the throne to marry the divorcee Wallis Simpson – and relations between countries grew increasingly fractious during the prelude to the Second World War.

EIGHT

——◆·◆——

Good Times and Bad Times

'You can imagine how thrilled I was,' said Caroline Haslett, 'when our Queen, then Duchess of York, made her first public speech in opening our conference at Wembley in 1925.'[1] Speaking many years later on BBC radio, Caroline was recalling the first International Conference of Women in Science, Industry and Commerce, organised by the Women's Engineering Society as part of the British Empire Exhibition.

The event – Caroline's brainchild – was described in *Woman Engineer* as 'a great and outstanding event in the history of the woman's movement' and by Caroline's sister Rosalind as 'the moment of arrival' for the engineering society.[2] Representatives from the worlds of academia, business and technology from several different countries appeared on the platform in front of an audience of 4,000. In a speech described by Caroline as 'an inspiration to women the world over', the Duchess of York stressed that it was the first occasion on which women involved in science, industry and commerce had met together on equal terms to discuss what they could contribute collectively to human endeavour.[3] The first session, on 15 July 1925, was chaired by Lady Astor MP, and conference speakers included Margaret Wintringham MP, Margaret Bondfield MP, Ellen Wilkinson MP, Dame Millicent Fawcett, Lady Rhondda, and the peace campaigner Ethel Snowden, a former member of the Labour Party's national executive committee, whose husband Philip had served as chancellor of the exchequer in the Labour minority government of 1924. Millicent Fawcett, who had led the campaign for women's suffrage before the war, introduced a sober note. 'One of the disappointments of my life is that women have not got a better position in industry now than they have actually got,' she said, urging the assembled company to do everything in their power to put that right.

In addition to lectures on technical and political issues, and debates on fair pay and welfare in the workplace, examples of women's work were on show in stalls around Wembley's Palace of Industry.[4] These ranged from demonstrations of chocolate making and ice-cream making 'on the most up-to-date hygienic lines' to a display of gas equipment in which 'women were making incandescent mantles, some acting as instructors to the public in domestic economy'. Educating women in business administration and the arts of salesmanship was another dominant theme.

One very popular element of the exhibition was its focus on opportunities for women in the fast-expanding electricity industry. A number of lectures on the subject were given by Caroline's friend Margaret Partridge, and visits were arranged to places of interest, including the All-Electric Home at Olympia, created by the Electrical Development Association.

The great success of the Wembley conference raised the national and international profile of the Women's Engineering Society and propelled its chief organiser, thirty-year-old Caroline Haslett, onto the world stage, establishing her as a leading advocate of women's rights in industry. It also marked a welcome turnaround in the fortunes of the engineering society, which three years earlier had only narrowly survived a funding crisis.

In early 1922 Katharine Parsons, who had been contributing £444 a year to keep the society going, said she could do so no longer.[5] A review revealed that expenditure for 1921 had amounted to about £900, including the cost of producing *Woman Engineer* magazine, while income was £650. Average yearly subscriptions brought in £107. Active membership was 337, but it was thought that only about 170 members would be able to afford an increased subscription. Katharine gave a warning that, unless other means could be found to keep the work going, the society would in all likelihood cease to exist by the end of March. Apart from worrying about the drain on her personal resources, Katharine may have been discouraged from continuing by her daughter's growing detachment from the project – for Rachel had other things on her mind and was becoming ever more immersed in political activities.

There was a powerful collective impetus to save the society from its financial plight. A provisional executive committee, led by Cleone Griff, was set up to review possible economies and to consider fund-raising activities such as balls and bridge parties. It discussed at length an appeal to potential donors, and Caroline suggested that the Industrial League, led by Lady Rhondda, could be a source of support. In the event, a variety of these measures were combined to put the society on a more secure footing, if only temporarily, but it was donations by rich benefactors that were the most crucial factor. Katharine Parsons agreed to make a reduced annual contribution of £100, and there were payments from her husband, Charles, and other industrialists. Important donors included Emma, Lady Beilby, who – to Caroline Haslett's delight – turned up one day at Dover Street and insisted that the secretary accept a contribution of £100, with no restrictions on how the money was spent. When Lady Beilby died, she left £500 to the society, in whose work she had taken a strong personal interest. With her support, her daughter Winifred became a prominent industrial chemist and, in partnership with her husband, Frederick Soddy, did groundbreaking research into radioactivity.

Rescued from the brink of oblivion, the Women's Engineering Society set about organising its first conference, which was held in Birmingham in 1923. Since the society was the only organisation of women engineers in the world, it had been decided to invite representatives of the profession from other countries. Among the foreign guests was Dr Lillian Gilbreth, a psychologist and member of the American Society of Mechanical Engineers, whose influence would have a lasting impact on Caroline Haslett's career. With her husband, Frank, Lillian Gilbreth had been carrying out pioneering work on 'motion study'; its purpose was to find the best way to do any job by analysing the processes involved and minimising the number of actions needed to carry it out. It was an early example of the application of scientific techniques to business management. In the words of Caroline's sister Rosalind, 'Scientific management as understood by the Gilbreths meant the study of all problems affecting the health, efficiency and happiness of human beings in industry.'[6]

Caroline's interest in the movement to 'humanise' industry was stimulated by another meeting with the Gilbreths at the first World Power Conference, held in London in 1924, where she had been asked to speak on the subject of 'Power in Domestic Use and Agriculture'. The purpose of the conference was to create an international forum on energy resources. Realising the urgent need to get the female voice heard in such discussions, Caroline began to consider assembling a group of women with views on, and experience in, the use of electricity.

Around the same time, Mabel Matthews, a Women's Engineering Society member, applied to join the Institution of Electrical Engineers

(IEE). As part of the application process, she wrote a paper about the use of electricity in the home, which included a scheme for setting up a women's electrical association. The submission was rejected by the IEE, but Caroline supported Mabel's ideas and raised them with Katharine Parsons.

Although Katharine instinctively opposed the involvement of the Women's Engineering Society in domestic electrification – whose significance was not yet proven – she initially gave her blessing to the scheme. On 12 November 1924 a large meeting was held at 1 Upper Brook Street, the Parsons family's London home, to hear Mabel Matthews read her paper – in which she argued convincingly that, as well as lightening the burden of housework, electricity in the home would bring enormous benefits in terms of health, hygiene and comfort. The men in the audience included Charles Parsons and Caroline's friend 'F. S.' Button, who had recently been co-opted onto the society's council. Also present were representatives from the Girl Guides, the Women's Co-operative Guild, the Garden Cities and Town Planning Association, the Headmistresses' Association, the National Union of Women Teachers, the National Council of Women and the National Women's Citizens' Association. The Matthews proposals were given an enthusiastic reception and the meeting culminated in a vote in favour of creating a women's electrical association.

A month later, when asked to become chairman of the new body, Katharine Parsons declined the invitation, saying that she did not have enough time to devote to the task. This was the first clear sign that she was uneasy about the enterprise, perhaps regarding it as a competitor to the engineering society, rather than complementary to it. She could not – or did not want to – recognise the far-reaching potential of such a group, as expressed by F. S. Button: 'While the Women's Engineering Society could only serve the few, the Electrical Association for Women had a scope which was nationwide.'[7] When

Caroline was appointed director of the association on 12 December, Katharine found it hard to accept that the young woman who had been with her from the very beginning of the society, and on whom she had come to depend, had now been elevated to the top position in a rival organisation. She apparently saw it as a betrayal – and her hostility grew.

Katharine may also have resented the growing influence on Caroline of Margaret Partridge, a prominent member of the society who had recently launched an electricity supply company in Devon under the name of M. Partridge & Company, Domestic Engineers. A mathematics graduate of Bedford College, part of London University, Margaret had been involved in engineering since 1915, when she started work in London with a small electrical firm, before transferring to a job in munitions.

After the war, Margaret had returned to her home county of Devon with the intention of providing rural settlements with electric lighting at a moderate price. Her firm employed both women and men, but she was particularly keen to encourage female applicants. In 1922 she put on an exhibition of electric models and machines in Exeter, including a range of labour-saving devices aimed at housewives.

Margaret had been a moving force behind the formation of the Electrical Association for Women and remained a staunch supporter of the organisation and an ally of Caroline Haslett. The affection between the two women is evident in their correspondence.[8] 'My dear Haslett,' wrote Margaret in February 1925. 'On or after 4 April, you and I will explore the beauties of Dartmoor and the south coast and the vagaries of Triumph and sidecar – making the new flat in Exeter our centre of operations.' She went on to make an intriguing reference to F. S. Button: 'If F. S. B. would like to explore too, there is the solo Triumph available for one of the party – but unless Mother happens to go away for Easter, there won't be a bed in my flat.' (She sometimes signed off her letters to Caroline with the words 'best of love to you both', and there are several suggestions that Caroline and F. S. may have been a couple.)

Margaret explained that her project to instal electricity in the village of Thorverton had been hindered by local prejudice. 'One man holds a queer suspicion that I am a wicked adventuress they should have no dealings with – or else that, as I offer light to publicans and sinners (bakers and farmers too), their only way of showing their superiority of birth and position is to pass by on the other side.'

Things had not improved by 25 April, when Margaret wrote again to Caroline:

> You know the Thorverton situation pretty well. They are all nervous, but the strange thing is they all agree that the more talk there is the more they all want electricity. I don't think there is the slightest doubt about the demand, but they don't trust me or anyone else far enough to be signatories to the registration of a company. They are a bit like sheep there.

There was no denying the satisfaction of overcoming such hurdles and bringing a project to fruition, however. When the electrification scheme in Bampton, another Devon village, was completed in 1926, Margaret wrote to tell Caroline of her satisfaction: 'My dear – for sheer exciting experience, give me a town to light – 70 miles an hour belts and 320 Volts on the board with a well-soaked cement floor – and then remember you are the responsible engineer for the whole lot, and there isn't another soul within 20 miles at least who understands the switchboard!!!' Electrifying Bampton had not been without its problems, again mostly derived from the conservative attitude of its inhabitants. In this case, there was concern about the propriety of women working at electricity plants because it involved evening work. 'Though gay, Bampton is proper!' wrote Margaret. 'The trouble is that it is not right for a young girl to be out late at night without a chaperone – specially not at power stations!'

Both Caroline and Margaret were carving out lives for themselves in a world where professional women were still a rarity, and they joked together about how to deal with conventional expectations of female status and behaviour. 'Please tell me, am I a lady or an engineer – what are you?' asked Margaret in a letter of 28 May 1925 about a conference they were both due to attend. 'Do you notice that at each of the papers there is a special stunt for ladies . . . What ho! I've made a new hat for that – don't be angry.'

Caroline's reply was unequivocal. 'We are both going as engineers or semi-engineers and not as wives,' she wrote. 'I am most interested in the news that you have made a new hat for the occasion. I do hope that it is the kind of hat which engineers and not wives would wear.'

On another occasion, Margaret wrote to Caroline about the legal rules affecting the administration of her firm. 'I'm having altercations about my absolute right to be married as many times as I please without altering any document or agreement in any way!' she said. 'I *won't* see why my status "married" or "spinster" should have any more bearing on the case than it would with a man.'

Roedean School in Sussex, where Rachel Parsons had been educated, was among the many bodies that invited M. Partridge & Company to submit a tender for an electrical installation – in this case for 800 lights – but Margaret thought she would be too busy to take on the job, suggesting that Caroline might do it instead. The approach by Roedean prompted Margaret to reflect on the singularity of her situation:

Of course, it really is a joke to contemplate a lone female in Exeter – without the first shadow of a staff – calmly saying she is going to light a town, a super school and incidentally have spare time to assist in one of the most important women's organisations of the day, but it can be done, I know. My reserves are in excellent order.

During the spring of 1925 the antagonism between Katharine Parsons and Caroline Haslett went from bad to worse. Katharine's sense of her own superiority – bolstered no doubt by her husband's pre-eminence in the industrial world and the huge success of the Parsons firm on Tyneside – blinded her to the fact that times were changing. 'I have been harried and worried by my president to the extent of a solicitor's letter,' wrote Caroline to Margaret on 9 May. 'She is behaving in a perfectly stupid way but it is wonderful how much damage an obstructionist can do even without brains.' A rift had opened up between the forward-looking, practically inclined society members, who were often trained engineers, and the more traditional idealists who remained loyal to Katharine. It would develop into a battle for the very heart of the society.

As plans took shape for the Wembley conference that summer, the most serious row of all erupted. As chairman of the conference committee, Katharine vehemently opposed the choice of a speaker on electrical engineering, insisting that, instead, Annette Ashberry should speak about Atalanta Ltd. When most of her colleagues on the committee, who favoured the original choice, refused to back down, she abruptly resigned the chairmanship and instructed her secretary to send a letter to the engineering society's council:

Lady Parsons wishes me to say that she retires from every committee on the WES and Wembley Conference, and severs all connection with the WES as at present constituted. She also desires that her name be removed from the advisory councils of the Women's Electrical Association and the Wembley Conference, and her name must not be used in any literature sent out.

A second letter was received from Charles Parsons requesting that 'in the circumstances prevailing' his name be removed from the society's documents.

'The president has resigned from the WES and has also, in addition, done her best to wreck the conference,' wrote Caroline to Margaret, 'but we are all going along quite merrily . . . I really think, taking everything into consideration, that we are very fortunate to be rid of any further muddle-headedness.' With time running short to find a replacement, she persuaded Nancy Astor to take the chair at the conference.

Stunned by this turn of events, council members were at a loss about how to proceed. Discussions descended into recriminations between the two factions, with Mary Selby and Annette Ashberry, both supporters of Katharine, resigning their positions. An investigation led by Laura Annie Willson into the cause of the crisis proved fruitless because – apart from insisting that she was fighting for the status of the society – Katharine refused to co-operate, turning down every invitation to explain what had led to her dramatic withdrawal from the organisation in which, over a period of six years, she had invested so much of her time, money and energy.

After a particularly tense meeting of the council on 18 July, at which Margaret was present, she wrote to Caroline of her suspicions that Katharine 'would far rather kill the society than let anyone else run it'. Explaining why she had had to leave the meeting early, Margaret characterised the dispute as a division based on politics and class. 'I do wish I could have stayed yesterday,' she said, 'but there was a £3,000 tender in question, so I just had to [go]. Worst luck –

that is rather where the society ladies get an extra pull over working members. I'm Bolshi!!!!'

The two women's correspondence reveals that Caroline had found it hard from the start to deal with Katharine Parsons' imperious and mercurial manner, and she was not alone in this respect. In November 1925, Herbert Schofield, the principal of Loughborough College, told Caroline about the difficulties he had faced when Atalanta Ltd had been based at Loughborough. 'I am prepared to believe anything is possible at a meeting when Lady Parsons is in the chair,' he wrote. 'During my own period on the Board of Directors, the most inexcusable decisions were arrived at, and the whole method of administration was so unconstitutional that I do not think I have ever had anything like a similar experience.'

A report in *Woman Engineer*, of which Caroline remained editor, made clear the society's regret at the departure of one of its main founders, but failed to mention an equally important figure – her daughter, Rachel. 'The mind which conceived the idea of the Women's Engineering Society is one of no mean order,' noted the report. 'The society was established in the immediate aftermath of the war-time period; its foundations were sufficiently truly laid, and its work so energetically and wisely carried on, to have withstood the buffets and the storms of the tremendous industrial depression which followed that period.' But the journal reassured its readers that 'Fortunately, those trained and technical women who have all along formed the backbone of, as well as the justification for, such an organisation remain loyally with us.'

A new era began for the Women's Engineering Society with the installation as president of Laura Annie Willson, a businesswoman whose enthusiastic support of the Electrical Association for Women, on whose council she also sat, allowed the two organisations to develop in productive harmony. At the time of her election, Laura

Annie, as she was known, had recently launched a revolutionary scheme to build sixty-four three-bedroom houses for working people, selling at £400 each (about £24,000 in today's money), in her home town of Halifax. 'The houses will be erected in the form of a horseshoe, with tennis courts, etc., in the middle and a road 10 ft wide round the backs of the houses. Each house will have its own private front garden,' according to *Woman Engineer*, which went on to highlight a plan inspired by the philosophy of the electrical association: 'Mrs Willson is considering providing facilities for an electrical service in these homes, so that when the estate is completed it will not only be the most artistic but the most efficiently equipped collection of working-class houses in Halifax.'[9]

Unlike most other members of the Women's Engineering Society, Laura Annie was married and the mother of two children, George (born in 1900) and Kathleen Vega (born in 1910), and for many years she and her husband had been joint directors of Smith, Barker and Willson, a lathe-making factory in Halifax, which had manufactured munitions during the war. Most of its wartime workers were women. In 1919, the company had, of course, fallen foul of the law when it tried to challenge the ban on women employees imposed by the Restoration of Pre-War Practices Act – an event that only fuelled Laura Annie's determination to fight for equality in the industrial world. Her presidential address, delivered at Leeds University on 3 September 1926, revealed her open-minded and visionary attitude towards women and employment, which went far beyond the immediate concerns of the engineering society. 'A woman should be allowed to choose her work (if she wishes so to do),' she said. 'So much time is spent in earning one's living that the work should be suitable to the individual engaged in it.'[10]

Born in 1878, Laura Annie had developed a view of the world that drew on her experience of a poverty-stricken childhood in a Yorkshire mill town, where she started work as a 'half-timer' in a factory at the age of ten. In her opening speech as president, she remarked on the great improvement in living standards that had taken place during her lifetime, attributing this to the growing use of 'engineering products and inventions' such as ovens fuelled by electricity or gas rather than coal. Working conditions were immeasurably better. 'Wages are higher and hours are shorter. Child labour has been abolished.' Looking back on her early life and comparing conditions then with now, she said, 'It almost seems as though a miracle has happened.'

In early 1907, as an active member of the Women's Social and Political Union and the Women's Labour League, Laura Annie had taken part in a weavers' strike at Hebden Bridge in Yorkshire, and been arrested for 'violent and inflammatory speech'.[11] She was found guilty and locked up in Armley Prison, Leeds, for fourteen days. 'I went to gaol a rebel, but I have come out a regular terror,' she told the *Halifax Guardian* on her release. Later that year, she was one of seventy-five women arrested after a suffragette rally in Westminster, which ended with an attempt to gain access to Parliament.[12] Found guilty of disorderly conduct, she was again sentenced to fourteen days, this time in London's Holloway prison. On their return to Yorkshire, she and others who had endured the same fate were welcomed as heroes.

Laura Annie's first-hand knowledge of trade unions and her political activities, in addition to her experience as a company director, had taught her the importance of treating workers fairly and rewarding them with good wages – which, as she argued, benefited the employer as well as the employee. 'I believe that a new spirit is coming into industry,' she said. 'It has been shown so often that the square deal pays, and that higher wages bring greater production.'

Her newfound interest in house-building was a response to the critical housing shortage in Britain after the war, particularly affecting poorer people in provincial towns. The most significant state intervention was the House and Town Planning Act 1919 – known as the Addison Act after the Minister of Health, Christopher Addison – which introduced council housing, but this and other government measures failed to meet the apparently limitless demand. It had become increasingly clear that a large-scale programme of private house building was also required.

Laura Annie had witnessed at first hand the dismal living conditions of working people in Halifax and wanted to do what she could to improve them. It was entirely appropriate for her to concern herself with this subject in her present role, she said, since housing was 'very much a woman's question, and a form of engineering of the domestic kind'. Her aim was to build moderately priced, well-designed, labour-saving houses for young couples who would otherwise have to live in furnished rooms.

The first two estates constructed according to the Willson principle, using Accrington brick and slate tiles, were begun close to the company's factory in Ovenden, followed by two similar estates elsewhere in Halifax.[13] 'It may interest you to know,' she said in her presidential speech of September 1926, 'that since 19 July 1925 I have built seventy-two houses, all of which are sold and occupied. I also have sixty houses built to the roof, many of them being slated, and about one hundred houses in course of erection.' In 1926 Laura Annie was admitted to the National Federation of Housebuilders as its first female member.

So successful were the Halifax estates that in 1927, taking deposits in advance to provide working capital, she began work on an estate of 210 houses and bungalows at Englefield Green in Surrey at the request of Egham Urban Council.[14] This was laid out with wide roads, grass verges and gravel footpaths, with four types of houses costing between £465 and £550 each. All the houses were designed to include installations of both electricity and gas. Her final building project was at Walton-on-Thames, also in Surrey, where she spent her last decade.

Towards the end of her life, Laura Annie reflected on her career as a house builder. 'Since 1925 I have done work to the value of about quarter of a million pounds,' she said, 'and am pleased to have done this for three very important reasons: financial ones to myself; the job was important and very much needed doing; I had an opportunity to demonstrate that business need not be confined to one sex.'[15] When she died in April 1942, excluding the houses sold earlier, she owned 185 houses in Halifax, Englefield Green and Walton-on-Thames, most producing rental income and estimated to be worth more than £71,000 (£3,282,000 in today's money).

Of equal interest to Laura Annie during her house-building period was promoting the installation of electricity in the home in order to reduce the burden of domestic chores. In 1927 she helped to found a company called Electrical Enterprise Ltd to take advantage of the opportunities offered by the Electricity (Supply) Act 1926, which had led to the creation of a national Electricity Board.[16] Among the other directors were Margaret Partridge and Caroline Haslett, and the chairman was Dr John Purves, who had played an important part in Margaret Partridge's schemes in Devon. They hoped to speed up the process of rural electrification by building small power stations in country locations. An equally important aim was to provide employment for women in the electricity supply industry, in the belief that, as described in the prospectus, 'the services of women will be particularly valuable in introducing to rural homes the benefits to be derived from these modern services'.[17]

When stepping down as president of the Women's Engineering Society in the autumn of 1928, Laura Annie Willson spoke of being at the start of 'a golden age' for women, especially those entering the business world. 'Industry has become fascinating and profitable to women,' she said, 'and we want to play a full part in that new life.'[18]

It was a view echoed by the writer and feminist advocate Vera Brittain, whose book on jobs for women was published in the same year.[19] While identifying engineering as second only to advertising in offering 'the finest opportunities to enterprising women', she insisted that 'the best openings for women are provided by new businesses and professions capable of alteration and expansion, rather than by the older and more circumscribed vocations with a long tradition of masculine authority' – which, in addition to its other attractions, is precisely what made the fast-expanding electricity industry such an irresistible prospect.

NINE

The All-Electric Home

The creation in 1924 of the Electrical Association for Women – and her appointment as its first director – was a pivotal moment in Caroline Haslett's life. It was the start of the realisation of her dream to transform human society through the power of science, as she explained in 1943: 'One of the greatest scientific discoveries is electricity, bringing light, warmth and power. Here then was a force which would lighten the housewife's labours, which would give us clean cities and would bring to the countryside the amenities of the town without spoiling the natural beauty. So we turned our attention to this most important side of engineering, because we felt that it held out so many hopes for humanity.'[1]

Caroline's intention was to assemble a group of expert women to whom other women and electrical engineers alike could turn for advice and instruction.[2] Education was a priority, with Margaret Partridge and others, including Caroline herself, giving lectures around the country and helping to raise awareness of the new venture in schools and among organisations such as the Girl Guides and the Women's Institute. Evening classes were arranged for members already working in the electrical industry and as domestic science mistresses, and an Electrical Housecraft School would eventually be set up at 20 Regent Street, which from 1933 became the site of the association's headquarters and clubroom. Caroline wanted all women to appreciate the wonders of science, to acquire electrical knowledge, and to have time to follow their own interests.

The backing of some well-established firms and individuals in the electricity industry helped to launch the new organisation, which began with very little money, though British Thomson-Houston Company, Metropolitan-Vickers Electrical Company and General Electric Company each provided a small amount of funding. Champions in Parliament included Lady Astor (Conservative) and Ellen Wilkinson (Labour) – and Caroline was thrilled when Lady Astor agreed to become the association's first president. Over the years, a warm understanding developed between Caroline and Nancy Astor, whom Caroline described as 'full of life and hope and joyous undertakings', even though she sometimes found her lacking in spontaneity. Reflecting later how much she appreciated Nancy's support for her various ventures, Caroline said, 'Many a time [has] her sparkle invigorated and cheered me, and life always seems to have much more flavour when tasted in her company.'[3]

In June 1926 Caroline launched a magazine called the *Electrical Age for Women* (later shortened to the *Electrical Age*), which she continued to edit as long as she remained director of the association. 'The Women's Engineering Society and later the Electrical Association for Women allowed me to share the trials and tribulations of Fleet Street in a small way,' she explained later. 'The *Woman Engineer* is a quarterly given up in the main to technical subjects and the *Electrical Age* is also a quarterly, run on rather more popular lines.'

The spread of the Electrical Association for Women was immediate and rapid. The first branch opened in Glasgow in November 1925, spearheaded by Elizabeth Kennedy, managing director of the machine-tool manufacturer J. B. Stone & Company. This was soon followed by branches in Birmingham and Manchester. The Manchester branch was led by Gertrude Entwisle of Metropolitan-Vickers – the first woman since Hertha Ayrton to be elected to the Institution of Electrical Engineers (IEE), of which she became an associate member in 1920. Elizabeth Kennedy and Gertrude Entwisle were both influential members of the engineering society.

Like other august scientific bodies, the IEE, which had actively supported the formation of the Electrical Association for Women, had a less than impressive record concerning the admission of women – as reflected in the story of Hertha Ayrton, an outstanding mathematician, engineer and inventor.[4] In 1899 the IEE had been the first body of its kind to admit a woman to full membership – based on Hertha's groundbreaking work on the 'hissing' of electric arc lights – but since then no other woman had enjoyed the same privilege. In 1904 Hertha addressed the Royal Society on the significance of patterns formed by sand ripples on the seashore, for which she received the society's Hughes Medal in 1906; but, as a married woman, she was barred from becoming a fellow of the society – a fact that she continued to complain about until her death in 1923. In the event, the Royal Society elected its first female fellow in 1945, and it was not until 1958 that the IEE admitted another woman to full membership.

In an early article on the activities of the Manchester branch of the Electrical Association for Women, published in the October 1926 edition of *Electrical Age*, Gertrude Entwisle reported that no public meetings had been possible because of the General Strike that had taken place that year, but arrangements for the autumn programme included visits to the Singer Sewing Machine Company, an instructional talk on 'Illumination and Wiring a House', and a lecture by Mrs de Ferranti entitled 'Ideas on Electricity in the Home'.

Gertrude Ziani de Ferranti, a new member of the association's council, was closely involved in the electrical engineering work of her husband, Sebastian, president of the Electrical Development Association, which had given crucial support to the Electrical Association for Women. 'He was the first man in the electrical world to believe in us,' wrote Caroline.[5] 'He saw from the beginning that it was through women that the domestic development of electricity would come and he urged me to go on.' Ferranti, the founder of what became a hugely successful engineering company, is particularly remembered as the designer of Deptford power station, which, when completed in 1891, was one of the largest generating stations in Europe.

Caroline used to enjoy staying with the Ferrantis at their Derbyshire home, which was full of devices invented by Sebastian. 'The beds were warmed electrically and the great scientist himself took personal delight in showing me the many electrical gadgets, often the result of his own fertile brain, and designed to ease the work of the house-wife,' she recalled.[6]

Another pair who liked to experiment with electrical equipment on home territory was Sir John and Lady Shelley-Rolls, the owners of Avington Park, near Winchester. Eleanor Shelley-Rolls was a founding signatory of the Women's Engineering Society, and had taken on the task of liaising between the society and the new electrical association. She and her husband had adapted an early type of water turbine, originally used to drive a pair of stones for grinding corn, into a small power station for producing electricity on the Avington estate.[7] As a result, according to an article in *Electrical Age*, 'Not only has the Avington estate an adequate supply of electricity, but a large number of surrounding villages have also been supplied.' Electricity was used for lighting the dairy and the cow byres on the nearby farm, 'and it is intended before long to use electricity for milking and other farm operations'.

The first meeting of the South Wales and Monmouthshire branch of the Electrical Association for Women took place on 24 March 1927 at Cardiff City Hall, with Lady Rhondda installed as president. Margaret Rhondda was described in *Electrical Age* as 'a woman of outstanding prominence in the industrial and feminist world'. The journal remarked on her tremendous energy and business ability: 'She is on the board of twenty-seven companies, including many colliery companies. She is also editor of *Time and Tide*, the weekly review, and is president for the current year of the Institute of Directors.' *Electrical Age* reminded its readers in its spring 1927 issue that, having inherited her father's title, Lady Rhondda had been excluded from the House of Lords on grounds of gender: 'In 1922 she tried by petition to the Committee of Privileges to obtain a writ of summons to the House of Lords, but failed on the interpretation of the Sex Disqualification (Removal) Act, on which her claim was based.'

Meanwhile, a selection of less elevated but no less able women were taking up similar positions in other parts of the country, including prominent women's suffrage activist Norah Balls in the northeast region and Margaret Partridge in the southwest, so that, by the time she came to write her third annual report in 1927, Caroline Haslett could say, 'We can truly claim to be a national organisation and entirely representative, in that we have amongst our members women of all shades of opinion and of all ranks in life.'

The association took over the premises of the Kensington and Knightsbridge Electricity Lighting Company Ltd, located on the site of one of the world's first power stations. Their landlord was Colonel R. E. Crompton, who had designed lighting systems for Windsor Castle, Vienna State Opera and the Savoy Theatre (a very early example of public lighting in London).[8] When the new premises were opened by Nancy Astor on 14 November 1927, she was presented with an electrically lit bouquet.

It was not all plain sailing for the female electricity pioneers, however, and they were soon embroiled in a challenge to the law that banned women from working in factories between the hours of 10 p.m. and 5 a.m. As had been the case in the earlier battle over the 1920 Employment Act, the argument was that restricting women's hours of work had a detrimental effect on female employment – the law did not apply to men – and on companies that employed women.

The focus of the dispute, which erupted in 1928, was a small power station in Devon – one of the group established by Margaret Partridge, whose company had undertaken the running and maintenance of the stations after they had been built.[9] Among the directors of M. Partridge & Company at this time was the former Tongland supervisor Margaret (Madge) Rowbotham, who had made a return to engineering the previous year. The two Margarets would manage the firm together for more than twenty years, becoming intimate companions as well as professional colleagues.

M. Partridge & Company employed several engineers and apprentices, including women, and day and night supervision of the stations was part of their normal training. One of their apprentices, Beatrice Shilling, was discovered by a factory inspector working in a power station after 10 p.m. – and the firm was held to have broken the International Labour Organization (ILO)'s Washington Convention on night working for women and children, to which the British government had subscribed. The Washington Convention had been introduced in 1919 with good intentions – to defend the rights of women working in sweated trades – but no account had been taken of its negative aspects. Caroline Haslett and the Women's Engineering Society backed Partridge in discussions with the ILO, an agency of the League of Nations, and lobbied the organisation to change its rules – but they faced trenchant opposition. Some of those who were against change cited the physical weakness of the female sex. Others insisted that women should devote at least the night hours to their domestic duties – which would have been impossible if they were busy in the factories – and that working at night exposed them to dangers from which they should be protected.

The controversy also affected a small electrical supply company that had been set up in 1926 in Bungay, Suffolk, with a majority of women as shareholders.[10] Caroline Haslett and Margaret Partridge were among the directors, and Caroline's sister Rosalind was the first company secretary. The firm aimed to provide openings for women and to encourage them to enter the electrical engineering profession – but the work of its female managers also fell foul of the Washington Convention.

The campaigners won a partial victory in 1934, when at a session of the ILO an amendment to the convention was accepted and the wording was altered to exclude 'women holding responsible positions of management'. The right of women to work at night was established – but only those women in management jobs. The restriction on female factory workers remained.

Margaret Partridge took pleasure in hiring young female apprentices and testing to the limit their resilience and capacity for hard work. More often than not, her high hopes for particular individuals were disappointed, but this was not the case with Beatrice Shilling, who had joined the firm at the age of nineteen and would go on to become a leading aeronautical engineer and inventor. 'I really think [Beatrice] is a great acquisition to the firm – able to enjoy any new experience, and not in the least superior or blasé – the fault of the very young at times,' wrote Margaret to Caroline.[11] 'She has a wicked joy in making all the YWCA hostel stand their hair on end by tales of her unladylike exploits when wiring.'

Margaret herself was not above the odd 'wicked' diversion. 'I've reached a whole series of alarming conclusions re electricity and women that I just daren't write down,' she admitted to Caroline. She and her partner, Madge Rowbotham, encouraged Beatrice to study at the University of Manchester, from which the young woman emerged in 1933 with an MSc in mechanical engineering, and three years later Beatrice was recruited as a scientific officer by the Royal Aircraft Establishment in Farnborough, Hampshire.

Throughout her career, Margaret Partridge continued to have a seminal influence on the development of women's role in engineering. She was the chief author of the *The Electrical Handbook for Women*, the flagship publication of the Electrical Association for Women, edited by Caroline and published in 1930. 'She had the ability to put technical problems and their solutions into concise and intelligible words for those not so knowledgeable,' reported *Woman Engineer* in a review of the book.

During the Second World War, Margaret founded Exeter Munitions Ltd and she was appointed women's technical officer for the southwest, advising on female employment in munitions factories.[12] She became vice president of the Women's Engineering Society in 1942 and served as its president from 1943 to 1945. After the war, she retired to live with Madge in the Devon village of Willand, where she had spent her childhood. An episode from this period fondly remembered for long afterwards by local people involved the wiring of the new village hall – which Margaret had decided should be completed by members of the Women's Institute under her supervision.

The Electrical Association for Women accepted an invitation from its northeast branch, headed by Norah Balls, to hold its fourth annual conference, in 1929, in Newcastle upon Tyne. The location was particularly appropriate because the North East Coast Exhibition, a world's fair, was also taking place in Newcastle that year. As explained in *Electrical Age*, the occasion had an international flavour, for it was the first time in the history of the industry that women from different countries had occupied a common platform, with delegates from the United States, the Netherlands and Austria, among other countries. This aspect of the association's work was very important to Caroline Haslett, who had been proud to write in 1927, in her annual report, that 'Evidence of interest in our work has reached us from America, Canada, South Africa, Japan, Germany and Austria, and requests received from Sweden and southern Ireland for help in forming similar associations in those countries.' The significance of the Newcastle conference was endorsed by a message of support from Margaret Bondfield, the newly appointed Minister for Labour – the first female Cabinet minister.

A special thrill for visitors to Newcastle that year was to see for the first time the spectacular King George V Bridge across the Tyne (now known as the Tyne Bridge), which had been opened by the king on 10 October 1928. Virtually none of them would have been aware that a Scotswoman, Dorothy Donaldson Buchanan, had played a large part in its design – and that she was, moreover, the first female member of the Institution of Civil Engineers, admitted in 1927, as well as a member of the Women's Engineering Society.[13] After graduating in 1923 from Edinburgh University with a BSc in civil engineering, Dorothy was employed by Dorman Long & Company of Middlesbrough, steelwork contractors who were working on the design of Sydney Harbour Bridge. She began in the design office, then moved to the drawing office to work on the bridge's southern approach spans. After a six-month spell in Northern Ireland, working for the Pearson company on the Silent Valley reservoir – where her mentor was Sir Ernest Moir, husband of Margaret – Dorothy returned to England to join the Dorman Long design team. She then worked on the design of the steelwork for King George V Bridge in Newcastle and Lambeth Bridge in London.

The president of the engineering society in 1929 was Margaret Moir, who had supported the society, practically and financially, from the very beginning. 'I should like to tell you how proud we are of this abnormal child of ours,' she said in a speech on its tenth anniversary. 'Every report tells of fresh branches being formed, fresh expansion in the branches already existing, and we look with pride and amazement at this young giantess we have brought into being.'[14] Although not herself a trained engineer, Margaret was steeped in engineering through the work of her husband. As a director of S. Pearson & Son, Ernest had won fame for his construction of the Blackwall Tunnel in London and various tunnels under the Hudson River and the East River in New York City. His other major feats included the Admiralty Harbour at Dover; harbour works at Valparaíso, Chile; and the Great Northern and City underground in London. Like his wife, Ernest Moir was a great advocate for women in engineering.

Having backed Caroline Haslett in her battle with Katharine Parsons over the formation of the electrical association, Margaret Moir would find her true métier in her work for the younger organisation, of which she became president in 1931. In this role she gave full expression to her belief that 'the dawn of the all-electric era' was at hand. She had no doubt about the importance of this development in freeing women to pursue careers outside the home. 'It is essential that women become electrically minded,' she wrote in an article published in the *Morning Post*.[15] 'By this I mean they must not only familiarise themselves with electric washing machines, fires and cookers, but possess sufficient technical knowledge to enable them to repair fuses and make other minor adjustment. Only by doing so will women learn to value electricity's cheapness and utility, and regard it as a power to rescue them from all unnecessary household labours.'

In 1930 the Electrical Association for Women, led by Gertrude de Ferranti, conceived and planned a life-size All-Electric Flat to display at the Bachelor Girls' Exhibition, which opened in November at the New Horticultural Hall, Westminster. The architect Edna Mosley, an association member, was commissioned to design the demonstration flat, which was paid for by the British Electrical Development Association. Characterised by clean, stark lines, the All-Electric Flat contained the latest electrical equipment, gadgets and ideas, along with built-in furniture, supplied by Heal's, the renowned London furnishing store. It conformed to the modernist ideal of 'form follows function', whereby utility and ease of operation were equated with beauty. Described by its creators as 'the first public expression of how the bachelor woman could live electrically', it proved to be the most popular attraction at the exhibition. A later display of a scale model of an All-Electric Working-Class Kitchen also created tremendous interest, with the Duchess of York and the Bishop of London among the eager onlookers.

On 14 April 1932 Margaret Moir presided over the seventh annual general meeting of the Electrical Association for Women, held at the Dorchester Hotel, using the opportunity to congratulate Caroline Haslett on her election as the first female Companion (or Fellow) of the Institution of Electrical Engineers. She also presented 104 diplomas in Electrical Housecraft – an award instigated by the association to raise the status of women in the electrical industry.

Domestic electrification offered obvious advantages to people who were accustomed to employing servants – and for the servants themselves – as Margaret made clear in her *Morning Post* article:

The servant problem will be simplified. Not only will the staff be decreased in numbers, but maids will have no cause to complain of backaching duties. The modern mistress anxious to secure faithful service will take a pride in equipping her house with the latest labour-saving devices. Thus the future home, with its thermostatically controlled heating and cooking arrangements, will enable her to go shopping or attend a matinée happy in the knowledge that work is being scientifically carried on at home, with the staff relieved of all but the minimum amount of drudgery.[16]

There were advantages, too, for less well-off families that needed a woman's income as well as a man's, in that a home equipped with labour-saving electrical appliances would make it easier for a woman to take up paid employment. 'Let the critics say what they will about married women working,' Margaret wrote. 'Many are proving already that a combination of duties is possible without one being sacrificed to the other.'

Margaret Moir's article, published on 11 July 1931, was entitled 'A Vision of the Home of the Future'. It culminated in a passage that, while considering some of the more outlandish possibilities consequent on the spread of domestic electricity, allowed her to give free rein to her fantasies. In fact, even she might have been surprised how prophetic some of her ideas have turned out to be:

The home of the future conjures up fascinating pictures to the most unimaginative. Think, for instance, of waking at seven and saying, 'Now, I must have my early morning sun-bath.' This is no wild castle in the air, but an actual possibility. Artificial sunlight lamps will eventually find their way into every home, so that we shall have little to fear from the vagaries of our climate. Light is flexible and in the future will be used not only for utilitarian purposes, but in decorative schemes as well. The hostess who wishes to display some originality can use alternative forms of lighting according to her mood, choosing blue one day and rose-coloured the next. Walls will be fitted with panels of warmly tinted Lalique glass so that on dull days the room can be flooded with artificial sunlight with the turn of a switch. Flowers will live longer in this scientifically lighted home, and it is safe to prophesy that colds will be chronicled as the plague of an unenlightened generation. Even the electric fire at present considered a luxury will be looked upon as a curiosity fit for a museum. Heat will be generated from heating panels behind walls, and thermostatically controlled according to the season of the year.[17]

On 23 October 1935, at the instigation of the Bristol branch of the Electrical Association for Women, a specially designed All-Electric House was opened in the city for public viewing by Catherine, Countess of Westmorland. Based on the results of a survey about what domestic improvements women most wanted, it included many new elements.[18] 'Naturally the house is all-electric,' remarked *Electrical Age*, 'but much more has been accomplished than the replacement of old-fashioned equipment with modern appliances . . . there have been fundamental changes out of which has emerged a house that is both well designed and excellently equipped.'

The building, described as a small house with a compact kitchen, was planned to be 'labour-saving', so that the housewife would 'not have to carry wood and coal, clean dirty grates with the resultant dust on floors and furnishings, wind any clocks, clean any metal used in the construction, buy any material for pelmets, clean windows frequently or have any chimney swept, and her cleaning, washing and decorating bills will correspondingly diminish'. It had a selling price of £1,000 (about £70,000 in today's money) and, it was estimated, would cost about £30 (£2,000) a year to run inclusive of heating, washing, cooking, cleaning, refrigeration and lighting. Although the house was designed to be managed without paid domestic help, provision was made for a maid 'if desired'. An electric clothes-drying room was later taken out of the design because it was too expensive and consumed a great deal of energy.

During the month when the All-Electric House in Bristol was open for viewing, more than 20,000 people passed through its doors, and most of them were apparently excited and inspired by what they saw. The original version was sold shortly after the opening ceremony and repeat orders were soon received. Enquiries about the revolutionary new structure came not only from many parts of Great Britain and Ireland but also from the United States, Bermuda, the Netherlands, Austria, France, India, Greece, Iceland and New Zealand.[19] It was enthusiastically reviewed in the national press and in many journals, including *The Architect and Building News*, *The Cabinet Maker*, *Design for Today*, *Homes and Gardens*, *Ideal Home*, *L'Art Ménager*, and the journal of the Royal Institute of British Architects. This liberating vision of a new domestic realm had undoubtedly captured the public imagination.

TEN

—◆—

Conquest of the Air

Airborne flight had been a subject of fascination to the Women's Engineering Society from its earliest days, largely at the instigation of Eleanor, Lady Shelley-Rolls, who organised a lecture in November 1921 on 'Women and the Conquest of the Air'. It covered flight from the balloon era, of which Eleanor had first-hand experience as the sister of Charles Rolls – a pioneering aviator as well as a founder of the Rolls-Royce car company. She had accompanied her brother on many of his 170 ascents, including taking part in the 1909 International Balloon Race from Hurlingham in west London to Billericay in Essex.[1]

Charles Rolls' death in an aeroplane crash in 1910, aged only thirty-two, had a lasting effect on his only sister, and Eleanor's grief intensified during the Great War, with the loss of two more brothers. As the only surviving child of John Allan Rolls, 1st Baron Llangattock, she became heir to the Hendre, the family estate in Monmouthshire, and a considerable fortune. Her lifelong interest in engineering and her support, both practical and financial, of the Women's Engineering Society had their roots in this period. Her husband, John, was also keen on aviation, becoming vice chairman of the Aerial League of the British Empire, founded in 1909.

Although the Montgolfier brothers had demonstrated the efficacy of hot-air balloons as early as 1783, and Jean-Pierre Blanchard had flown in a balloon across the English Channel two years later, more than a century passed before ballooning really caught on. A major change occurred during the first decade of the twentieth century, when it became a fashionable pastime for those who could afford it. As explained in the 'Conquest of the Air' lecture, the most famous female balloonist in Britain was May Assheton Harbord, with a record that included five trips across the Channel.[2] After casually joining friends in an ascent in 1906, May became an enthusiastic aeronaut and piloted her own balloon on more than 200 voyages, some of them in the company of Eleanor and John Shelley-Rolls.

Among her many lucky escapes was the occasion when, having crossed the Channel in a storm, she was thrown out of the basket in a violent landing. 'I can claim, therefore, to be the only woman who has landed on the Continent on her head,' she said wryly. After making a journey of seventy-eight miles in a balloon on 11 September 1909, May was awarded a prize by the Aero Club, and in 1912 she became the first woman in Britain to obtain an aeronaut's certificate.

Aeroplane flight was also gaining in popularity. Two years earlier, Hilda Hewlett, an aviation enthusiast from London, had joined forces with the French engineer Gustav Blondeau to open the first flying school in Britain, at Brooklands motor-racing circuit in Weybridge, Surrey. Many people had their initial experience of flying at Hewlett and Blondeau's school, including T. O. M. (Tommy) Sopwith, who would go on to become chairman in the 1920s of the Hawker Aircraft company. In August 1911, after completing her test in a Farman III biplane at Brooklands, Hilda Hewlett became the first woman in Britain to be granted a pilot's licence.

As part of the discussions following the 'Conquest of the Air' lecture in 1921, Major-General Sir Sefton Brancker, a pioneering aviator in the newly formed Royal Air Force, referred admiringly to work done by women during the war in the construction of aeroplanes. Other speakers included Hilda Hudson, a designer in the Air Ministry during the war, who pointed out that many of the firms that had done such good work on aeroplanes were now having to dismiss their staff, and the country was thereby 'losing the nucleus of its design brains'.

In 1926 the Women's Engineering Society and the Air League of the British Empire sponsored a lecture on aviation as a career for women. It aroused so much interest that in 1927, as part of the society's fifth annual conference, a dinner was held in honour of women aviators and motorists. In the same year, Cleone Griff, a member of the Birmingham Metallurgical Society and herself a qualified pilot, began a long-running series of 'Aviation Notes' for *Woman Engineer* magazine.

One route for educated women into the world of aviation was the Royal Aircraft Establishment (RAE) at Farnborough in Hampshire, which had evolved in the early twentieth century from the Army Balloon Factory into the Royal Aircraft Factory, and then went on to become the pre-eminent centre of aeronautical research in the world.[3] The RAE had its roots in the late 1870s, when the army had recognised that hot-air balloons had potential military applications, especially for spying and reconnaissance.

By 1915, about 5,000 men and women were working at the Royal Aircraft Factory (which became the RAE in 1918) as scientists, technical staff, test pilots and administrators.[4] Aircraft manufacture was a major part of the establishment's work, but this declined after complaints from private companies about unfair competition. Since many aircraft were crashing without their makers or pilots having understood what had gone wrong, the Royal Aircraft Factory turned its attention to scientific work, building two wind tunnels for experimentation and testing purposes. The resulting improvements in aerodynamics and structures made Britain a leader in the field of powered flight.

Mathematicians capable of carrying out detailed analyses were in great demand at Farnborough. Since many of the brightest young men had volunteered for the armed services, Oxford, Cambridge, Imperial College and other leading educational institutions were asked to identify their best female mathematics graduates and current students to work at either the Royal Aircraft Factory or its sister organisation, the Admiralty Air Department.[5] Among the young recruits to the Air Department was nineteen-year-old Letitia Chitty, an outstanding school maths student who, after the war, went on to study engineering at Newnham College, Cambridge – the alma mater of several other women who shone at Farnborough. Letitia later worked on structural stresses in airships for the Air Ministry before joining Imperial College as a researcher and lecturer. She was the first female fellow of the Royal Aeronautical Society and in 1969 she became the first woman to receive the Telford Medal of the Royal Institution of Civil Engineers.

In the event, women worked at Farnborough as analytical engineers from 1917 until the RAE closed in 1988, helping to save thousands of lives – and many of them joined the Women's Engineering Society. An outstanding example of the brilliant women mathematicians recruited by the RAE in the early 1920s was Hilda Lyon, who designed the transverse framework for the R101 airship, and whose research into related technologies led to a design of US submarines known as 'the Lyon Shape'. Another was Frances Bradfield, who became a specialist in aerodynamics and stability; in

1934 she was appointed head of the wind tunnels section, where she remained until the end of the Second World War.[6] Frances then worked on Hawker jet fighters and in 1948 was awarded the Royal Aeronautical Society's bronze medal.

In the first half of the twentieth century, the aeronautical field proved more welcoming to women than other areas of engineering, perhaps because large-scale aircraft production was relatively new, and the technology was developing so fast, that there was less opportunity for entrenched prejudices to come into play. In fact, the Royal Aeronautical Society had been open to women long before other comparable engineering institutions. The society was founded in 1866, and the first female member is thought to have been admitted in 1874.

Of all the names associated with the RAE at Farnborough, perhaps the most familiar today is Beatrice (Tilly) Shilling, who is celebrated for her work, before and during the Battle of Britain, on the Rolls-Royce Merlin engines that were used to power Spitfire and Hurricane aircraft, and for solving a dangerous defect in them by inventing a device that became known as 'Miss Shilling's orifice'.

After doing her apprenticeship at M. Partridge & Company in Devon, in 1929 Tilly had embarked on a course of electrical engineering at Manchester University. During her student years, she worked briefly in the transformer department of Ferranti in Hollinwood, and then, following her heart, she went on to do a master's degree at Manchester in Mechanical Engineering. In 1934 she bought a second-hand 490 cc Norton motorcycle and started racing at Brooklands. Having tuned the engine to make it go faster, she finished sixth in her first race and third in her second. 'She transformed her standard motorcycle into a racer whose speed impressed professional riders,' wrote her biographer, Matthew Freudenberg.[7] In

1935 Tilly became the fastest woman to complete the Brooklands circuit, reaching 106 mph on her way to victory.

It was motorcycling that brought Tilly together with George Naylor, another racing enthusiast, whom she married in 1936, soon after joining the RAE at Farnborough, where George was employed in the mechanical test department. Tilly had been taken on at Farnborough as an author of technical manuals, but the work gave her no satisfaction and after a few months she managed to transfer to the engine experimental department.

Her groundbreaking work on the injection carburettor earned her a series of promotions and on 1 November 1939, two months after the outbreak of the Second World War, she was appointed technical officer in charge of carburettor research and development. In this role, she began to investigate the tendency of the Merlin engines in Spitfires and Hurricanes to hesitate or cut out just as the pilot entered a dive in pursuit of, or in retreat from, an enemy plane, sometimes resulting in a fatal crash. Tests and calculations revealed that the phenomenon was caused by 'negative gravity' – when the aircraft started to dive, anything that was not fastened down, including fuel in the carburettor float chamber, surged upwards, depriving the engine of fuel and ultimately causing it to cut out.[8] Tilly's solution was to insert into the engine a disc-shaped brass restrictor that prevented the fuel from flowing away from where it was needed during a dive. It was this simple device, which could be fitted to an engine while it was still in an aircraft without removing the carburettor, that came to be known as the 'orifice' – and it was reckoned to have saved many lives.

After the war Tilly Shilling continued her research on engines, including, in the late 1950s, engines for Blue Streak missiles, part of a government defence programme that was eventually cancelled, and she worked with the Aeronautical Research Council on accident investigations. In 1958, when the British European Airways Ambassador aircraft carrying the Manchester United football team crashed on take-off at Munich, killing seven team members and eleven journalists and club staff, Tilly was able to show that the accident had been caused not by pilot fault, as had been thought, but by drag from slush that had prevented the plane from reaching its correct take-off speed.[9]

Speed was an interest – and an obsession – that stayed with Tilly throughout her life. 'Her idea of relaxation was to drive a fast car at full throttle,' according to Freudenberg, 'and if the car was not fast enough, her workbench was there in the back room to machine new parts to make it faster.' From the mid-1950s she and her husband raced cars as members of the British Automobile Racing Club, and they maintained a whole stable of motorcycles for their use.

Independently of activities at Farnborough, two other remarkable women, both in their early twenties, were carving out careers for themselves in aviation. They were Pauline Gower and Dorothy Spicer, who had met in 1929 while learning to fly at the London Aeroplane Club based at Stag Lane aerodrome in Edgware, Middlesex.[10] As well as qualifying to fly as a chief pilot on any of the major air routes, Pauline gained her commercial pilot's licence, which allowed her to carry passengers 'for hire or reward', and Dorothy became only the second woman (after Amy Johnson) to qualify as a ground engineer. To secure the practical experience required to gain the necessary Air Ministry licences, Dorothy had spent six months with Saunders-Roe Ltd of Cowes, Isle of Wight, to learn aircraft construction, and six months with the Napier Engineering Company in Acton, London, to learn about engines. Possession of all four Air Ministry licences – a unique achievement for a woman – authorised her to build every element of an aircraft, air frame and engine from scratch, and to approve the materials required for the work.

In 1931 Pauline and Dorothy decided to pool their flying and engineering talents by setting up a business to provide flights for pleasure and an air-taxi service; they hired a three-seater Simmonds Spartan aeroplane for the purpose.[11] The intention, as described in Pauline's book *Women With Wings*, was to 'give joy-rides to the public, to take anyone anywhere by air at any time, to service private owners' planes'. They later bought a De Havilland Gipsy Moth for use in the business, but they struggled to survive financially. In 1932 they toured the country with an 'air circus', putting on shows in 200 towns, and in the same year they joined the aeronautical section of the Women's Engineering Society, newly formed at the prompting of the Irish aviator Mary, Lady Bailey.

Since securing her pilot's licence in 1927, Mary Bailey had astonished the world by making a solo return flight in a Cirrus Moth from Croydon airport to Cape Town. She had reached home on 16 January 1929 after a return journey of 18,000 miles that involved flying across the Congo, along the southern edge of the Sahara and up the west coast of Africa. It was at the time the longest solo flight and the longest flight achieved by a woman – for which Lady Bailey was awarded a DBE. During the Second World War she served in the Women's Auxiliary Air Force (WAAF).

When the Civil Air Guard scheme was set up in October 1938 to subsidise the training of pilots through civilian flying clubs, Pauline Gower was one of the five commissioners appointed to administer it.[12] The scheme was open to anyone between the ages of eighteen and fifty, of either sex, and proved tremendously popular – but there were few jobs available for the pilots after they had completed their training. In addition, women pilots had to contend with a great deal of prejudice, as exemplified in a letter of 1928 to Lady Bailey from C. G. Grey, editor of *The Aeroplane* magazine. 'We quite agree . . . that there are millions of women in the country who could do useful jobs in war,' he wrote. 'But the trouble is that so many of them insist on wanting to do jobs which they are quite incapable of doing. The menace is the woman who thinks she ought to be flying a high-speed bomber when she really has not the intelligence to scrub the floor of a hospital properly.'

On the outbreak of war, Pauline Gower proposed the establishment of a women's section in the new Air Transport Auxiliary (ATA), set up under the management of Gerard d'Erlanger of the British Overseas Airways Corporation (later British Airways).[13] The task of the ATA was to ferry military aircraft from factory or repair facility to where they were needed for operational purposes, freeing service pilots for combat duty. After several obstacles had been overcome, it was agreed to form a small pool of women pilots to ferry De Havilland Tiger Moths from Hatfield air base to sites where the planes could be stationed for future use.

Pauline was appointed commanding officer of the ATA women's section at an annual salary of £400 (about £22,000 in today's money). She was initially allowed to employ only eight women, who took up their jobs on 1 January 1940. All had considerable flying experience and all were qualified flying instructors. They included Margaret (Margie) Fairweather, the daughter of the liberal politician Lord Runciman, who had completed 1,000 hours as a private owner and worked as an instructor for the Civil Air Guard at Renfrew; and Rosemary Rees, a former ballet dancer who owned her own plane and had done a great deal of air touring.

Although Pauline herself was, at twenty-nine, younger than most of her team, she had held a flying licence for nine years and had accumulated 2,000 hours of flying experience. She also showed leadership qualities beyond her years, as recorded in *Woman Engineer* by the British aviator Amy Johnson, an early ATA recruit, who remarked that, although Pauline was well known for her 'high-flying capabilities', she was admired even more as 'a clever psychologist, studying and understanding to no mean degree the temperaments of the girls under her care'. Poignantly, in view of how she would come to die, Amy commented on the need for the ATA pilots to avoid undue risks.[14] 'After all, the work of the ATA is to deliver machines safely and in one piece,' she wrote. 'Whether it be today or tomorrow matters far less than the condition in which a brand-new, highly expensive machine arrives.'

As time went on, the recruitment rules were relaxed and during the Second World War as a whole 166 women took to the air as ATA pilots, one in eight of the total; they came from Britain, Canada, Australia, New Zealand, South Africa, the United States and several other countries.[15] Among the American recruits was Jacqueline Cochran, who returned to the USA and started a similar all-female organisation known as the Women Airforce Service Pilots. The female ATA pilots were initially restricted to non-combat aircraft, but they were eventually allowed to fly virtually every type of aircraft flown by the RAF and the Fleet Air Arm, including four-engined heavy bombers. Hurricanes and Spitfires were first flown by women pilots in July and August 1941. From 1943 the women pilots received the same pay as their male counterparts in the ATA; this was the first time that the British government had sanctioned an equal pay arrangement in an organisation under its control.

Fifteen of these women lost their lives in the air, among them Margie Fairweather, who was killed in 1944 while landing a Proctor aircraft. Pauline Gower survived the war, and in 1945 she married Wing Commander Bill Fahie, but she died in 1947 giving birth to twin sons, who survived. Dorothy Spicer also met a tragic end. In 1938 she had married Richard Pearse, who became a test pilot at the RAE in Farnborough. In late 1940 Dorothy joined him at the RAE, taking on flying work as an air observer and research assistant, and helping to develop new types of aircraft. After the war Richard worked in Rio de Janeiro as South American representative for British Aviation Services Ltd. He and Dorothy were aboard a flight from England to Brazil in December 1946 when bad weather forced their Avro York to divert from a scheduled landing at Rio. In thick fog, the plane flew into a mountainside, killing all on board.

The first member of the ATA to die in service was Amy Johnson, whose Airspeed Oxford aeroplane mysteriously plunged into the icy-cold Thames estuary near Herne Bay in Kent in January 1941. The circumstances of Amy's death, at the age of thirty-seven, caused a storm of controversy that still refuses to die down. According to the official record, neither the body of this highly experienced air-woman nor the wreckage of her plane has ever been found.

In the popular imagination, Amy Johnson was a brave, glamorous and largely lucky daredevil who finally overreached herself. She made history in 1930 by becoming the first woman to fly solo from England to Australia – the first of several extraordinary achievements – but she was not doing it only for thrills. 'My flight was carried out for two reasons: because I wished to carve for myself a career in aviation, and because of my innate love of adventure,' she said after-wards.[16] In fact, her flying success depended on hard-won engineering expertise – knowing how to patch up and repair her planes when things went wrong. She was the first woman to gain a British Air Ministry ground engineer's licence (soon followed by Dorothy Spicer), and from 1935 to 1937 she served as president of the Women's Engineering Society. In the opinion of her friend Caroline Haslett, 'It was not just luck and courage but real engineering skill that brought her through.'[17]

Amy also betrayed strong feminist instincts, although she may not have acknowledged them as such. 'We women are on the threshold of another career which has so far been regarded as the strict province of men – aeronautical engineering,' she said in a speech of 1932, going on to ridicule the idea that men's physical strength gave them a decisive advantage:

> In engineering there are many jobs beyond a man's strength. When faced with such a job, what does he do? He fetches an instrument. What did I do when I found a job beyond my strength? At first, I used to fetch a real man engineer, and if he couldn't do the job he'd fetch some tool that would do it. I soon learned that it saved time to fetch the tool right away.[18]

Amy was convinced that women shared with men the vital qualities needed in aeronautical engineering – 'patience, skill, delicate fingers and a fertile mind' – and there was no reason that they could not succeed, whether it was in the design department, the workshops or the repair shops.

Born in Hull in 1903, Amy Johnson graduated with a BA from Sheffield University in 1925 before moving to London, where she worked as a secretary in a solicitor's office and developed an interest in flying. During the winter of 1928–9 she learned to fly at the technical school of the De Havilland aircraft company at Stag Lane, Edgware, where, through the London Aeroplane Club, she met Pauline Gower and Dorothy Spicer.[19] She also met Sir Charles Wakefield of Castrol, who, along with the Royal Dutch Shell Oil Company, helped to finance her attempt to break the light-aeroplane record in a solo flight to Australia. Amy's father, John Johnson, a herring importer, shared with Wakefield the £600 purchase price of a single-engine De Havilland Gipsy Moth.

Amy set off alone in the Gipsy Moth, which she called *Jason*, from Croydon airport on 5 May 1930 and landed in Darwin in Australia's

Northern Territory nineteen days later, on 24 May, after an epic flight of 11,000 miles.[20] Even though she had failed to break the England to Australia record of fifteen and a half days set in 1928 by Squadron Leader Bert Hinkler, it was an astonishing triumph, which earned her the congratulations of King George V and the award of CBE; she also received a gift of £10,000 from the *Daily Mail*. As a qualified ground engineer, Amy had joined the Women's Engineering Society shortly before her flight to Australia, and on her return she gave a talk to the Society of Engineers entitled 'The attention I gave to *Jason*'s engine during my flight', for which she was awarded the society's gold medal.

Eleanor Shelley-Rolls invited Amy to give a lecture about her epic journey in the drawing room of her London home. 'It was a memorable and rousing evening,' said Claudia Parsons, who was one of the guests. 'There was to be supper afterwards but the lecture got so out of hand with the combined enthusiasm of audience and lecturer that Lady Shelley-Rolls had to keep withdrawing to get supper postponed.'[21]

Reminiscing in a BBC radio programme about Amy's courage and resilience, Caroline Haslett recalled their conversation when she was Amy's passenger during a flight along the Thames in the early 1930s.[22] 'The planes [she flew] would seem very frail to us. She said she used to nurse them and put patches on when things fell off. When she spoke of *Jason*, it seemed as if she was talking about a pet – not something in which you crossed oceans and deserts.'

Amy Johnson secured a succession of triumphs in the air, most of them in aircraft built by De Havilland.[23] In July 1931, accompanied by a mechanic called Jack Humphreys, she achieved a record flight from England to Japan in a Puss Moth. A year later, flying solo, she set a record from England to Cape Town, also in a Puss Moth. In

1933, with her husband, Jim Mollison, she completed a thirty-nine-hour nonstop flight in a Dragon across the North Atlantic – the first ever such flight from the UK to the USA – and in the England to Australia air race of 1934 the Mollisons flew nonstop in record time to India in a Comet.

Amy set another solo record on the England-to-Cape-Town route in 1936, on this occasion in a Percival Gull, designed by the new Percival Aircraft Company. On her return, a reception was held in her honour at the House of Commons. Organised by the Women's Engineering Society – of which Amy had become president the previous year – and hosted by Irene Ward, the Conservative MP for Wallsend, it consisted of a reception attended by the nine current female MPs, and several senior members of the British Federation of Business and Professional Women. Representatives of the engineering society included Caroline Haslett, Verena Holmes, Elizabeth Kennedy, Margaret Moir and F. S. Button. Also among the guests was Herbert Morrison, leader of the London County Council and Labour MP for Hackney South. Following the success of this event, a new note of intimacy entered the correspondence between Caroline Haslett and Amy Johnson, who agreed to continue as the society's president for another term. It was clear, however, that Amy was suffering from severe psychological stress at the time and she took a rest cure in Switzerland. There were hints of serious problems in her relationship with Jim Mollison, a Scottish aviator whom she had married in 1932, and in 1938 the Mollisons were divorced.

Amy joined the ATA in early 1940 and rose to the rank of first officer. During a routine ATA flight on 5 January 1941, while flying an Airspeed Oxford from Blackpool to RAF Kidlington near Oxford, she went off course in bad weather and her plane, which may have run out of fuel, crashed into the Thames Estuary near Herne Bay.[24] Amy bailed out and a parachute was observed floating downwards through the snow. Several sailors reported seeing two figures in the water and hearing calls for help. Lieutenant Commander Walter Fletcher, the captain of a nearby vessel, HMS *Haslemere*, dived into the icy water, but his rescue attempt failed and he died later from exposure and shock.

Neither Amy's body nor the wreckage of the plane has ever been recovered, though some of her possessions, including a pigskin travel case, washed up nearby. Theories abound about what actually happened that afternoon, and it has never been satisfactorily explained why such an experienced pilot had strayed so far off course. The identity of the 'second body' has prompted speculation that, against ATA rules, Amy could have been carrying a passenger – but, more plausibly, her travel bag may have been mistaken for a human shape.[25] In 1999, Tom Mitchell, who served during the war with an anti-aircraft regiment in Kent, said that her plane was shot down by friendly fire – implying an official cover-up. In 2014, at a ceremony in Herne Bay to celebrate Amy's memory, David King, who had been based at nearby RAF Detling during the war, insisted that her aircraft had been secretly retrieved – and that, soon after she disappeared, he had seen the plane, 'a yellow Oxford', on a low-loader RAF truck in which he had hitched a lift near Maidstone.

Since her death, the story of Amy Johnson has been retold and reinterpreted in films, songs and fictional accounts, and her life has been commemorated in many different ways, from the erection of statues to the naming of buildings and aircraft. In 2011 the Royal Aeronautical Society established an annual Amy Johnson lecture to celebrate a century of women in flight. Whatever the details of her tragic end, her most important legacy is her record as a pioneering airwoman, as she herself would have wished, according to Caroline Haslett.[26] 'Amy sincerely believed in progress – technical progress, progress in human relations, and progress of the human spirit,' wrote

Caroline after her death. 'She wanted to help other women make their mark in aviation.' Amy's inspirational qualities were recognised soon after her death at a memorial service in London, when representatives of some forty women's organisations came to pay tribute.

While reflecting on her career in engineering during a BBC radio broadcast of 1943, Caroline Haslett spoke about the peculiar satisfaction it had given her to work with the female adventurers who had set out to conquer the air. 'The younger generation of women aviators personify the godlike quality of courage,' she said. 'Utterly feminine, completely charming, strong, clear-visioned, without care but always careful, they have taken life calmly in their stride. Amy Johnson, Pauline Gower, Dorothy Spicer, all of them impressing you first that they are unspoilt children of their age; these are one of the gifts of the Women's Engineering Society to me.'

ELEVEN

Conflicts and Dreams

The late 1920s ushered in a strange period in the life of Rachel Parsons. With her political ambitions thwarted, she was left feeling disorientated and alone. Since severing links with the Women's Engineering Society she had moved on, and she probably found the evolving philosophy of the organisation – and that of the Electrical Association for Women – at odds with her own interests. Her mother's feud with Caroline Haslett and the new generation of professional women engineers made a resumption of her earlier career even more unlikely. Although Katharine Parsons put in an occasional appearance at the society's events, her daughter's name was rarely mentioned in an engineering context, except in 1934, when Rachel was admitted to membership of the North East Coast Institution of Engineers and Shipbuilders.

There was also a growing estrangement between Rachel and her parents, which had its roots in the emotional turmoil caused by the death of Tommy. In any case, her parents were often abroad, either inspecting the installation of Parsons steam turbines in power stations around the world, or – a favourite diversion as they grew older – enjoying cruises to the West Indies and other exotic locations. Rachel retained some shares in C. A. Parsons and Company, but otherwise demonstrated little interest in the Tyneside company, from which she had apparently been ostracised. She was now firmly established in London.

Despite the family differences, Rachel's parents were generous enough to ensure that she was never short of money, and by the summer of 1923 – the year she stood for Parliament – she was the owner of a large Georgian house in Portman Square, where she began to entertain on a grand scale, perhaps in the hope of advancing her political fortunes. In 1926 she moved to an even bigger house, 5 Grosvenor Square, which had a ballroom that could accommodate 500 guests. Here, over the next thirteen years, she hosted receptions, concerts and charity balls for the rich and famous, including aristocrats, diplomats and members of the British and foreign royal families.

The press reported Rachel entertaining guests on her chartered yacht, *Narcissus*, at the annual Cowes regatta in the Isle of Wight and participating in many events of the London Season. For several years she invited friends and acquaintances to join her in a box at Covent Garden opera house, prompting the *Observer* newspaper to comment that 'Miss Parsons, with Lady Ravensdale, is London's best-known spinster hostess'.[1] In 1938 she was invited to join the committee of the Bath Festival of Drama and Music, whose luminaries included film producer Sidney Bernstein, socialite Diana Duff Cooper, actor John Gielgud, diplomat Lord Gerald Wellesley and the Earl and Countess of Rosse. Rachel was never truly happy in this new life, it seems, and, although she got to know many influential people, she developed few deep friendships.

Following the deaths of both her parents in the early 1930s, Rachel became even richer. Charles died in 1931 while on holiday in Bermuda, leaving an estate worth £810,000 (well over £54 million today) – though, after the distribution of legacies, only a relatively small proportion of this went to his daughter.² When her mother died in 1933, and was buried beside Charles in the churchyard at Kirkwhelpington, near Ray Demesne, Rachel failed to attend the funeral, pleading illness. Holeyn Hall in Wylam was sold after Katharine's death, but Rachel inherited the 10,000-acre Ray estate, which she reputedly never visited. After many years of neglect, the estate was given up to the Land Commission in 1947 and the house was demolished. The estate was planted and managed by the Forestry Commission – apart from the agricultural elements, which were bought in 1954 by the trustees of the first Viscount Devonport, a Liberal politician and retail magnate. Meanwhile, Rachel retained her Grosvenor Square home until early 1946, when she sold it to purchase the equally opulent 43 Belgrave Square; she soon moved on from there to buy 3 Belgrave Square, which had been put up for sale in August 1946 by the widowed Princess Marina, Duchess of Kent.³

With neither a husband nor children nor any close blood relations to consider, this fabulously rich woman now decided to throw her energies into an exciting but unfamiliar activity: horse racing. Inheriting a love of horses from her mother, she had ridden often over the Northumberland moors during her childhood, and attended the odd race meeting, but what had once been a pastime now became a passion. Rachel began to buy racehorses and had them trained at Stockbridge in Hampshire by a well-known figure in the racing world, H. S. 'Atty' Persse. This new fascination brought her into frequent contact with her mother's family, the Bethells of Rise Park, who had a long-established interest in racing, and she was advised by the bloodstock expert Marcus Wickham-Boynton, a distant relative and neighbour of the Bethells in the East Riding of Yorkshire. Between 1937 and 1940, at which point wartime restrictions were imposed on horse racing, Rachel attended numerous race meetings all over the country and enjoyed particular successes with horses named Battle Cruiser and Davy Doolittle. Her racing colours were light blue and violet stripes with a violet cap.

Writing in 1956 about her cousin by marriage, Anne Parsons, Countess of Rosse, speculated about Rachel's frustrated career and lack of personal fulfilment – a combination that profoundly affected Rachel's character and created the public perception of her as a 'difficult' and eccentric woman. 'Had she been young today, when full equality in careers for men and women exists, what fields of honour in the world of science might not have been hers, with all eccentricities accepted?' wrote Anne.[4] 'Had she married, on the other hand, the unselfishness that is demanded of a wife and mother would have surely softened and moulded the thousand jagged abnormalities that crowded so technical a brain.'

Having little alternative, Rachel turned to a socially conventional life that neither suited nor satisfied her, and as she grew older she was beset by suspicion about other people's motives, which could make her behaviour seem hostile. 'There must be many, though, like myself, who accepted great hospitality from her in the past, and many who can recall acts of sincere kindness,' said Anne. 'She had good friends; but sycophants and fortune-hunters galore collected increasingly, whispering in her ear sweet flatteries that must have sickened a woman of her maturity.'

A few days before the outbreak of the Second World War, Rachel boarded the fabulously luxurious French liner SS *Normandie*, bound for New York. Four years earlier, *Normandie* had won the Blue Riband for the fastest westbound crossing of the Atlantic on her maiden voyage, making the journey from her home port of Le Havre to New York at an average speed of 29.92 knots (55.52 kmph); this overtook *Mauretania*'s record, held from 1909 to 1929, by almost four knots. Rachel repeated the journey on *Normandie* the following

April, then sailed on from New York to Bermuda. Passenger lists reveal that, on both occasions, she described herself as fifteen years younger than her actual age of fifty-five.[5]

The *New York Times* of 11 February 1941 records her hosting a society luncheon at the Palm Beach Biltmore in Florida. Since her presence in England during the conflict could serve little purpose, Rachel must have wondered whether she might spend her time more rewardingly in the United States. However, in 1940, to escape the bombing of London, she bought Little Court, a Georgian-style house with twenty-five acres of land at Sunningdale in Berkshire. There she sat out most of the war and experimented with self-sufficiency by growing her own vegetables and rearing ducks. 'It was the only reason I bought the place,' she told friends.[6]

Caroline Haslett's war could hardly have been more different from Rachel's. On 4 March 1940, with Caroline now installed as president, the Women's Engineering Society marked its twenty-first birthday with a celebration at the Park Lane Hotel in London attended by more than 300 people. The chief speaker was Ernest Brown, Minister of Labour and National Service. Caroline read a letter from the Queen,[7] which congratulated the society on having opened up a new field of employment for educated women, and for having persuaded technical bodies and engineering institutions all over Britain to admit female members. 'These enlarged opportunities are of especial value today, when the engineering skill of women may soon prove of such infinite value to the country,' said the Queen.[8]

Concern had been mounting among members of the British Federation of Business and Professional Women, headed by Nancy Astor, about the number of women who had lost their jobs since the outbreak of war, when many ordinary peacetime activities in business and the professions were superseded by national defence exigencies.

In an echo of events in the 1914–18 war, women began to demand 'the right to serve' and the right to be trained, along with men, in the new skills required to manufacture munitions. Following informal meetings at Nancy's home in St James's Square, a Women Power Committee was set up, chaired by Irene Ward MP. Consisting of ten MPs, three trade-unions representatives and eight leaders of women's organisations, including Caroline Haslett, its main purpose was to lobby for 'the fullest utilisation of womanpower in the war effort'.[9]

In September 1940 Caroline was asked by the Minister of Labour to take strategic responsibility for the training of women. At the same time the leading mechanical engineer Verena Holmes was appointed technical officer of the Ministry of Labour, attached to the training department. The situation concerning women seemed to be improving, but it was not until March 1941 that the ministry set up a specialist committee to advise on recruiting and registering female workers. Caroline broadcast a series of talks encouraging women to sign up for the war effort, and to publicise government schemes for training women and men in skilled work.[10] She travelled about the country visiting factories, observing the working conditions and welfare of thousands of women, and in 1942 co-wrote a handbook called *Munitions Girl*, telling prospective recruits everything they needed to know about what it meant to work in a munitions factory.

Meanwhile, Verena Holmes had devised a three-month course in workshop practice for munitions workers, which was taken up by technical colleges around the country. Claudia Parsons – who had completed her circumnavigation of the world by car in 1938 – did the course at the Beaufoy Institute in Lambeth, south London, as she recounted in *Century Story*.[11] It included lessons in machine drawing and in how to make simple metal devices using machine tools. 'There were all types of professional women from architects to actresses, mingling with housewives and society women, all delighted to find that, given the tools, they could make things in metal as much as in cloth,' wrote Claudia.

At Caroline's instigation, the Beaufoy was visited by the Queen, who said she wanted to take the course herself. 'The Queen was told of my former Loughborough training, and I described myself as a reconditioned engineer,' said Claudia, whose job was to assemble hydraulic pumps. Claudia later joined Verena at the Ministry of Labour, where she visited factories to identify women doing 'sensible' work (as opposed to mundane and repetitive tasks), which was then recorded and photographed, for later compilation into a handbook.

When the two women toured Scottish factories together, Claudia realised that Verena was exhausted from overwork, and that her extraordinary contribution to mechanical engineering had not been properly recognised. 'Her profession had long been exposed to some of the meanest male prejudices,' she said. 'She was only now winning the merits she had long since earned because they could no longer be withheld.'[12]

Claudia was later employed as part of a team led by the writer C. P. Snow, who was employed as technical director at the Ministry of Labour, to review working practices at the Admiralty drawing offices, which were beset by staff shortages and disaffection. She regarded it as 'an awesome ordeal'. Although in the dockyards women were fitting out ships and doing welding and wiring jobs, and the WRNS had taken over a lot of men's work, at the headquarters in Bath 'a woman was an inferior to whom no one of importance spoke'.[13] As the staff dining room was reserved for men, she was asked to have her meal with the tracers. 'I learned at this lunch of the women's loathing for the wiring diagrams they had to trace, and the consequent shortage of tracers,' she said. 'My only contribution to that survey was a page of portraits of our team, which I did for my own amusement.' Although Claudia had had several serious relationships with men during her travels round the world, she treated the male sex generally with disdain. When asked why she never got married, her response was: '[Men] very often threatened to stop me doing what I wanted to do.'[14]

None of the magnificent women associated with the first thirty years of the Women's Engineering Society – least of all Claudia Parsons – had a life that could be described as conventional. Few of them married, and even fewer had children. Many were well educated and used their education to forge independent lives and careers for themselves that would not have been possible for their predecessors. Remaining single and outside the mainstream of society exposed them to suspicion and ridicule – and Caroline Haslett herself was not immune from such treatment. A year after founding the Electrical Association for Women in 1924, she had been characterised in the *Westminster Gazette* as the epitome of 'Miss All-Alone, the self-sufficing bachelor girl of 1925, [who] working hard in trade or profession finds time to equip and run a little home'.[15] The reporter who visited the 'little home' noted, 'Everything in it is the expression of her independent personality.'

In fact, the flat, which had been electrically wired by Caroline and her friend Margaret Partridge, was full of the most up-to-date appliances. 'Lonely? Not a bit of it!' the article continued, remarking that Caroline invited friends round to listen to music on her homemade gramophone. 'Miss All-Alone is now the head of a new engineering organisation for women,' the report concluded admiringly, 'with all the world before her and the friendship of women who are doing things in the trades and professions.'

Caroline herself was acutely aware of the conflict women faced in choosing between family life and rewarding employment. Writing in 1938, when the marriage bar was still in force, she insisted that society would be 'happier, more sanely balanced and interesting' if women were given full opportunity to express and use their gifts by combining marriage and a career.[16] 'To those who do not wish to marry, society must afford full scope for employment – employment that can give shelter, clothing and food and take away the fear of a lonely old age of poverty,' she said. Introduced in response to the economic depression and high unemployment of the 1920s, the marriage bar meant that certain occupations were closed to married women – or, if married women were admitted, they were obliged to give up work when they became pregnant. The bar was gradually lifted from 1944 onwards, but the belief that women would be unable to give a job their full attention because of domestic demands remained widespread, as did the exclusion of women from many trades and industries.

It is not clear whether Caroline ever contemplated marriage to her friend F. S. Button, or whether she decided to sacrifice a marriage to her career, but her words on the subject appear to come from the heart. As her professional star rose, she continued to depend on the guidance of F. S., who reliably voiced his support for her endeavours. In a twenty-first-anniversary edition of *Woman Engineer*, F. S. argued in 1940 that women's work in engineering was only just beginning, and that the society had a vital role to play. 'Every woman with technical and administrative training is helped by the work of the Women's Engineering Society, and each and every one of them ought to belong to it,' he wrote. F. S. was twenty-two years older than Caroline; his death in 1948, at the age of seventy-five, must have hit her very hard.

One of the qualities that made Caroline Haslett stand out from the crowd as a manager was the importance she attached to the happiness and wellbeing of her workforce – an approach championed by the American psychologist and engineer Lillian Gilbreth. This concern was evident in the collaborative spirit that permeated the Kensington headquarters of the Electrical Association for Women, of which Caroline remained director until 1956 – by which time the organisation had 14,000 members in 160 branches throughout Britain. Caroline had absorbed the results of Lillian Gilbreth's studies into time and motion in the workplace, and this remained an important influence, encouraging her to advocate the introduction of scientific management techniques into the home.[17]

'My knowledge that [women] can work together successfully is a formula which I continually put to the test, for my staff of thirty is made up entirely of women and girls,' she wrote in 1938,[18] explaining that no new venture at the Electrical Association for Women was ever undertaken without the full knowledge and approval of her senior colleagues. 'My staff work with me, not for me, and we sow and reap and glean together in great comradeship and harmony.' Their regular work included running conferences, publishing magazines and editing books, as well as organising branches of the association and keeping in touch with its many thousands of members. A thriving 'housecraft' school had been set up, and diplomas and prizes were administered to reward a host of achievements associated with electrical engineering. 'We are recognised by government departments and there are very few fields of public service upon whose committees we are not represented.'

Another clue to Caroline's success came from the pen of the American feminist writer Crystal Eastman, who encountered her in the mid-1920s at a meeting of the Women's Freedom League, where Caroline was speaking, and was dazzled by her physical presence: 'Big mouth, strong nose, shining eyes, a grave and lovely face. Maternal, too, I thought, in that rich universal way in which some women's faces are maternal – suggesting strength, security, happiness.'[19] Crystal was surprised when Caroline said that she was not an engineer, and nor had she ever studied engineering, but that she had had some excellent training at the Cochran Boiler Company during the 1914–18 war, followed by four months' practical experience in the engineering shops. Then, at the age of twenty-three, she had been offered the job of secretary at the Women's Engineering Society: 'There were sixty-odd applicants, all of them older and many with university degrees, but for some reason Lady Parsons chose me.'

Caroline believed that one of her great achievements was to have secured admission for women to all the engineering societies. 'Every branch of engineering has its own society: mechanical engineers, marine engineers, civil, electrical, automobile, etc.,' she told Crystal. 'And professional standing requires membership in one of these societies and the right to print its initials after one's name.'

During the 1939–45 war, when Caroline was working for the Ministry of Labour, the leaders of all the main women's services, including the WRNS, the WAAF and the ATS (Auxiliary Territorial Service), consulted her about the welfare of their female employees.[20] The wide scope of her interest was reflected in the network of International Women's Service Groups she set up to foster goodwill among refugees from various countries and to represent the interests of non-British business and professional women. Within a year, 546 women from twenty-six countries were registered with the scheme, which helped them to find training and employment in Britain.

The Electrical Association for Women was very active during the Second World War, especially on the propaganda front. Since electricity was rationed at 75 per cent of normal consumption, it was vital to encourage economy of use, so the association spread the word through leaflets, poems, films and talks, and Caroline co-authored a book with Elise Edwards entitled *Teach Yourself Household Electricity*. The association also set up a mobile canteen service for people in need that went into action in 1940. Within a year, there were twelve mobile canteens in service, one of them all-electric. Caroline was the only woman member on the twenty-strong committee convened by the Institution of Electrical Engineers (IEE) to plan electrical installations in postwar Britain; an important recommendation based on its findings was a new plug and socket standard.

During the war Caroline represented the British government on business missions to the United States, Canada, Sweden and Finland, and to the British forces in the Middle East; and afterwards she took a leading role in conferences organised for women in Germany by the British and American authorities.[21] While on a tour of North America in 1944, she highlighted the large number of women doing essential war work in Britain: 87 per cent of single women aged eighteen to forty and 76 per cent of married women without children were in full-time employment. She later reported that during the war years 7.5 million women had been mobilised for active service, and 10 million more had helped the war effort by performing essential household duties.

In 1945 the first Women's Electrical Exhibition was held in London and attended by the Queen, who expressed her satisfaction that, as well as celebrating technical work done by women in the services during the war, the event 'offered hopes for a happier future for mothers and housewives by exhibiting many improvements in the home'.[22] In the same year, with financial backing from the Central Electricity Board, the Electrical Association for Women set up the Caroline Haslett Trust to promote the education of women 'with regard to electrical housecraft and electrification in all its applications to domestic problems'. It provided scholarships and travelling fellowships for aspiring teachers of domestic science.

As a mark of her uniqueness, Caroline had been the sole woman delegate to the World Power Conference in Berlin in 1930 and she went on to represent Britain at later international power conferences. The extent of her public activities over the next twenty years was quite extraordinary, as described by Margaret Partridge: 'She was a member of council of the British Institute of Management 1946–54, of the Industrial Welfare Society, of the National Industrial Alliance, of the Administrative Staff College, and of King's College of Household and Social Science.'²³ She was on the governing boards of three university colleges, a member of the Central Committee on Women's Training and Employment, a member of council and vice president of the Royal Society of Arts 1941–55, and chairman and later president of the British Federation of Business and Professional Women.

Apart from editing *The Electrical Handbook for Women* and *Household Electricity*, and authoring a feminist manifesto called *Problems Have No Sex*, she showed another kind of concern for the well-run home by chairing the home-safety committee of the National Safety First Association and becoming vice president of its successor, the Royal Society for the Prevention of Accidents. She played a part in the postwar planning of Britain on the board of the Crawley New Town Development Corporation, and she served as vice president and first female chairman (1953–4) of the British Electrical Development Association.

Caroline's election in 1950 as president of the International Federation of Business and Professional Women put her in a position to influence the spread of feminism all over the world. By this time, the organisation, founded in 1930 by the American lawyer Lena Madesin Phillips to promote opportunities for women everywhere, had groups active in twenty countries. Caroline's inspirational conduct in this role, and her contribution to 'international friendship' was singled out for praise by Isobel Cripps, the wife of the Labour Cabinet minister Stafford Cripps, who described her as 'one of the most warmly human people I have ever known'.

Caroline's friendship with Isobel Cripps led to her appointment as the first female chairman of a government working party. This was the Hosiery Industry Working Party 1945–6, one of the committees set up by the Labour government to review the production, supply and distribution of various commodities that had been neglected during the war. Caroline was able to explain to her fellow committee members that stockings were an essential article of clothing for a woman and that, in the words of her sister Rosalind, 'Women derived deep psychological satisfaction from being able to obtain with ease a sufficient supply of stockings of attractive quality that both fitted and wore well.'[24]

On a more practical level, she helped to overcome the shortage of stocking-making machinery by encouraging the Bentley Engineering Company to manufacture a specially designed range of Bentley-Cotton machines, each of which 'produced thirty-two stockings at a time, in approximately thirty-five minutes, using forty-four miles of silk thread in the process'. Workers were needed to operate the new machinery, and Caroline encouraged women to apply for the job vacancies, especially in Nottingham and Leicester, which had strong links with the hosiery industry. She also advocated the use of women on a part-time shift basis, so that they could cope with the demands of a home and do a useful job at the same time.[25]

In 1931 Caroline had been made a CBE for her services to women, and in 1947, in recognition of her work for the Ministry of Labour and the Board of Trade, she was promoted to the rank of Dame Commander of the Order of the British Empire. Later that year – in what was widely seen as the crowning achievement of her career – she was appointed to the board of the British Electricity Authority (BEA), newly formed to manage the electricity industry under national ownership. The BEA named one of the ships in its collier fleet *Dame Caroline Haslett* in honour of its first female member.

While throwing her energies into this part-time role, Caroline continued to fulfil her commitments as director of the Electrical Association for Women.

Work for the new body – which became the Central Electricity Authority in 1954 and evolved into the Central Electricity Generating Board in 1957 – was extremely taxing, involving the merger of some 560 separate undertakings into one unified system. 'I don't think anyone, except those who directly participated in the work, could possibly know the strain, mental and physical, which pressed so heavily upon us,' said Walter, Lord Citrine, reflecting on his time as head of the BEA, when he got to know Caroline well.[26] Citrine remarked on his colleague's magnetic personality and lively sense of humour, and praised her moral courage and wise counsel.

Henry Self, chairman of the Electricity Council, attributed the fast growth of the industry since nationalisation in 1947 partly to Caroline's 'extraordinary flair' for productive negotiations with government ministers, trade unions and representatives of private industry, both in Britain and abroad.[27]

The writer and social reformer Violet Markham, who had led the Central Committee on Women's Training and Employment, believed that Caroline had 'burned herself out in the work which was the mainspring of her existence'. In the spring of 1954 Caroline was diagnosed with nephritis, a kidney disease, and later that year she moved to Bungay in Suffolk for a period of recuperation at the home of her sister Rosalind. In the event, a series of health crises meant that by the end of July 1956 she was forced to resign from many of her roles.

Caroline died on 4 January 1957, three days after suffering a coronary thrombosis, at the age of only sixty-one, having expressed a desire to be cremated by electricity. An obituarist in *The Times* highlighted her valuable work in 'breaking down the prejudices of employers against taking on female labour'.[28] In a tribute in *Woman Engineer*, Margaret Partridge identified her friend's outstanding characteristics as 'indomitable courage and determination; an intense interest in people, particularly women; and a flair, amounting to genius, for picking out a fundamental point from amongst a confusion of extraneous details', which made her a brilliant committee chairman.[29] Although Caroline had not founded the Women's Engineering Society, said Margaret, it was she who had given the organisation its character and independence of spirit. 'Her courage and determination surmounted what would today be considered insurmountable difficulties of straitened means and the narrow Victorian upbringing of her early years.'

Even before reaching the peak of her professional career, Caroline had been confident enough to assess her own achievements. 'If I have made a small contribution to modern thought – it is that the new world of mechanics, of the application of scientific methods to daily tasks, especially in the home, need have no fear for the lay mind,' she wrote in 1938.[30] 'I see in this new world a great opportunity for women to free themselves from the shackles of the past and to enter into a new heritage made possible by the gifts of nature which science has opened up to us.'

TWELVE

———

Jagged Abnormalities

It was Sunday 1 July 1956, two days after Marilyn Monroe married Arthur Miller, and a week before the House of Lords decisively threw out a parliamentary bill to abolish the death penalty for murder. Precisely one year earlier, the nightclub manager Ruth Ellis had gone to the gallows for killing her violent lover.

The evening was still balmy when an animated crowd emerged from the late show at Newmarket's Kingsway cinema, but it was almost dark. 'Sometimes you can't tell who's good and who's bad!' trumpeted the billboards, seizing on a general fascination with James Dean's first screen triumph. '*East of Eden* is a story of explosive passions and Elia Kazan has made it into a picture of staggering power.'

As couples and small groups dispersed, a solitary flame-haired figure made her way along the dimly lit high street towards the world-famous Rowley Mile racecourse. Younger in body and spirit than her seventy-one years might suggest – and she had, of course, successfully pretended to be fifteen years younger than she actually was – Rachel Parsons would later be portrayed in the press as 'the woman who walked alone'. A movie enthusiast, she made a habit of going to the cinema two or three times a week. The familiar home-ward route took her uphill past Black Bear Lane and the White Lion pub to the stone drinking fountain at Birdcage Walk. Shortly after 10.20 p.m., she turned right into Falmouth Avenue, a crescent-shaped cul-de-sac on the edge of town.[1]

Some eighteen months earlier, Rachel had bought Lansdowne House, a detached Victorian villa in Falmouth Avenue, where she lived in solitary isolation, and installed her top racehorses in its sprawling stable yard – an area bordered by the broad exercise track known as The Rows, leading up to Newmarket Heath. Dozens more animals had been stabled over the years at Branches Park, a 2,600-acre stud farm at Cowlinge, ten miles to the south, which she had acquired soon after the Second World War, after selling Little Court in Sunningdale to the playwright Terence Rattigan.[2]

Since taking up racing in the 1930s, Rachel had gradually acquired more and more horses, including numerous brood mares, and she now owned a total of seventy-two, including sixteen foals and ten yearlings.[3] She had horses in training in Newmarket with C. H. 'Harry' Jellis and Fred Armstrong, and an outstanding prospective stallion, Le Dieu d'Or, at Glasgow Stud in Enfield, Middlesex.

On reaching Lansdowne House, the last building in the street, Rachel's first mission, despite the lateness of the hour, was to attend to the horses. She took the gravel path to the left of the house, enter-ing the yard through a gate in the wattle fence. A young man was waiting for her in the shadows. He silently watched as she fetched a bucket of oats from the barn and made her way round the stables, adding handfuls of feed to each trough and allowing the sleepy ani-mals to nuzzle her arms and legs. She was wearing a lightweight green coat rather than her usual mink, the man noticed.

Her task finished, Rachel picked up a leather bag from the mounting-block and made her way to the house. As she opened the gate into the garden, the intruder was ready. He stepped in front of her and barred the way, pleading for help. Terrified by this approach from the dark – something of which she lived in constant fear – and scarcely able to make out the face of the man who accosted her, Rachel shouted at him to go away. He repeated his demands more insistently, while she tried to ward him off. 'She hit me with her handbag across the head. I told her not to be silly and pushed her away,' said her assailant later. 'She was fuming and still she came at me. She called me a tramp and a guttersnipe.'

Caught up in an increasingly violent struggle, the young man grabbed hold of a six-inch-long, one-inch-diameter iron bar, used to maintain machinery in the oat-crushing loft. 'She hit me again with the handbag and I hit her with the iron bar . . . I picked it up and told her to stop it and still she came for me.' As Rachel fell backwards onto a patch of grass, her attacker dropped his weapon. He put his hands under her shoulders and noticed that she was struggling to breathe. 'I didn't know whether to run away or not,' he said. He stayed with her for a while, but, as he tried to sit her up, 'She gave a heavy gasp like a gurgle or a giggle, and then she stopped breathing.'

He dragged Rachel on her back along the gravel path and in through the rear door of the house, leaving her body on the kitchen floor while he went upstairs with keys taken from her handbag. He unlocked her bedroom door and entered the room, closing the curtains and switching on the light before filling a small suitcase with valuable items. He then went back downstairs, stuffed banknotes from Rachel's purse into his coat pocket and dragged her body into an empty larder, concealing it under a pile of sacks. Before leaving, he retraced his steps through the house, locking all the doors behind him and leaving by the same way he had entered. Near the fence was the bloodstained iron bar, which he picked up and concealed in a dark corner of the stable yard. Early next morning, the iron bar would be moved to a more secure hiding place – a shed used for coal storage.

At 12.45 p.m. the following day, the manager of Morley's pawn-brokers in Cambridge, thirteen miles from Newmarket, called the police to report a scruffily dressed customer who had offered him a pair of expensive Ross binoculars in a leather case. The alert led to the arrest of Dennis James Pratt, a twenty-five-year-old stable man, who was also found to be carrying two cameras and two travelling clocks. In his wallet were eighteen ten-shilling notes and fourteen £1 notes, which he claimed to have won at the races.

Pratt broke down under interrogation. 'How long will you keep me if I tell you?' he asked DC Kenneth Procter. 'Will you look after my wife and let her know?' When pushed to explain the source of the valuables, he said, 'They're from Lansdowne House – Parsons – Rachel's.' After giving Rachel's full name and address, he insisted on dictating a statement. 'This will shock you,' he began. '*I have done her in.*'

Later that afternoon, a police search of Lansdowne House revealed a locked entrance to a larder leading off the scullery. When two officers forced their way in, they saw a heap of old sacks lying on the floor behind a wooden screen. The shape of Rachel's legs and feet was visible beneath the coverings. 'I felt her wrist and found that it was cold and stiff,' said DC Mark Connelly in a statement. The upper part of Rachel's body and her head were covered with the green overcoat – now saturated in blood – that she had been wearing at the time of the attack. 'The body was fully dressed in a green two-piece suit, blouse and stockings,' reported Connelly. 'The jacket, blouse and brassiere were dragged up slightly, and the left breast was partly exposed and bloodstained.' Rachel's right arm was slightly bent and the hand was on her right hip, revealing five carefully varnished crimson fingernails. Her injuries were so bad that her head and face were virtually unrecognisable.

There were three deep parallel wounds on the left side of the scalp, and the forensic pathologist who later examined the body concluded that the cause of death had been shock and haemorrhage due to bruising of the brain and fracture of the skull. The pathologist also noted 'a trivial graze on the right cheek, bruising on the left side of the centre of the lower lip . . . and a fracture of the sixth rib on the left side'. There was no evidence of sexual assault. The dead woman's general health was judged to be exceptionally good for her age.

Within twenty-four hours of the discovery of Rachel's body, Dennis Pratt had been charged with her murder. The accused man had been living with his pregnant wife and their two young daughters at 18 Portland Road, Newmarket – a ten-minute walk from Lansdowne House, beyond The Rows exercise track. An able rider with frustrated ambitions to become a jockey, Pratt had worked at Rachel's stables for a year before leaving of his own accord in May 1956. He said that Rachel owed him money in lieu of holidays not taken, and he had been back to the stables a number of times to ask for it – but Rachel refused to pay. The total amount owing turned out to be £4 10s 8d.

It emerged that the holiday-pay issue had developed into a bitter row between employer and employee, as noted by, among others, a taxi driver who regularly drove Rachel from Cambridge station to Newmarket. A few days before her death, he saw Pratt on the doorstep at Lansdowne House and watched Rachel confront him. 'I've come to see you,' said Pratt. 'I've got no money.' She told him to leave, threatening to call the police. Other witnesses revealed that several people had a grievance against Rachel. She could be very generous at times, they said, happy to lend large sums to those in need; on other occasions, she teased and taunted her male staff in public and called them names.

John Maloney, a racehorse trainer once employed by Rachel, who had moved into a cottage at the rear of her stable yard in October 1955, complained about her interference in his work. He said that Rachel would habitually go round the yard at night and give the horses food they didn't need. Pratt was working there as a stable lad when he first arrived, said Maloney, and, if Rachel criticised him, he would argue with her. 'Pratt always stuck up for himself and answered her back, but I never heard him threaten her, although she used to call him "a dirty rat" and "a dirty urchin".'

Maloney said the young man did his job well and was kind to the horses, but he was a habitual gambler who made a habit of borrowing cash from friends and acquaintances. 'I have often seen him go to Miss Parsons on his own and I know many times she lent him money.' While on remand, Pratt admitted to winning or losing up to £50 a day (well over £1,000 today) from gambling. Once, after a row, he had walked out on Rachel, but two weeks later he returned. 'Miss Parsons thought a lot of Pratt,' said Maloney, 'and when he left she hoped he would come back.' There seems little doubt that – in spite of their publicly tempestuous relationship – a mutual affection, or dependency, had developed between Rachel and Pratt.

The ferocious killing made front-page news across the country – not only on account of the murky circumstances in which it occurred, but also because Rachel Parsons was at the time one of the richest people in Britain. 'MILLIONAIRESS FOUND DEAD AT HER HOME' read one of the splash headlines, 'STABLEMAN CHARGED WITH MURDER'.

Among the national newspapers, it was the *Daily Express* that could lay claim to the most lurid coverage. In a story headed 'TURF

HEIRESS DEATH RIDDLE', the paper revealed that 'Miss Rachel Parsons, racehorse owner, daughter of a great engineer, grand-daughter of an earl, a glittering hostess turned eccentric recluse', had been found dead with head injuries in the mansion in which she lived alone in Newmarket. 'This was a nightmare come true,' wrote the reporter. 'For seventy-one-year-old Miss Parsons, in her red wig and clothes of twenty years ago, had a habit of locking and barring herself in her bare, cobwebbed home and phoning police to say she had seen intruders prowling in the grounds. The signs last night were that she had been attacked with an iron bar in the tangled garden, then dragged indoors.'

The newspaper noted that in the early 1930s Rachel had inherited a fortune from her father, as well as some of his genius, for she herself was a qualified engineer and a naval architect. 'As a girl among the Edwardian gallants, she was one of Mayfair's most eligible heir-esses. But she died with only one love. A love of animals.'

Establishing a theme that recurred often in the months to come, the *Express* sought to highlight the victim's eccentricities, painting her as a Miss Havisham figure: 'At Lansdowne House, where they found her last night, only one of the fourteen rooms was furnished – and that barely. But the stables were modern and comfortable. At Branches Park, her 2,600-acre estate and stud farm not far away, Bruno the guard dog had the forty-room mansion to himself.' Warming to its subject, the newspaper devoted the next day's front page to a follow-up story, 'THE LOVE AND FURY OF MISS RACHEL': 'For forty years, until she was killed . . . Rachel Parsons kept the bitter secret of her life. She was a woman scorned. In her youth her flowing red hair made her a picture of fury. In her old age she wore a brilliant red wig.' The colour of her hair and the wearing of a wig loomed large in character sketches of the dead woman.

Forty years earlier, reported the *Daily Express*, Rachel had been a director of the engineering works founded by her father on the Tyne. During that time she had fallen in love with one of her colleagues in the firm. 'But the man turned her down. Turned down the boss's daughter. He married another. Rachel Parsons of the red hair did not forget or forgive.' No further clues were given about the identity of the mysterious lover. Alexander Law, the former managing director at Heaton (see pages 108–9) – who may have been the man referred to – had retired in 1945 after a long and successful career with English Electric Company in Rugby.[4] He died on 24 March 1956 and was survived by his wife, Isabel, and three children. Less than three months later, Rachel herself was dead.

Other newspapers focused on Rachel's life of wealth and privilege, her career as a racehorse owner and her strange, impetuous behaviour. The *Newmarket Weekly News* traced 'the beginning of her eccentricity' to the time of her purchase in 1947 of Branches Park, the eighteenth-century mansion and estate in Cowlinge that had allegedly been neglected. Farm managers, stable workers and domestic staff had come and gone in quick succession, and tied cottages on the estate stood empty. None of the news media gave any prominence to her career as an engineer, her role in the Women's Engineering Society, or her involvement in politics.

Even the engineering society itself adopted a muted tone in its brief note of condolence to the Parsons family:

Miss Parsons was a brilliant pioneer in academic engineering training for women, and it is to her and to the enthusiasm of her mother, the Hon. Lady Parsons, that the society owes its being. The charter of the Women's Engineering Society bears the signatures of Miss Parsons and her mother.

The tremors caused by the killing were felt not only in Great Britain but also on the other side of the Irish Sea – at Birr Castle, County Offaly, Rachel's ancestral home. Laurence Michael Harvey Parsons, 6th Earl of Rosse, had inherited the earldom and the demesne of Birr from his father in 1918, at the age of twelve. Michael, as he was known, had since gone on to thrive as the master of Birr and taken a leading role on the Historic Buildings Committee of the National Trust. In 1935 he married Anne Armstrong-Jones (née Messel), sister of the fashionable theatre designer Oliver Messel. Michael's easy charm and extraordinary good looks – qualities he shared with other members of his family – would later lead *The Age* newspaper in Melbourne to describe him as 'the Adonis of the Peerage'.[5] As the grandson of Charles Parsons' eldest brother, Michael Rosse was one of Rachel's nearest surviving relatives.

The shock and confusion felt by the Parsons family at the calamity of Rachel's unexpected death was reflected in a letter from the redoubtable Nora Robertson of Huntington Castle in Clonegal, County Carlow, to her old friend Michael Rosse.[6] 'This fantastic melodrama just takes one's breath away!' she wrote. 'But one dreads the corroborative details that may emerge at the trial.' Sympathising with Michael for the 'embarrassing notoriety' that his association with the case might bring, Nora admitted that she had conflicting thoughts about Rachel. 'Of course she was crackers – but not nice crackers; yet in her young days she was really congenial – and good.'

Theories and wild rumours abounded about Rachel's death. To the amazement of many, and the incredulity of some, she had failed to make a will, so the task of distributing her considerable riches fell to Michael Rosse and John (Johnnie) Randal Parsons, another cousin. Since Rachel had died unmarried and childless – and without parent, brother, sister, grandparent, uncle or aunt surviving her – the residue of her estate had to be divided between her immediate and distant cousins on both sides of the family. Michael and Johnnie set out to establish the nature and extent of Rachel's assets, including houses, land, horses, furs, jewels, furniture and family heirlooms, and then to establish the number of those entitled to a share – a figure that would eventually rise to twenty-eight. It was a huge and difficult task – and it was not made any easier by the cavalier attitude of the executors at Barclays Bank.

'I had a letter from Barclays yesterday and they will be writing to you,' wrote Johnnie to Michael in May 1957.[7] 'They appear to have found "voluminous papers of no value" [going back to 1926] amongst Rachel's furniture at the Pantechnicon and Mr Madeley seems to have given orders for it to be burnt. They also found three oil paintings which they presume are portraits of Rachel from about four to twenty years of age.'

When challenged about its decision to burn Rachel's papers, the bank sought to dismiss the two men's concerns. 'Most consisted of applications for the payment of accounts and actual accounts, but there were also very large numbers of paid cheques, invitations to various functions, acceptances and refusals of invitations apparently issued by Miss Parsons, and sundry odd correspondence with dressmakers and various tradesmen,' wrote the manager. 'Mr Madeley spent two and a half hours going through all the papers to make perfectly certain that there was nothing among them which would be of any assistance to the administrators in dealing with the estate or to members of the family as being of any interest to them.'

Stung by the bank's insensitivity, Johnnie resolved to keep a closer eye on the activities of its officials. The following month, he wrote again to Michael about the three portraits of Rachel, opposing the idea of their being sold at auction. 'If no member of the family or any Bethell wants them, I should like to see them destroyed,' he said, presumably fearing that the pictures – showing Rachel as a child and young woman with a mass of red hair – might be used unscrupulously to discredit their subject still further. 'I think I have made Mr Sharp very cross over the destruction of all the papers. But it was a very wrong action in principle, and especially in an administration, and even more so in the case of violent death. It is just a year since you saw her at Ascot – poor Rachel.'

In moving her home after the war to Newmarket, the birthplace and headquarters of thoroughbred horse racing, Rachel had not envisaged becoming the target of a form of misogyny even more painful than she had encountered during her engineering career. Under the rules of the Jockey Club, the governing body of British racing, women were not allowed to be trainers or jockeys, and female owners were barely tolerated.[8] In short, most women were formally barred from the racing scene, and those who tried to circumvent the barrier were often treated with contempt. One who had broken through, in the early 1930s, was Dorothy Wyndham Paget, who achieved a string of triumphs over a twenty-year period, but whose unconventional behaviour led to her being derided and belittled as 'the original barmy owner'. Dorothy's most successful horse was Golden Miller, five times winner of the Cheltenham Gold Cup and the only horse to win both the Gold Cup and the Grand National in a single year (1934). According to scornful critics in the press, Rachel was cast in the same mould. She would arrive at the races 'dressed as shabbily as her predecessor' and sit in the back of her Rolls-Royce 'eating sardines out of a tin'.[9]

Although Rachel had been the victim of a terrible crime, much of the press coverage after the killing amounted to a character assassination of the dead woman, revealing unsavoury details that would later be exploited by Pratt's defence at the trial. Initially, it was Rachel's appearance and way of life that prompted disparaging comments. According to one local paper, she always wore the same clothes, even when attending Royal Ascot: 'Victorian-style hat complete with "fruit salad" . . . and down-at-heel shoes often caked with mud.'[10] While she had 'no close friends and few callers', she was a familiar sight at race meetings around the country.

People who penetrated Rachel's homes were apparently amazed at what they found there. At Branches Park, her Suffolk mansion, she occupied just one room, cooking on an oil stove in the corner. 'Egg shells, bacon rinds and pieces of bread were strewn about the floor, and the room gave the appearance of not having been cleaned for years,' while the swimming pool was used for storing bales of straw and oats for the horses. Animal feed was also kept in the house, which was overrun with vermin.

A similar story was told by the police officer who had found Rachel's body at Lansdowne House in Newmarket. The outside area was 'neglected and unkempt', he said, and the inside was dirty. Another officer mentioned that 'some thousands' of keys had been found in the house. Fearful of intruders and distrustful of almost everyone around her, especially after a series of break-ins at Branches Park, Rachel had kept everything locked up and carried the keys with her. Several times in the months before her death, she had made complaints to the police. The possibility of Dennis Pratt's involvement in the break-ins does not seem to have been investigated.

Among those who claimed to have witnessed Rachel's tyranny at first hand was Henry Verschoyle, a retired colonel once employed as a stud manager at Branches Park, who said he had sometimes seen her 'lash out with a dog whip at some luckless labourer'. Verschoyle claimed later in an interview with the *News of the World* that Rachel had foretold her own violent death, saying, 'I know that one day someone will kill me. I know that as surely as I am standing here.'[11] It seemed to the colonel as if she were challenging him to go ahead and do it. 'She knew she was hated by the men on her staff – men

Both images: Tyne & Wear Archives & Museums

Above and below: Female employees at Heaton Works carry out some of the intricate tasks required in the manufacture of turbines for electricity generation, including (above) fitting gills to conductors.

IET Archives

Women's Engineering Society and IET Archives

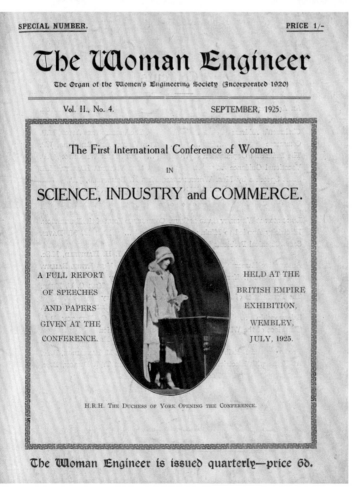

SPECIAL NUMBER.   PRICE 1/-

The Woman Engineer

The Organ of the Women's Engineering Society (Incorporated 1920)

Vol. II., No. 4.   SEPTEMBER, 1925.

The First International Conference of Women

IN

SCIENCE, INDUSTRY and COMMERCE.

A FULL REPORT   HELD AT THE
OF SPEECHES   BRITISH EMPIRE
AND PAPERS   EXHIBITION,
GIVEN AT THE   WEMBLEY,
CONFERENCE.   JULY, 1925.

H.R.H. THE DUCHESS OF YORK OPENING THE CONFERENCE.

The Woman Engineer is issued quarterly—price 6d.

Above: The inaugural conference of the Women's Engineering Society, held in 1923 at Birmingham University. Katharine Parsons is seated fifth from left.

Wembley, July 1925: the First International Conference of Women in Science, Industry and Commerce was launched by HRH the Duchess of York, who became Queen in 1936, on the accession of her husband as George VI.

Women's Engineering Society and IET Archives

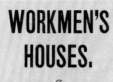

WORKMEN'S HOUSES.

Modern.
Attractive.
Durable.

Can be built in quantities of 48.

Price £400 each (Freehold).

ENQUIRIES SOLICITED.

LAURA A. WILLSON, M.B.E., Jumples, Halifax.

Laura Annie Willson designed and built hundreds of high-quality homes for working people, describing housebuilding as 'a form of engineering of the domestic kind'.

IET Archives

Three presidents of the Women's Engineering Society: (left to right) Laura Annie Willson (1926–28), Caroline Haslett (1940–41), Margaret Partridge (1944–45).

IET Archives

Impressions of Some Well-known People at the Birmingham Conference of the E.A.W. (See page 666)

The most prominent individuals at the 1933 conference of the Electrical Association for Women provided a rich subject for caricature.

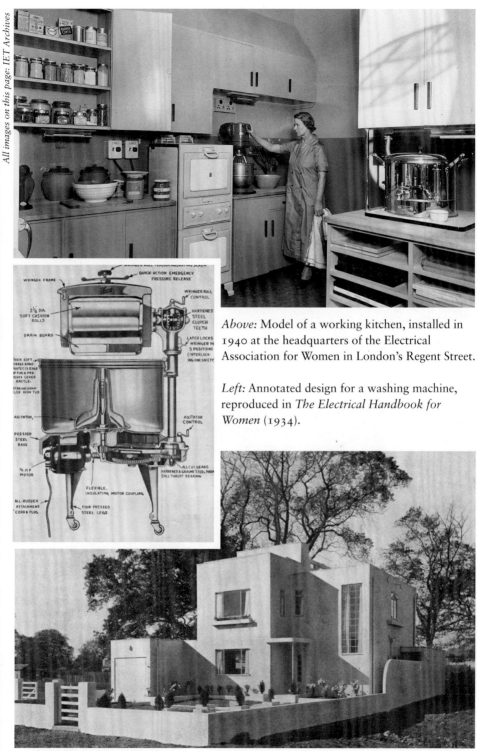

All images on this page: IET Archives

Above: Model of a working kitchen, installed in 1940 at the headquarters of the Electrical Association for Women in London's Regent Street.

Left: Annotated design for a washing machine, reproduced in *The Electrical Handbook for Women* (1934).

The All-Electric House in Bristol, designed by the Bristol branch of the Electrical Association for Women, attracted huge crowds when it opened to the public in 1935.

Above: Some of the female pilots of the Air Transport Auxiliary (ATA), formed in 1940. The women's section of the ATA was established and led by Pauline Gower.

Above: Amy Johnson in the cockpit of *Jason*, the Gipsy Moth in which she flew solo from England to Australia.

Right: Dorothy Spicer (left) and Pauline Gower, who together ran an air-taxi business in the 1930s.

Courtesy of Negative Gravity by Matthew Freudenberg

© *Illustrated London News / Mary Evans*

Above: Beatrice (Tilly) Shilling astride a Norton, one of her many motorbikes, as shown in the 1935 Norton catalogue. Behind her is an image of a Spitfire, whose engine safety was much improved by the insertion of 'Miss Shilling's orifice'.

Right: Disappointed in her professional and political ambitions in the late 1920s, Rachel Parsons became a society hostess, staging concerts and lavish parties at her grand homes in Mayfair and Belgravia.

News UK / News Licensing

The Fantastic Miss Parsons

● *Behind the cob-webbed windows and locked doors of her gloomy country home Rachael Parsons, wealthy race-horse-owner, lived alone in a weird world. She left its shadows only to scream abuse at her staff and tradespeople. She was feared, hated, shunned. Once almost a millionairess, she begrudged parting with even a halfpenny.*

● *It was her meanness that brought her fantastic existence to a sudden and violent end. When she refused Dennis Pratt, an ex-stable lad, a few pounds holiday money, he struck her down with an iron bar and killed her. For this he stood his trial at Essex Assizes at Chelmsford and was sentenced to 10 years' imprisonment for manslaughter.*

● *Pratt did more than kill Rachael Parsons. He killed a fantasy. Now a "News of the World" special investigator unlocks the doors to the strange world in which she lived. He reveals how, over the years, this brilliant daughter of a famous man forsook the gay life of a gracious hostess to become an eccentric recluse living in abject squalor.*

With £600,000 To Spend She Lived In Squalor

By NORMAN RAE

RACHAEL PARSONS was one of Britain's wealthiest women. Yet she lived in almost indescribable squalor behind locked doors in a gloomy 40-room mansion. And she died because she begrudged an employee a paltry pound or two.

She left £623,617 (duty paid £400,539)—and no will. Because she had no close next of kin, 30 relatives share the residue of her estate.

I have been investigating this extraordinary woman's strange life, seeking the reasons for her incredible meanness and her wretched existence; probing the secrets behind the locked doors.

It is a fantastic story of a woman who predicted her own death.

Rachael Parsons was the daughter of Sir Charles Parsons, inventor of the marine turbine engine. And in days when people in her social circle thought women should be beautiful rather than brainy, she decided to become an engineer herself.

It was not until her father's death in 1931—when she inherited almost £1,000,000—that she began to play any part in society. And then it was on a grand scale.

She became a regular racegoer and was as knowledgeable as any member of the Jockey Club. Her house in Grosvenor-square, London, became the rendezvous of famous people, including members of the Royal family.

The Whispers

Was She Frustrated In Love?

But it was whispered that she was showing "signs of eccentricity."

Some said she was frustrated in love; that she intended marrying a young diplomat, and that the young man took fright at the last moment, fearing he was to become a "rich woman's darling."

She abandoned her plans to buy a large house at Goodwood, where she was going to set up racing stables after their marriage.

And with the passing years Rachael Parsons became something of a recluse.

She bought her first string of racehorses just over 20 years ago and by the start of World War II had had several wins with horses trained by "Atty" Persse. Among her winners were Doctor Dolittle and Battle Cruiser, Golden God and his half-brother Le Dieu D'Or.

Soon after the war Rachael Parsons bought Branches Park estate, some eight miles from Newmarket, with its great dark red rambling mansion and stables, and several farms.

Time was when the villagers from nearby Cowlinge played cricket in the park and their children enjoyed many a jolly party in the grounds. At night the windows of the great house were ablaze with light and its lovely rooms filled with music and laughter.

Rachael Parsons ended all that.

Life Was Chaos

Not Even Enough Spoons For Her Guests

What went on behind the locked doors of the vast house in the last gloomy years of Rachael Parsons's life is best told by Mrs. Ida Stubbings, of the Park Farm. For nearly eight years she was Miss Parsons's daily help, her cook, waitress, keeper of the records—and companion both to Miss Parsons and her dog, Bruce.

"It was not long before I realised I was working for a very strange woman," she said. "At first she was still quite cultured. Then, slowly, I saw her deteriorate.

"In the early days there were still fine parties. All the best people attended. There were plenty of staff to cope then. But at the very end Miss Parsons lived alone in one room. Even at her other home, Lansdowne House, in the heart of Newmarket, she lived without any staff or companions.

"I sometimes wondered if some of the distinguished guests who stayed at Branches Park realised what went on behind the scenes.

"At first there was a full staff and a butler but there was never enough cutlery, and conditions in the kitchen were chaotic — and not too clean.

"Sometimes I had to dash into the guests' bedrooms grabbing the teaspoons from their early morning cups of tea because there weren't enough spoons for the breakfast table.

"Sometimes the water supply went wrong and the butler had to fetch water from a disused well for the guests' wash-bowls—and tea.

"The parties became fewer and fewer — and then they ended.

"The men Miss Parsons employed to manage her horses and estate were hard-working and honest. But she regarded them as thieves, rogues and vagabonds.

"She deluded herself that the stable lads were stealing and selling the linseed, the corn and other foodstuffs. So she linen cupboard. The mice, attracted by the food, played havoc with beautiful sheets and eiderdowns. They chewed them to pieces to make their nests.

In time she hid everything. Door after door was locked. And as Det. Mark Connolly told the jury at Pratt's trial he found thousands of keys in the house when he went there to investigate Miss Parsons's death.

Not even the law was immune from the fiery Miss Parsons—or her dog—as Det. Connolly also revealed at the trial.

Once she reported to him the theft of her furniture. Another time she said she had lost 2,000 pheasants. Asked by the detective if she suspected poachers she snapped back, "I did not say poachers, you damn fool. I said stealing."

He was ordered off the premises and chased by her Airedale dog.

As the days went by Rachael Parsons's meanness and suspicions increased. One missing rabbit bone set her off on another crazy system, as Mrs. Stubbings recalls.

"One day Miss Parsons asked me how many pieces there were in a rabbit," said Mrs. Stubbings. "She had counted the bones and pieces of flesh of a rabbit cooked for her supper and concluded that one of the staff had filched a piece.

"Her suspicions started a new habit. She would carry any rabbit or chicken straight from the pot in the kitchen to her bedroom. The remains would be allowed to mildew in pans or on plates for weeks.

"Sometimes — and towards the end quite frequently—she cooked eggs and bacon in her bedroom. Eggshells and greasy rind were left in heaps on the floor until the day she unlocked the door and stood on guard over me while I swept them up.

Pratt, the man who brought the fantasy to an end.

"She would keep biscuits and butter all mixed up in a drawer with face powder, cosmetics and hairpins."

And when Rachael Parsons went to Lansdowne House she took her squalor with her. In the Assize Court at Chelmsford Det. Sgt. Ronald Bigmore said he found the house dirty and neglected. In Miss Parsons's bedroom were masses of old eggshells and tea leaves choked up the bath.

And she roamed around almost in rags—*with a dirty, old, fabulously expensive mink coat over them.*

"Her clothes, smart at first, were held together with safety pins and bits of string," said Mrs. Stubbings. "She would deliberately wear odd shoes, examining several pairs and selecting the best two shoes irrespective of style or colour.

"Whenever tradesmen called she quarrelled with them and called them thieves and robbers. Electricians and plumbers were accused of theft. I thought sometimes she staged these rows so the men would walk out and she could avoid payment.

"Servants arrived and left as regular as clockwork. When a new servant was due I would be told at the last minute to get a meal ready. Usually there was only stale bread.

"She had a curious way of paying wages. She would keep the staff waiting until Monday. 'That way they have to stay another week. If I paid them on Saturday they'd be gone by evening,' she said.

"It was a cruel way to treat folk who were not well-off. Yet she had a streak of kindness in her—reserved for animals. She loved horses and was devoted to her dog, Bruce.

"When Bruce went lame once he lay for days in a stupor. I discovered she had been doping his food with a strong sleeping draught to ease his discomfort.

"And I have been told she used to get up in the middle of the night to give her horse Golden God an extra feed in absolute defiance of the trainer's wishes.

"I hope I haven't drawn too harsh a picture of Rachael Parsons. For all her wealth, I was sorry for her and did what I could for her."

In and around Newmarket they still talk of a dapper Colonel whom Rachael Parsons appointed as stud and farm manager — and how for months he fought a losing battle for the men she employed, and for sanity in dealing with the estate and the horses.

He is Col. Henry Cosby Verschoyle, ex-Regular R.A.S.C. officer—and I found him leading a quiet life in his home on the banks of one of the West Country's most famous salmon fishing rivers.

"Rachael Parsons was unlike any other woman I have known," he told me. "I believe she was unique—a woman who could have been so wonderfully kind, who could have done so much good in this world, but who, in fact, was a she-devil.

Her Fear

"One Day Someone Will Kill Me"

"As she screamed her insults at me and others it was as much as I could do to keep my self-control.

"She would look at me and say: 'Colonel, I know that one day someone will kill me. I know that as surely as I am standing here.'

"It seemed as if she was taunting me to go ahead and do it.

"She knew she was hated by the men on her staff. Men she had goaded and taunted almost beyond endurance.

"To start with I was left alone to do the best I could. Then she began cracking the whip.

"Her farm had been neglected and was in danger of being taken away from her. To gain time I ordered one large field to be sown with wheat.

"But no sooner was the ground ready, with the tractors out on the final stages for sowing, than she was down there shouting and raving and ordering all work to stop and the men to leave the field.

"'I will be the boss around here,' she would scream—often at no one in particular. And sometimes I have seen her lash out with a dog whip at some luckless labourer.

"When she kept people waiting for their wages and they protested, she would threaten to set her dog on them.

"There was a grim scene in the stable yard one day. She had threatened a stable lad who thereupon grabbed a pitchfork and retorted: 'If you set your dog on me I'll rip you and him to bits.'

"Miss Parsons was so sure she was surrounded by thieves she would not buy feed in bulk. I had to drive into Newmarket for a bag or two at a time.

"It was typical of her that when a field of oats was being harvested she stood by the threshing machine counting the bags as they were driven off to her home, where there was a second check to ensure none had disappeared on the way.

"She laughed like anything one week-end when a new employee arrived with his wife and young family to find the comfortable house he had been promised leaked like a sieve and had no domestic water supply.

"I Can See Her Now . . ."

"When I protested it was not very funny for a mother with young children to care for she just laughed again and said I had no sense of humour.

"I can see her now in a dirty, bedraggled skirt, dirty blouse, torn stockings and down-at-heel shoes—and a mink coat —almost in hysterics over her joke.

"To her all the people in her employ were so much trash, to be driven at her slightest whim. Yet all the time, behind all her bluster, was that gnawing fear of sudden death.

"'Do you know, Colonel,' she once told me, 'I always sleep with a loaded gun in my bedroom. They will not kill me easily. You know I am quite aware that a number of people would like to murder me.'

"I think that fear sprang from her medieval outlook. She would have liked to have lived in days when no one dared answer her back; when her employees would have been serfs.

"And of some who knew her she would say this to me: 'They are vultures waiting to pick my bones.'

"Stood It For A Year"

"I stood it for a year before I got my marching orders. I had held on hoping to get some of the money I felt she owed me. But I had no written agreement.

"I remembered her words on the first day we met: 'Such things are for ordinary folk, not for people like us. . .'"

Three Pictures That Span The Years

1919 1946 1950

'SHE CALLED ME A GUTTERSNIPE'

"YOU killed an old woman in a most brutal fashion. The jury have taken a merciful view of your case, but that cannot disguise the fact that this was a very brutal crime."

Mr. Justice Diplock said this when he sentenced 26-year-old Dennis Pratt, of Portland-road, Newmarket, to 10 years' imprisonment.

Pratt was acquitted of murdering Miss Parsons and was found guilty of manslaughter.

Miss Parsons's body, with severe head injuries, was found under sacks in a locked pantry at Lansdowne House. Pratt was alleged to have told the police, "I have done her in."

Pratt, giving evidence, said he was married with three children. again on July 1 she started arguing straight away and called him and his wife guttersnipes.

She hit him twice with her handbag though he told her to stop. While they were arguing he noticed an iron bar and hit her with it.

"She still came for me and I could not help it. I don't know how many blows I struck," said Pratt.

Mr. Michael Havers, defending: Did you intend to kill her?

Pratt: No; I cannot realise now that I have done it.

"Still In A Dream"

Mr. W. T. Wells, Q.C., prosecuting, recalled that in a statement to the police Pratt said: "I cannot realise that this

In covering the trial of Dennis Pratt for the killing of Rachel Parsons, the *News of the World* quoted a farm manager's claims that the dead woman had been 'wicked' and 'a she-devil'. Rachel's cousins expressed their deep shock to the editor, insisting that the article gave 'a totally wrong impression to all who read it'.

she had goaded and taunted almost beyond endurance,' he said. 'Rachel Parsons was unlike any woman I have known. I believe she was unique – a woman who could have been so wonderfully kind, who could have done so much good in this world, but who was, in fact, a she-devil.'

Michael Rosse and Johnnie Parsons, who displayed an instinctive loyalty towards their late cousin, even though they had not been particularly close to her, were unprepared for the press onslaught. In the early days, they turned a blind eye, attempting to brush aside the accusations of disgruntled employees, but when the *News of the World* published its 'she-devil' interview with Henry Verschoyle, they could no longer remain silent.

With the support of Elizabeth, Lady Cayley, a prominent journalist who was Rachel's cousin on her mother's side, the two men composed a letter of protest to the editor, expressing the family's deep dismay and claiming that a one-sided and exaggerated picture had been drawn, giving a completely wrong impression to anyone who read it.

'Miss Parsons, like many elderly people living alone, in later years admittedly developed eccentric habits; but to describe her as "wicked" and a "she-devil" is untrue and shameful,' wrote the cousins.[12] 'In her youth she possessed a brilliantly clear brain and mind, and until recently she was of perfectly normal behaviour. She was always a person of strong will and determined views; but she also had a distinct sense of public service and was capable of great kindness, as many can testify.'

The letter received an obsequious but unrepentant response from the *News of the World*'s editor, Reginald Cudlipp. 'Our story was based on information given by named people who had worked for Miss Parsons and knew her intimately – possibly, as so often happens, quite as intimately as her own relations,' wrote Cudlipp crisply.

The most sympathetic and eloquent account of Rachel's troubled life came from the pen of Anne Parsons, Countess of Rosse, Michael Rosse's wife, published in the obituaries column of *The Times* on 18 July 1956. Anne was well known as a society hostess and she and her husband were influential advocates for the preservation of British heritage; in February 1958 Anne would go on to found the Victorian Society. Her son by her first marriage was Anthony Armstrong-Jones, who married Princess Margaret in 1960.

Although Anne had not known the young Rachel personally, she had heard adulatory accounts within the family of her character and talents – talents that had clearly not been allowed to blossom to the full in adult life. She believed that the many disappointments that Rachel had encountered, and the internal contradictions – the 'jagged abnormalities' – with which she had had to grapple did much to explain her unconventional, sometimes aggressive behaviour in later years.[13] This lack of fulfilment, Anne believed, was inextricably linked with what it had meant to be an educated woman growing up in the early twentieth century – and she took what now seems an optimistic view about how much the situation had improved in the years since the First World War.

Dennis Pratt was remanded in custody at Bedford prison and later moved to Brixton in south London, where he underwent psychiatric and medical tests. While described as 'a rather facile, weak and immature man of below average intelligence', he was pronounced sane and fit to stand trial. Clinical examination revealed one very curious fact. He had a complete transposition of the organs of his chest and of his abdominal cavity – that is, his heart was on the right side, his liver was on the left side, and his stomach was on the right – but this had not apparently caused him any disability.

Letters from Pratt to various family members during his time on remand reveal tantalising details about his relationship with Rachel.[14] 'I want to let you know what happened I didn't want to happen,' he wrote to his sister Madge. 'It would never have happened if she had been sensible . . . [On Judgement Day] she will have to face up to the Lord our God in answer for her actions, for they were madman's actions. She was unable to control herself weather [*sic*] in mind or self.'

In a letter to his grandmother, Pratt claimed that Rachel had wanted to kill him. 'What I have done, she entended doing to me or trying to do,' he wrote. 'I want to tell you Gran she was so very silly in herself and in her ways so childish and stupid in her everyday way of things. I can with truth only say her and her ways were fit only for something out of this world.'[15]

When the case came to trial at Chelmsford Assizes four months after the killing, in November 1956, Martin Jukes QC was engaged to lead for the defence, with an inexperienced but brilliant young barrister called Michael Havers as junior counsel. Since Pratt denied murder, the defence set out to show that the killing had constituted manslaughter on the grounds of provocation. To build their case, the defence lawyers set about a forensic dissection of Rachel's character, calling a string of hostile witnesses and omitting to reveal a number of salient facts about the relationship between Pratt and the dead woman. On the opening day of the trial, Havers asked Pratt whether he had intended to kill Rachel. 'No. I cannot realise now that I have done it,' he replied. It was recalled in court that he had said something similar in his original statement to police: 'I cannot realise that this has happened. It is like a dream.' Asked by the prosecuting counsel, 'When did you come out of the dream?' Pratt replied, 'I have not come out of it even now.'[16]

One of the most sensational court cases of the mid-1950s, it would prove to be not only a trial of the accused but also a posthumous public humiliation of the victim and a denigration of her extraordinary achievements.

THIRTEEN

—◆—

A Defence of Provocation

'You killed an old woman in a most brutal fashion. The jury has taken a merciful view of your case,' said Mr Justice Diplock in November 1956 before sentencing Dennis Pratt to ten years' imprisonment for the manslaughter of Rachel Parsons. Although a mass of evidence had pointed to murder, the prosecution case had been badly mishandled, and Pratt's defence lawyers succeeding in persuading the jury to accept a plea of provocation – with the result that their client had been spared the hangman's noose. Michael Havers had painted a picture of Pratt as a man of 'quiet demeanour' and below-average intelligence who had been grossly abused and called a 'guttersnipe' by an old woman in a temper: 'She swings her bag at him, and this time hits him. He still tries to calm her down. She swings and hits him again – and there to hand was the iron bar.'[1] Pratt had gone to Lansdowne House to ask for the money to which he was entitled, said Havers, omitting to explain why the defendant had found it necessary to visit Rachel late in the evening, after dark, or how it came about that the iron bar was fatefully 'to hand'.

Many witnesses, most connected with the racing world, had been called to testify that Rachel lived a life of wretchedness and squalor, treating her staff with meanness and contempt. This was presented as inexcusable in view of her great wealth and privilege. No consideration was given to the series of thefts and break-ins at Branches Park, nor to the fact that Rachel had moved into the centre of Newmarket because she was too frightened to live on her own in a remote country house. Even Rachel's love of fast cars, including Bentleys and Daimlers, was held against her. 'Miss Parsons had a fleet of eight expensive cars which she drove fearlessly,' reported the *Newmarket Weekly News*, 'but they were all in need of repair, for she thought nothing of driving across ploughed fields on her estates to talk to one of her workers.' It was emphasised that, after a number of motoring offences, Rachel had been disqualified from driving, since when she had paid others to chauffeur her around.

Crucially, no connection had been established at the trial between Dennis Pratt and Branches Park, a place he knew well, since some of Rachel's racehorses and many of her brood mares were stabled there. And no mention was made of the fact that – even though they were very different in character and social class – Rachel and Pratt had, in a rather complicated way, come to depend on each other.

In his summing-up, Mr Justice Diplock told the jury that, in reaching a verdict of manslaughter, they had to be satisfied that the provocation was serious enough to cause the accused to lose mastery of his mind and a reasonable man to lose his self-control. He reminded them that they had been given a picture of 'an eccentric, quarrelsome, unpleasant old woman, dirty in her habits and uncontrolled in her language' – someone who, it was implied, most probably deserved what was coming to her. It was a case of what would later come to be identified as 'victim-blaming' – a tactic that evidently produced the desired result for the defence.

A year after Pratt's reprieve from a murder conviction, the defence of provocation and other manslaughter defences were modified by the Homicide Act 1957, which also restricted the use of the death penalty. Capital punishment for murder was abolished in 1965 in Great Britain and in 1973 in Northern Ireland. Provocation was finally abolished as a defence for manslaughter in 2010.

Michael Havers, the thirty-three-year-old junior defence counsel in the trial of Dennis Pratt, would go on to become Attorney General in the Conservative government led by Margaret Thatcher. He held this post from 1979 to 1987, making his the longest unbroken tenure of the office since the eighteenth century. In June 1987 he was appointed Lord Chancellor, but resigned a few months later owing to ill health.

Havers' period as Attorney General was marred by controversy. On one occasion, this involved his comments about women. At the trial in 1981 of Peter Sutcliffe, the Yorkshire Ripper, on thirteen counts of murder, Havers said of Sutcliffe's victims: 'Some were prostitutes, but perhaps the saddest part of the case is that some were not. The last six attacks were on totally respectable women.' This apparent condoning of the murder of prostitutes led to furious protests, suggesting as it did a disturbing prejudice on the part of the Attorney General in relation to the female sex. Havers later represented the Crown in two of the most notorious miscarriages of justice in British legal history: the trial and appeal of the Guildford Four and also of the Maguire family (known as the Maguire Seven), all of whom were wrongfully convicted.

Michael Havers was the son of the High Court judge Sir Cecil Havers, who is remembered for presiding over the 1955 trial of Ruth Ellis for the killing of her lover David Blakely, and being the last judge in Britain to sentence a woman to death. The actor Nigel Havers, Michael's son, revealed in 2010 that his grandfather had written to the Home Secretary asking for a reprieve for Ruth Ellis because he regarded her action as a *crime passionnel*, but this was refused. Afterwards Cecil Havers provided money annually for the upkeep of Ruth Ellis's son. In 1988 Elizabeth Butler-Sloss, Cecil Havers' daughter, was the first female judge of the Court of Appeal and in 1999 she became the first woman to be appointed president of the Family Division of the High Court, making her the highest-ranking woman judge in the UK.

The involvement in Dennis Pratt's defence of a man from such a prominent legal family has led to speculation about a conspiracy to discredit Rachel Parsons' reputation[2] – but it was surely pure chance that the relatively inexperienced Michael Havers, who had not yet made his mark on the law, came to act on behalf of her killer.

Although the death of Rachel Parsons was a singularly dramatic event that could be attributed to extreme misfortune, it had – and still has – powerful symbolic value. A highly intelligent, independent, unmarried woman who had refused to conform to social convention had been silenced in the most brutal way imaginable, and this was particularly relevant in an era such as the 1950s, when there was a backlash against the great advances made by women during the first half of the twentieth century. Rachel was never one to keep quiet about her beliefs and motivations; she was forceful and articulate, and her outspokenness, especially on feminist issues, had got her into trouble throughout her life.

She was quite different in this respect from Caroline Haslett, who had used tact and charm, as well as wily intelligence, to achieve her professional aims. '[Miss Haslett] was not a brusque or aggressive character and did not appear or behave like the typical woman executive of fiction,' said *The Times* in its obituary of Caroline, who died precisely six months after Rachel.[3] 'She was a person of methodical mind who yet contrived to avoid being enslaved by system. Her work was her life. She shone as an organiser, and knew the virtues of judicious delegation.' Caroline was accepted and admired in the influential echelons of mid-century Britain in a way that Rachel was most decidedly not.

The public vilification – and destruction – of intellectual and articulate women has a history that goes back to Hypatia of Alexandria, who was born in the second half of the fourth century. Hypatia was a mathematician who taught philosophy and astronomy at the Neo-Platonist school in Alexandria. Although she was a non-believer, she was tolerant of all faiths, including Christianity, and she was widely respected for her wisdom and her teaching abilities – but in 415, for complicated and obscure reasons, she was stripped naked, brutally murdered and torn to pieces by a mob of Christians.

This ancient atrocity was recalled by the author and campaigner Dora Russell in her book of 1925 on women and knowledge.[4] Dora was writing about the feminist struggle that had begun in the late nineteenth century and culminated in the suffragette movement of the early twentieth century, during which 'ugly or intelligent women, for the most part, paid a heavy price'. Not only were they rejected during their youth, and starved of what Dora called 'natural joys', but as 'old maids' they became the object of general scorn and derision. 'Was it astonishing that the revolt [of the early feminists] had in it something frenzied and ascetic – that it seemed to express the anger of the spinster thwarted and despised in the current scheme of values?'

Given that the first company founded by women for the employment of women was called Atalanta Ltd, it is intriguing that Dora Russell chooses the story of Atalanta – a swift-footed virgin huntress from Greek myth – to illustrate the pitfalls that awaited professionally ambitious women who entered into marriage and conventional sexual relationships. Atalanta had sworn an oath of virginity to the goddess Artemis. Responding to pressure from her father, she finally agreed to marry a man who could outrun her in a race. Many tried and failed, but Hippomenes succeeded with the help of Aphrodite, who gave him three golden apples. Every time Atalanta got ahead of him, Hippomenes rolled an apple in front of her and she would run after it, allowing him to win the race – and ultimately obliging Atalanta to marry him and to submit to the limitations imposed on a wife.

Responding to the theory that some feminists had relinquished sex because of their 'Puritan' instincts, Dora Russell wrote:

> I do not think the pioneers were so much Puritan as votaries, hanging the tablet of each achievement in the temple of Athene or of Artemis, pressing on, breathless, swift of foot, sure of aim, in dread of the fate of Atalanta whom the Golden Apples lured to destruction and the marital embrace.[5]

In order to secure rewarding jobs and fulfil their dreams, many of the individuals involved in the early years of the Women's Engineering Society and the Electrical Association for Women had to overcome the stigma of 'spinsterhood'. Older women such as Margaret Moir and Laura Annie Willson had established their families before the First World War, but very few of the young women who joined the society in the 1920s and 1930s were married, though some, such as Dorothée Pullinger and Tilly Shilling, went on to marry later. The aeronauts Amy Johnson, Pauline Gower and Dorothy Spicer, who entered into marriages in the 1930s, all died tragically early – in Amy's case, after a divorce – so they had little opportunity to explore the possibilities of combining a career with family life.

While the marriage bar was in force (as it remained until 1944), it was impossible in many professions for a woman with family commitments to have a job. Ambitious and powerful women were often in same-sex relationships, though they did not generally identify themselves as 'lesbian', a pejorative term at the time. Female homosexual behaviour was never illegal in Britain, though there had been vain attempts to make it so in 1921. A role model for some was Margaret, Viscountess Rhondda, who divorced her husband, Humphrey Mackworth, in 1923 and lived with Helen Archdale, editor of *Time and Tide* magazine, for several years.[6] She then forged close links with Winifred Holtby, the novelist and intimate friend of Vera Brittain, another influential feminist writer. Lady Rhondda subsequently spent twenty-five years living with Theodora Bosanquet, who was literary editor and later director of *Time and Tide*, as well as an amanuensis to the American novelist Henry James.

Margaret (Madge) Rowbotham, the engineer who had managed the Tongland factory at Kirkcudbright, and then moved to Devon to work with Margaret Partridge in her electrical engineering firm, went into hotel management in the 1930s, becoming managing director of the Osborne Hotel in Exeter.[7] During the last ten years of her life, she lived with Margaret Partridge at the latter's family home in Willand, a village north of Exeter; the two Margarets were recognised locally as a couple.

There had been opposition to spinsters before the First World War – especially to those women who had chosen not to marry, including members of the Women's Social and Political Union, from which the suffragette movement was born. The decision to remain single was seen as a provocative act that undermined social stability. According to Sheila Jeffreys, the author of *The Spinster and Her Enemies*, this hostility grew during the war, when women's new work role in industry created renewed anxiety, and got even worse in the 1920s.[8] 'The promotion of the ideology of motherhood and marriage together with the stigmatising of lesbianism helped to reinforce women's dependence upon men,' wrote Sheila Jeffreys.

A new theory took hold, promoted by sexologists of the time, that celibacy was dangerous for women because it denied them an appropriate outlet for their sexual instincts. Such repression, it was argued, would cause them to be 'man-hating', 'destructive', 'fanatical' and, in extreme cases, 'a threat to civilisation'. Women who failed to respond to sex with enthusiasm were classified as frigid, and the fear of being labelled in this way was used as a weapon. 'The attack on the resisting women within marriage was combined with a massive renewed onslaught of propaganda against spinsters, feminists, "manhaters", lesbians, all those categories of women who were seen as rejecting not only sexual intercourse but marriage itself.'[9]

The extreme social pressures that existed during the 1920s and 1930s throw into relief the singular achievements of the Women's Engineering Society in its early years. The society provided a rallying point for independent-minded, visionary women who sought not only a good education and secure employment for themselves and others but also a better, fairer world for all members of the female sex. These pioneers met many obstacles on the way, but they were united in their determination to bring about change. The fact that they had come together to form an organisation with a clearly defined mission, as Rachel Parsons had advocated from the start, gave them a unique strength – and allowed them to do important work that would prepare the ground for the equality legislation, notably the Equal Pay Act and the Sex Discrimination Act, that came into force in the 1970s.

One of the outstanding qualities of the Women's Engineering Society has always been the diversity of talent it encompasses and encourages – reflecting both the wide diversity of the engineering profession itself and the number of different strands of engineering in which women have had the opportunity to demonstrate their intellectual and practical skills. As the pace of technological advancement grows ever faster in the 21st century, the wealth of choice has increased exponentially, but even in the mid-1950s it gave Gertrude Entwisle plenty of material for her talk in Portsmouth on 'Engineering as a Career for Girls'.[10] Gertrude was the first secretary of the Manchester branch of the Women's Engineering Society and had served as national president from 1941 to 1943. In the following extracts from the influential Portsmouth speech, she highlighted the achievements of individual women engineers – although she chose not to name names – during its first thirty-five years of existence.

We have a Women's Engineering Society started in 1918 by Lady Parsons, and I myself am continually astonished at the variety of work done by its members. There are several hundred of them and it is rare for two to be doing the same thing. It will give you some idea of the opportunities for girls if I tell you about a few of these.

I think it's true that the three women who studied engineering at Cambridge before the First World War (Lady Parsons' daughter was one of them) all became naval architects, but I've not heard of any doing that since.

One of the earliest members of the Women's Engineering Society's council was a fully qualified civil engineer. Civil engineering is the oldest branch of the profession and covers the building of bridges, making roads, tunnelling through mountains and many similar things, but does not seem to appeal to women as strongly as do other branches. However, a few have qualified and one is a lecturer at the Imperial College of Science. I also know of an Indian one and have met a Chinese woman who was doing research at Liverpool University.

The one who was on the council is Irish and was for many years a land surveyor under the Irish Land Commission.

Another member with an engineering degree, in addition to being a full member of the Institution of Mechanical Engineers, is also a member of the Locomotive Engineers and the Institute of Metals and an associate member of the Institute of Marine Engineers. Before the last war, she was in charge of a drawing office doing work for the Admiralty, and later in the war became the senior woman technical officer with the Ministry of Labour. She now runs a small engineering works of her own, in addition to doing consulting work.

As far as I know, there has been only one British seagoing engineer, though there have been lots of Russian ones. The one only got the chance because her family owned or had great influence with the shipping line. I remember the first notice of her in the *Daily Mail* was headed "Daughter of a Peer and God-daughter of a Queen". But whatever her ancestry, she undoubtedly made the grade. It was said of her that during her long apprenticeship she never failed to keep her watch. She went to Dunkirk and later was given an MBE for her courage and ability on an occasion when, in a raid, she coaxed a higher speed out of the engines than they had ever been known to give previously, ordered the stokehold and engine-room staff above to give them a chance and stayed alone in the engine-room where she had little hope of escape. She was also awarded Lloyds' War Medal for bravery at sea.

Did any of you read the books or see the films *Cheaper by the Dozen* and *Belles on Their Toes*? If you did, you may or may not have grasped that they were biographically true and that Mrs Gilbreth, when her husband died suddenly on his way to Europe, left her dozen children (the eldest was then eighteen), took her husband's berth on the ship, and delivered in Prague and London the lectures which should have been given by him. She had to do something to provide for the dozen, so she then returned to the States and began the struggle there to get herself taken seriously as an engineer. That she succeeded is proved by the fact that finally she was made a professor in one of the American universities.

A woman who is a member of the Institute of Heating and Ventilating Engineers is the senior partner in a consulting firm who have just been responsible for the reconstruction of the Central Criminal Court at the Old Bailey. Another, who took a Cambridge tripos and then became an electrical apprentice at Metropolitan-Vickers, joined a firm of consulting engineers and was concerned in lighting the reconstructed House of Commons.

Women engineers have also been employed on railways and on general transport, in the Post Office, by the BBC on radio and television, as illuminating engineers, by the Central Electricity Authority (some even in power stations) and by the Ministry of Supply as senior experimental officers.

Then there are quite a number of women who are now directors and some managing directors of small engineering works. As far as I know, however, there are not any on the directorate of any very large engineering works in this country, but that is a chance which still remains for some girl to make history!

Automobile engineering is another branch in which women have been very successful, but the two branches which have proved most attractive to girls have been electrical and aeronautical engineering.

One electrical engineer who lives in Devonshire was once chased by a London policeman on the roof of a building in Piccadilly Circus. Actually, she was fixing one of those neon signs, which was not, of course, a thing the policeman was likely to think of, nor to believe. She also formed a company to light Devon villages, and with her staff got together the capital, planned the power station, did the wiring and supplied the current to the villages.

Among aeronautical engineers, a woman was awarded the R38 prize for stress calculations on the airship and became the head of the stability section at Farnborough. Another there is a principal scientific officer and in the war was responsible for the work of a hundred people, and you probably saw the discussion in the papers about the one who went up to try to solve the trouble on the Comets.

Then there were the famous women pilots Amy Johnson and Dorothy Spicer. Amy was not the untutored girl the papers suggested. She was a university woman and, before she flew to Australia, had worked hard to learn aeronautics, and when she came back read a paper to the Association of Engineers on the repairs she had had to do en route. Dorothy Spicer looked a lady of fashion and the last person willing to dirty her hands. She met Amy and said she wanted to be an engineer. Amy looked at her and expressed her doubts, but she told us later, at a dinner, that Dorothy Spicer had got every licence there was to get, not only for flying but also as a ground engineer. It was ironic that she was killed flying as a passenger.

While acknowledging the huge difficulties that had been created by the marriage bar, Gertrude Entwisle did not dwell on the negative aspects of the employment situation for women; nor did she refer to the misgivings that persisted in many quarters of society about the idea of a woman combining a career with the raising of a family. Following the lifting of the marriage bar, she said, a more optimistic vision was possible, in which a rapidly mechanising world would create an ever-growing demand for skilled workers, both men and women. It was a reason to rejoice that girls were now admitted to engineering courses in all universities and technical colleges on the same terms as boys. Apprenticeships, too, especially in the electrical industry, were now increasingly open to girls. 'Most of the training schemes of the government and nationalised industries, such as the

Central Electrical Authority, specifically mention that girls are eligible,' said Gertrude. 'The only point with these is that government schemes, when giving figures for salaries, say "women somewhat less", whereas industrial apprenticeship schemes make no distinction in pay.'

In addition to openings in the traditional electricity industry, another type of electrical work that offered exciting prospects for women was the rapidly expanding new area known as 'radio engineering', which was in urgent need of trained staff. 'Research workers with degrees are required not only for radio and radar but also for electrical work on guided weapons, gas turbines, rocket propulsion, etc. – in fact, for anything where electronics are used,' said Gertrude. 'They are needed at Harwell for atomic energy research and at Farnborough for work on the generation and distribution of electrical power in aircraft.'

Working for a large firm offered women (and men) broad opportunities, whether in the field of design, salesmanship, research, erection or manufacture. Gertrude herself was an advocate for design, on which she had spent most of her professional life while working at the Metropolitan-Vickers firm at Trafford Park in Manchester. '[Design] is a most fascinating and satisfying job,' she said, predicting that manufacturers would be putting more and more emphasis on the aesthetic qualities of designed objects, so that workers with artistic skills would be in high demand. 'This means training at a school of art in addition to an engineering training, with the chance of a job depending almost solely on one's own personality and push.'

Research – both academic research and practical work, involving tests on materials – was another area in which women could excel. Gertrude personally was less interested in pure science than in practical activities, but she clearly recognised the importance of academic endeavour and valued it highly. 'One research worker who took a

Cambridge tripos and then a two-year engineering college apprenticeship is designing an X-ray Geiger counter spectrometer and is also a part-time lecturer at a technical college,' she mentioned as an example. 'I see from the programme of this week's events that a film is to be shown of "The Electron Microscope", and this same girl was concerned with developing [the microscope] in its modern form.'

Gertrude explained that pure science had not appealed to her as a career because it lacked 'the close association with the works and interest in the finished product which mean so much to an engineer'. She was pleased that the working environment for women had improved considerably – 'We are no longer at the stage when the appearance of a woman in the shops makes the whole place stop work, as it did when I started' – but for those who cared about social progress there was still pioneering work to be done.

Gertrude's rousing finale highlighted the rewards offered by engineering in all its forms. While acknowledging that not all the work was exciting – every occupation, after all, had its humdrum aspects – she described the intense pleasure of knowing that 'everything contributes to making something, something real that can be put to use, and for which you can see the use, and which you know will last'. There was also a matchless thrill in feeling an integral part of a large organisation where 'the most vital and revolutionary developments' were taking place all the time.

AFTERWORD

——◆——

Dawn Childs

The stories of the individuals featured in this book are truly inspirational. Those magnificent women who dared to defy popular opinion about women's innovative spirit and technical abilities created the foundation for all of us who followed. As Gertrude Entwisle related in the last chapter, by the 1940s there were women working and surging forward in different and varied areas of science and engineering, but they were still very much the exception in the almost entirely male engineering sector. As the Women's Engineering Society marks its centenary, the breadth and depth of the roles in which female engineers now excel are truly staggering. Women are represented in every engineering discipline and sector: aeronautical, space, electrical, electronic, mechatronic, automotive, rail, biomedical, mechanical, civil, building services, environmental, agricultural, systems, nuclear, renewable energy, maritime, oil and gas, acoustic, leisure and entertainment, communications – and more.

In taking up the reins of president of the Women's Engineering Society in 2018, I felt proud to follow in the footsteps of people such as Caroline Haslett, Amy Johnson, Laura Annie Willson and Margaret Moir. But I was acutely aware that, despite the rich history of women in engineering, and our current representation in so many sectors, there are still far too few females entering the profession. The cause of this seems to be a fundamental lack of understanding about how wide-ranging and interesting engineering can be, the great career prospects it offers, and the benefits it brings to society. Indeed, my own route into engineering was unplanned, and I had no idea what I was really setting out to do or what my job would entail. It is important, therefore, that all girls get the opportunity to appreciate what a career in engineering can be and what they could achieve. We must take inspiration from past pioneers, support those women who currently work in engineering, and nurture those who could be the engineers of the future.

Although I read Mechanical Engineering at university, I took the opportunity to go into the aeronautical field as an engineering officer in the Royal Air Force (RAF), where I oversaw the maintenance and airworthiness of various aircraft fleets. When I chose to leave the RAF, I became head of engineering at Gatwick Airport; this job meant maintaining the airport itself, which entailed a blend of three types of engineering – facilities, civil and infrastructure. Today, I am director of engineering at Merlin Entertainments, in charge of technical governance and delivery in more than 120 theme parks and attractions across four continents with a huge range of equipment including rollercoasters, ski lifts, large ocean-tank aquariums and historic castles. I use my own diverse experience to broadcast the message and to promote a better understanding of engineering careers, in the hope of encouraging an increase in the number of women going into engineering and a closing of the skills gap.

In spite of the best efforts of the Women's Engineering Society, progress has been painfully slow. By 1969, after the society's first fifty years of existence, women made up just half a per cent of engineers in the UK. When I studied engineering at university in the early

1990s, I was one of very few girls on the course; statistics show that, even then, women accounted for only 7 per cent of engineers. I fully expected this figure to creep up during the course of my career, but some twenty years later the February 2014 edition of *Professional Engineering* had on its cover '7%' in massive type with the words 'Damning statistic – only seven in every one hundred engineers are women'. So there had been no progress at all in two decades!

More recently, there has been a small movement in the right direction. In 2017 a series of conferences with the tag line '9% is not enough!' indicated that women had advanced 1 per cent a year through 2015 and 2016. A 2017 study by the WISE (Women into Science and Engineering) campaign to increase the participation of women in science, technology, engineering and mathematics reported that 11 per cent of professional engineers were women. If this rate is sustained, there may be just a chance of reaching the target of the Women's Engineering Society that, by 2030, 30 per cent of engineers will be women.

If you are inspired by the remarkable accounts in this book and elsewhere, or intrigued by the promise of engineering and the significant impact that women can have in the profession, then please pass the message on. If you are already an engineer, please speak openly and often about your own fascinating story. If you know girls who are currently in education, suggest that they explore what a career in engineering could offer them. In response to the slow progress, we are gradually building up momentum – and with your help we can accelerate. What better tribute to the magnificent women of the past could there possibly be?

Remember the past. Celebrate the present. Transform the future.

Dawn Childs, MA, MDA, BEng, CEng,
FICE, FIMechE, FRAeS, FWES
President, Women's Engineering Society

Milestones for Women in Technology, Engineering, Politics and Society

Unless otherwise indicated, entries generally refer to events in the UK.

1805 The French aeronaut Sophie Blanchard is the first woman to pilot a hot-air balloon. In 1819 she also becomes the first woman to be killed in an aviation accident, when fireworks ignite the gas in her balloon.

1811 Sarah Guppy designs a chain bridge and patents a method of making safe piling for bridges.

1833 Oberlin College, Ohio, USA, is the first university in the world to admit women.

1835 Mary Somerville, mathematician, and Caroline Herschel, discoverer of many comets and author of star catalogues, are the first women elected to the Royal Astronomical Society.

1843 Ada Lovelace publishes the first algorithm specifically designed for use on a computer (Charles Babbage's difference engine), making her the first computer programmer. The Ada computer language, devised in 1979, is named after her.

1865 Elizabeth Garrett Anderson is the first woman to qualify as a medical practitioner, having passed the necessary examination and obtained a licence from the Society of Apothecaries. She opens her own practice in London.

1869 Girton, the first university college for women, is founded by Emily Davies with the support of Frances Buss, Dorothea Beale and Barbara Bodichon. Initially based at Hitchin in Hertfordshire, it moves in 1873 to the outskirts of Cambridge.

1870 Margaret Knight is the first woman to be awarded a US patent, for a machine for making flat-bottomed paper bags. She goes on to acquire more patents, including some for rotary and internal combustion engines.

1883 Emily Roebling completes the construction of Brooklyn Bridge, New York City, USA, designed by her late father-in-law, John Roebling. Emily took over as chief engineer from her husband, Washington, when he developed decompression sickness (also known as the bends) from working on the supports for the bridge. She is regarded as 'the first woman field engineer'.

1890 Philippa Fawcett is the first woman to obtain the top score in the Cambridge Mathematics tripos, but she is not acknowledged as 'senior wrangler' (as the top-scoring student is known) because only men are included in the ranking. It is not until 1992 that a woman, Ruth Hendry, is given the title senior wrangler.

1897 Actress Minnie Palmer is the first woman in Britain to own and drive her own car, a French-made Rougemont.

1898 Hertha Ayrton becomes the first female member of the Institution of Electrical Engineers. In 1904 she is the first woman to read a paper on her work at the Royal Society. In 1906 she receives the Hughes Medal of the Royal Society – another first.

1899 Edith Stoney is appointed a physics lecturer at the London School of Medicine for Women, becoming the first woman medical physicist.

1903 The Women's Social and Political Union is founded in Manchester by Emmeline Pankhurst and her daughters Christabel and Sylvia.

1903 Marie Curie is the first woman to win a Nobel Prize – in Physics. In 1911 she is the first female recipient of a Nobel Prize in Chemistry.

1904 The Ladies' Automobile Club is founded in Britain. By the end of the year it has 300 members.

1905 Nora Stanton Barney is the first Englishwoman to gain an engineering degree, from Cornell University, USA; she is Cornell's first female engineering graduate.

1906 The National Federation of Women Workers is set up by Mary Macarthur.

1906 Alice Perry is the first woman in Europe to graduate with a degree in engineering, from Queen's College, Galway, Ireland.

1907 Florence Nightingale is the first woman admitted to the Order of Merit, set up in 1902 by King Edward VII to recognise individuals who 'have rendered exceptionally meritorious services . . . towards the advancement of the Arts, Learning, Literature and Science'. She was a pioneer of medical statistics as well as nursing methods.

1910 Raymonde de Laroche is the first woman to receive a pilot's licence.

1910 The Anglo-Irish journalist and pioneer aviator Lilian Bland is the first woman in the world to design, build and fly an aircraft – the Bland Mayfly.

1910 Rachel Parsons is the first woman to embark on the course for the Mechanical Sciences tripos at Cambridge University. The sisters Elsie and Eily Keary soon follow in her footsteps. All three enter Newnham College.

1910 The Girl Guides movement is formed.

1911 Hilda Hewlett is the first British woman to earn a pilot's licence, a year after opening the first flying school in Britain, at Brooklands motor-racing circuit in Surrey.

1912 Nina Graham is the first woman to gain a degree in engineering from a British university, a BEng in civil engineering at the University of Liverpool.

1912 Harriet Quimby, the first woman to hold a pilot's licence in the USA, scores another female first by piloting an aircraft across the English Channel.

1915 Ethel Jayne works with the Minister of Munitions, David Lloyd George, to introduce female welfare superintendents into munitions factories, opening up managerial roles in engineering to many women.

1915 The Women's Institute is formed to revitalise rural communities throughout Britain and encourage women to become more involved in producing food during the 1914–18 war. It later expands to become the largest voluntary women's organisation in the UK.

1916 The Women's Royal Naval Service (WRNS), the first armed forces group to recruit women, is formed. In 1917 Katharine Furse is named director.

1917 Agnes Borthwick becomes works manager of Georgetown's No. 2 factory at the National Filling Factory at Paisley, Renfrewshire. She is the only woman to reach such a senior technical position in the national factories.

1917 Eily Keary is the first woman to be elected a fellow of the Royal Aeronautical Society. She is researching aeronautics at the William Froude National Tank at the National Physical Laboratory, Teddington, Middlesex, where she stays for fourteen years.

1917 In the year in which the Order of the British Empire honours are instituted, engineer and businesswoman Laura Annie Willson is awarded an MBE.

1917 Margaret Rowbotham is appointed works supervisor at the Galloway Engineering Company, Tongland, Kirkcudbrightshire, a factory with a largely female workforce.

1918 The Women's Royal Air Force (WRAF) is established, with Gertrude Crawford as its commandant.

1918 The Representation of the People Act gives women in Britain aged over thirty with certain property qualifications the right to vote in parliamentary elections. The Parliament (Qualification of Women) Act allows women aged over twenty-one to stand as prospective Members of Parliament.

1919 Elizabeth Georgeson becomes the first female engineering graduate in Scotland. She goes on to become an expert in fire safety in mines, at the Safety in Mines Research Laboratory.

1919 The Women's Engineering Society is founded by Katharine and Rachel Parsons and several others, with Caroline Haslett as secretary.

1919 Nancy Astor becomes MP for Plymouth and is the first woman to take her seat in the House of Commons.

1919 The Sex Discrimination (Removal) Act allows women entry into some professions. For the first time, women can become lawyers, veterinary surgeons and civil servants.

1919 The Restoration of Pre-War Practices Act severely restricts the employment of women in industry.

1919 Rachel Parsons, Eily Keary and Blanche Thornycroft are the first three women admitted as associate members of the Royal Institution of Naval Architects.

1920 Dorothée Pullinger and Cleone de Heveningham Benest, who calls herself Miss Clayton Griff at the time, become the first female associate members of the Institution of Automobile Engineers.

1921 Margaret Partridge sets up a power supply enterprise, M. Partridge & Company, Domestic Engineers, offering to instal electrical power in rural homes in southwest England.

1921 Victoria Drummond is the first female member of the Institute of Marine Engineers.

1921 Carlia S. Westcott is the first woman to be granted a licence to work as a marine engineer in the USA.

1921 Letitia Chitty is the first woman to qualify for first-class honours in the Mechanical Sciences tripos at Cambridge University, although she does not receive a degree. (Cambridge does not award degrees to women until 1948.) She goes on to become a noted aeronautical and structural engineer.

1922 Galloway Engineering Company starts manufacturing the Galloway car designed by Dorothée Pullinger specifically for women drivers. Dorothée races Galloway cars successfully in Scottish time trials.

1922 Pearl Young becomes the first female technical employee of the US National Advisory Committee for Aeronautics (NACA, later NASA), going on to be chief technical editor at NACA's Langley Instrument Research Laboratory and an engineering professor.

1924 The Electrical Association for Women, proposed by Mabel Matthews, is founded to pioneer the use of electricity in the home. Caroline Haslett is appointed director.

1924 Verena Holmes becomes the first female associate member of the Institution of Mechanical Engineers and of the Institute of Marine Engineers, having worked for the New London Ship and Engine Company.

1925 Annette Ashberry, founder manager of Atalanta Ltd, an all-female engineering company, is the first woman to be admitted to the Society of Engineers, a learned body.

1925 Ilse Knott-ter Meer, electrical engineer, is the first female member of the Association of German Engineers. On the occasion of the World Power Conference in 1930 in Berlin, she organises the first meeting of German female engineers.

1926 Mary, Lady Heath is the first woman in Britain to obtain a commercial pilot's licence.

1926 Dorothy Rowntree is the first woman to qualify as a naval architect, gaining her BSc Engineering (Naval Architecture) from the University of Glasgow and working with her father, a Lloyds ship surveyor.

1927 Dorothy Buchanan is the first female member of the Institution of Civil Engineers and works on Sydney Harbour Bridge. She becomes part of the design team at Dorman Long, based in Middlesbrough, for the Tyne Bridge in Newcastle.

1928 The Representation of the People (Equal Franchise) Act gives women electoral equality with men, allowing all women over twenty-one to vote, regardless of property qualifications.

1928 Amelia Earhart is the first woman to pilot an aircraft across the Atlantic.

1928 Christine Stickland, a researcher in mathematical physics at King's College, London University, works on radiowave propagation with Robert Watson-Watt, the inventor of radar.

1929 Margaret Bondfield is appointed Minister of Labour, making her the first female Cabinet minister.

1929 Maria del Pilar Careaga, Spain's first female engineer, is the first woman in Spain to drive a train. She later takes up a political career, becoming the first female mayor of Bilbao.

1929 Speedway rider Fay Taylour represents Britain in the Australian Speedway Championship – and wins.

1930 Amy Johnson, the first woman to qualify as a ground engineer, makes the first solo flight by a woman from England to Australia.

1930 The International Federation of Business and Professional Women is founded in the USA by Lena Madesin Phillips.

1931 Verena Holmes registers her eleventh patent and becomes the first woman to be admitted to the Institution of Locomotive Engineers.

1933 Elizabeth Kennedy, managing director of J. B. Stone & Company, machine tool manufacturers, wins an award from the Institution of Electrical Engineers for her paper 'An analysis of the cost of electrical supply and distribution in Great Britain'.

1934 Yüksek Mühendis Mektebi is Turkey's first woman engineering graduate.

1935 The All-Electric House is exhibited in Bristol under the auspices of the Electrical Association for Women.

1935 Marie Kubaszewska, a Polish civil engineer, is responsible for tunnel and viaduct construction, and the supervision of repair and maintenance in connection with the new Warsaw railway line.

1936 Anne Shaw, an expert in industrial efficiency and motion studies, becomes the first female member of the Institution of Production Engineers.

1938 The Auxiliary Territorial Service (ATS), the women's army, is formed.

1940 The Air Transport Auxiliary (ATA) is formed by members of the Women's Engineering Society, including Pauline Gower, who becomes its commandant. During the Second World War it employs 166 female pilots.

1940 Lesley Scott Souter is the first woman to receive a BSc in Engineering at Glasgow University. In 1951 she becomes team leader at General Electric Company, working on the properties of germanium for radar and TV.

1941 Netta Harvey becomes one of only four women to be trained as shipyard electricians on Clydeside. She wires ships under construction at Harland and Wolff and later at John Brown & Company.

1943 Ayyalasomayajula Lalitha is the first female engineering graduate in India. She goes on to become a senior commissioning engineer for hydroelectric generators at Associated Electrical Industries.

1943 The Amalgamated Engineering Union (formerly the Amalgamated Society of Engineers, which opposed the admission of women after the First World War) votes to admit female members; 100,000 women join almost immediately.

1944 Verena Holmes becomes the first female member of the Institution of Mechanical Engineers.

1945 Of the 10,000 wartime code breakers at Bletchley Park in Buckinghamshire, three-quarters are women, many of whom have a degree in mathematics, physics or engineering; the vital contribution of these women to the war effort is not recognised until many years later.

1945 Kathleen Lonsdale and Marjory Stephenson are the first women to be elected Fellows of the Royal Society.

1945 Completion of Waterloo Bridge in London – it is known as the Ladies' Bridge because it was largely built by women.

1947 Caroline Haslett is the first female member of the British Electricity Authority (later the Central Electricity Authority).

1948 Cambridge University admits women to membership and degrees (twenty-eight years after Oxford University did likewise).

1950 The Society of Women Engineers is founded in the USA.

1950 Caroline Haslett becomes president of the International Federation of Business and Professional Women, having been vice president of the organisation 1936–50.

1951 The chemist Rosalind Franklin lectures at King's College, London on her pioneering research into the structure of DNA. In 1962 Francis Crick, James Watson and Maurice Wilkins, her colleagues at King's College, are awarded a Nobel Prize for discovery of the DNA double helix, but Rosalind's contribution is not acknowledged.

1953 Jacqueline Cochran, flying a Sabre 3 aircraft, is the first female pilot to break the sound barrier.

1953 Ann Davison is the first woman to sail single-handedly across the Atlantic Ocean.

1957 Molly Fergusson is the first female fellow of the Institution of Civil Engineers. In 1948 she was appointed Britain's first female senior partner in a civil engineering firm, Blyth & Blyth.

1958 The Life Peerages Act entitles women to sit in the House of Lords for the first time. The Act comes into force a few months after the death of Viscountess Rhondda, who had campaigned for the legislation for forty years.

1958 Irene Ferguson, a chief experimental officer at the Air Ministry and former ATA pilot, transitions to become Jonathan Ferguson. Jonathan's civil service employers elevate him onto the male pay grade.

1959 Kathleen Booth publishes *Programming for an Automatic Digital Calculator*, an early book on computer design and programming. She is the designer of one of the world's first three operational computers.

1960 Yvonne Pope becomes Britain's first female air traffic controller.

1961 Lucy Oldfield is presented with a glass slipper to commemorate her year as chairman of the London section of the Society of Glass Technology. She works at General Electric Company's Hirst Research Centre in Wembley, Middlesex.

1963 The Russian cosmonaut Valentina Tereshkova becomes the first woman in space, completing forty-eight orbits of the Earth in seventy-one hours in the spacecraft Vostok 6.

1964 Dorothy Hodgkin wins the Nobel Prize in Chemistry for the development of protein crystallography. In 1965 she becomes only the second woman since Florence Nightingale in 1907 to be admitted to the Order of Merit.

1964 Mary Cartwright is the first woman to win the Sylvester Medal of the Royal Society for the encouragement of mathematical research. In 1968 she is the first female recipient of the De Morgan Medal of the London Mathematical Society.

1964 The International Conference of Women Engineers and Scientists is founded by the Women's Engineering Society. Thereafter, the conference continues to be held every three years.

1965 Barbara Castle is appointed Minister of Transport, becoming Britain's first female Secretary of State.

1966 Sheila Scott is the first British woman to fly solo around the world. Two years earlier, the American aviator Geraldine 'Jerrie' Mock became the first woman in the world to achieve this feat.

1966 The Jockey Club allows women to hold training licences.

1967 Margaret Weston, electrical engineer, is promoted from deputy keeper of electrical engineering and communications at the Science Museum in London to become the museum's first female keeper.

1967 Jocelyn Bell Burnell observes the first discovered radio pulsars.

1969 A new Representation of the People Act extends the franchise to all women and men over the age of eighteen.

1969 The American computer designer Evelyn Berezin sets up a company in Long Island, New York, to manufacture and sell her invention, the Data Secretary – the first electronic word processor for secretarial use.

1970 The Equal Pay Act enshrines in law the principle of equal pay and working conditions for women and men.

1970 The first National Women's Liberation Conference, held in Oxford, seeks abortion on demand, free contraceptives, equal pay, equal employment and educational opportunities, and free twenty-four-hour nurseries.

1972 The Jockey Club allows women to be jockeys.

1972 The American astrophysicist Margaret Burbidge is appointed director of the Royal Observatory, Greenwich.

1972 Jackie Smith joins the parachute regiment of the Women's Royal Army Corps (WRAC) and becomes the first woman to fly with the Red Devils.

1972 Yvonne Pope is the first British woman to pilot a commercial jet aeroplane.

1975 The Sex Discrimination Act protects men and women from discrimination in employment, training and education on the grounds of sex or marital status.

1975 The Women and Manual Trades organisation is founded to promote the building trades as a career choice for women.

1976 Clare Francis is the first woman to cross the finishing line in the Transatlantic Yacht Race.

1978 Girl Technician of the Year Awards are launched by the Institution of Engineering and Technology (IET). In 1988 the name of the competition is changed to Young Woman Engineer of the Year Awards.

1979 Margaret Thatcher becomes Britain's first female Prime Minister.

1980 The South African driver Desiré Wilson is the first woman to win a Formula One race, at Brands Hatch in Kent.

1980 The American pilot Lynn Rippelmeyer is the first woman to captain a jumbo jet – a Boeing 747 – across the Atlantic Ocean.

1983 Barbara Sabey is awarded the Imperial Service Order for her contribution to road safety during a forty-year career at the Transport and Road Research Laboratory, where she was recruited as a young physics graduate in the 1940s.

1984 Sue Aldcock becomes the first woman to fly RAF fast fighter jets; she is a civilian test pilot specialising in the testing of anti-gravity suits at RAE Farnborough.

1985 The Daphne Jackson Trust is established to provide fellowship funding for women employed in the science, technology, engineering and maths (STEM) sectors to return to work after career breaks.

1986 An amendment to the Sex Discrimination Act 1975 allows women to retire at the same age as men and lifts the legal restrictions that prevent women from working night shifts in factories.

1990 Women in the Royal Navy are allowed to go to sea for the first time but they are not allowed on submarines or to be deep-sea divers.

1991 Helen Sharman becomes Britain's first astronaut and the first woman to visit the Mir space station.

1991 Julie Ann Gibson becomes the first female pilot in the RAF.

1992 Jo Salter qualifies as the first female RAF fast-jet combat pilot, flying Tornados.

1993 Aeronautical engineer Sheila Widnall becomes the first female Secretary of the US Air Force.

1994 Carole Jordan is elected the first woman president of the Royal Astronomical Society.

1997 For the first time, some army frontline jobs in the Royal Engineers, Royal Artillery and Royal Electrical and Mechanical Engineers are open to women.

1997 Pamela Liversidge becomes the first female president of the Institution of Mechanical Engineers.

1998 Susan Greenfield becomes the first female director of the Royal Institution.

1999 Astronaut and test pilot Eileen Collins becomes NASA's first female commander of a space shuttle.

1999 Elizabeth Butler-Sloss is the first woman to be appointed president of the Family Division of the High Court, making her the highest-ranking woman judge in the UK. In 1988 she became the first female judge in the Court of Appeal.

2000 Jennifer Murray is the first woman to fly solo round the world in a helicopter.

2004 Martha McSally is the first woman to command a US Air Force fighter squadron.

2004 Patricia Galloway is the first woman president of the American Society of Civil Engineers.

2005 Ellen MacArthur becomes the fastest solo round-the-world sailor.

2007 Sarah Buck becomes the first woman president of the Institution of Structural Engineers.

2008 Jean Venables is the first woman president of the Institution of Civil Engineers.

2010 Chi Onwurah is elected MP for Newcastle Central, becoming the first woman engineer to sit in the House of Commons.

2013 Sheila Holden becomes the first female president of the Chartered Institution of Highways & Transportation.

2014 Ann Dowling becomes the first female president of the Royal Academy of Engineering.

2014 The first National Women in Engineering Day celebrates the achievements of women in engineering.

2014 Maxine Stiles, Alexandra Olsson and Penny Thackray become the first women to serve in the Royal Navy's Submarine Service.

2014 Mary Barra, electrical engineer, becomes chief executive officer of

General Motors, making her the first female chief executive officer of a major global car manufacturer.

2015 Naomi Climer becomes the first female president of the Institution of Engineering and Technology (IET).

2015 Nora Stanton Barney, the first female junior member of the American Society of Civil Engineers (in 1905), having been refused full membership on gender grounds alone, is posthumously advanced to a fellow of the society.

2016 The film *Hidden Figures*, based on a book of the same name by Margot Lee Shetterly, reveals the largely unacknowledged roles played by NASA mathematicians Mary Jackson, Katherine Johnson and Dorothy Vaughan in helping the USA to win the Space Race, and their battles, as women and as African Americans, to overcome discrimination.

2016 Isobel Pollock-Hulf becomes the first female master of the Worshipful Company of Engineers.

2018 The astrophysicist Jocelyn Bell Burnell receives the Breakthrough Prize in Fundamental Physics for her scientific achievements and inspiring leadership. She donates the £2.3 million prize money to the creation of scholarships to help women, under-represented minorities and refugees who are pursuing the study of physics.

2018 Mary Ellis, the last surviving British female pilot to have flown in the Second World War, is celebrated on her death at the age of 101. As a member of the Air Transport Auxiliary (ATA), Mary flew more than 1,000 planes of seventy-six different types, including Hurricanes, Spitfires and Wellington bombers.

2018 Janet Harvey, aged ninety-six, is awarded an honorary doctorate in engineering by Glasgow Caledonian University in recognition of her work as an electrician during the Second World War in the Clydeside shipyards of Harland and Wolff and John Brown's.

Notes

A complete digitised set of *Woman Engineer* journal 1919–2014 is available in the online archives of the IET (Institution of Engineering and Technology): www.theiet.org/resources/library/archives

Chapter 1: Leading Ladies (pages 1–15)

1 Katharine Parsons, 'Women's Work in Engineering and Shipbuilding during the War', *Proceedings of the North East Coast Institution of Engineers and Shipbuilders* (NECIES), vol. XXXV, Newcastle upon Tyne, 1918–19.

2 Jill Liddington, *Rebel Girls, Their Fight for the Vote*, Virago, London, 2006.

3 Carroll Pursell, 'Am I a Lady or an Engineer? The Origins of the Women's Engineering Society in Britain, 1918–1940'. Essay published in Annie Canel, Ruth Oldenziel and Karin Zachmann (eds), *Crossing Boundaries, Building Bridges, Comparing the History of Women Engineers 1870s–1990s*, Harwood, Ontario, 2000.

4 Christopher Addison, *Four and a Half Years*, vols 1–2, Hutchinson, London, 1917.

5 David Lloyd George in a speech at Bangor, Wales, on

28 February 1915, quoted in Roger Lloyd-Jones and M. J. Lewis, *Arming the Western Front: War, Business and the State in Britain 1900–1920*, Routledge, London, 2017.

6 Deborah Thom, *Nice Girls and Rude Girls, Women Workers in World War I*, I. B. Tauris, London, 1998.

7 *Daily Chronicle*, London, 19 July 1915.

8 *Newcastle Journal*, 19 July 1915, 'Women and War Work'.

9 Some details of women's work in the munitions factories and its social consequences are reproduced from 'For England's Sake', an article by Henrietta Heald published in *History Today*, October 2014.

10 Gilbert Stone (ed.), *Women War Workers*, Harrap, London, 1917.

11 *The Times*, London, 3 August 1915.

12 Katharine Parsons, 'Women's Work'.

13 *The Official History of the Ministry of Munitions*, vols. 1–12, 1922.

14 F. G. H. (Gordon) Bedford, *Sixty Years with C. A. Parsons & Co., 1901–1961* (unpublished), Tyne & Wear Archives.

15 L. K. Yates, *The Woman's Part, A Record of Munitions Work*, Hodder & Stoughton, London, 1918.

16 Katharine Parsons, 'Women's Work'.

17 Yates, *The Woman's Part*.

18 Ibid.

19 Ibid.

20 Katharine Parsons, 'Women's Work'.

21 *Official History of the Ministry of Munitions*.

22 Katharine Parsons, 'Women's Work'.

23 Rachel Parsons, 'Engineering for Women', *National Review*, vol. LXXIV, 1919–20.

24 Rosalind Messenger, *The Doors of Opportunity, A Biography of Dame Caroline Haslett*, Femina Books, London, 1967.

25 Essay by Caroline Haslett in Margot Asquith (ed.), *Myself When Young by Famous Women of Today*, Frederick Muller, London, 1938.

Chapter 2: A Brilliant Inheritance (pages 17–35)

1 Randal Parsons, *Reminiscences*. Many details of Parsons family history and life at Birr come from this memoir by Randal Parsons, a brother of Charles, probably written soon after the death in 1908 of their eldest brother Laurence, fourth Earl of Rosse, and privately printed. Birr Castle Archives, Birr, Ireland.

2 Quoted in Patrick Moore, *The Astronomy of Birr Castle*, Tribune Publishing, Birr, Ireland, 1971.

3 Moore, *The Astronomy of Birr Castle*.

4 Ibid.

5 W. Garrett Scaife, *From Galaxies to Turbines, Science Technology and the Parsons Family*, Institute of Physics Publishing, Bristol, 2000.

6 Moore, *The Astronomy of Birr Castle*.

7 Scaife, *From Galaxies to Turbines*.

8 Moore, *The Astronomy of Birr Castle*.

9 John Timbs, *Curiosities of Science*, Kent & Company, London, 1858.

10 Rollo Appleyard, *Charles Parsons, His Life and Work*, Constable, London, 1933.

11 David H. Davison, *Impressions of an Irish Countess, The Photography of Mary, Countess of Rosse*, Birr Scientific Heritage Foundation, Birr, Ireland, 1989.

12 Susan McKenna-Lawlor, *Whatever Shines Should be Observed*, Samton, Dublin, 1998.

13 Charles Mollan, William Davis and Brendan Finucane (eds), *Some More People and Places in Irish Science and Technology*, Royal Irish Academy, Dublin, 1990.

14 Randal Parsons, *Reminiscences*.

15 Scaife, *From Galaxies to Turbines*.

16 Randal Parsons, *Reminiscences*.

17 Obituary of Sir Charles Parsons, *Proceedings of the Royal Society*, vol. CXXXI, June 1931.

18 Moore, *The Astronomy of Birr Castle*.

19 Randal Parsons, *Reminiscences*.

20 Charles Mollan, William Davis and Brendan Finucane (eds), *Some People and Places in Irish Science and Technology*, Royal Irish Academy, Dublin, 1985.

21 Ibid.

22 Ibid.

23 Scaife, *From Galaxies to Turbines*; Birr Castle Archives, Birr, Ireland.

24 Appleyard, *Charles Parsons*.

25 Obituary of Sir Charles Parsons, *Proceedings of the Royal Society*.

26 Obituary of Katharine Parsons by Mary Houstoun, *Transactions of the North East Coast Institution of Engineers and Shipbuilders*, vol. L, Newcastle upon Tyne, 1933–4.

27 Appleyard, *Charles Parsons*.

28 Obituary of Sir Charles Parsons, *Proceedings of the Royal Society*.

29 Report in *The Times*, London, 29 July 1933.

Chapter 3: Fires of Ambition (pages 37–53)

1 The exploits of *Turbinia* during the review of the fleet were covered in detail in *The Times*, London, 28 June 1897.

2 Christopher Leyland in *Heaton Works Journal*, June 1935, Tyne & Wear Archives.

3 Rollo Appleyard, *Charles Parsons, His Life and Work*, Constable, London, 1933.

4 George Baden-Powell, letter to *The Times*, London, 29 June 1897.

5 Ibid.

6 G. James, 'Turbinia: the experiment which transformed the world's navies', in *Rolls-Royce Magazine*, no. 48, 1991.

7 Ken Smith, *Turbinia, The Story of Charles Parsons and His Ocean Greyhound*, Tyne Bridge Publishing, Newcastle upon Tyne, 2009.

8 Appleyard, *Charles Parsons*.

9 G. L. Parsons (ed.), *Scientific Papers of Charles Parsons*, with a memoir by Lord Rayleigh and appendices, Cambridge University Press, 1934.

10 Rayleigh memoir in *Scientific Papers of Charles Parsons*.

11 Obituary of Katharine Parsons by Mary Houstoun, *Transactions of the North East Coast Institution of Engineers and Shipbuilders*, vol. L, Newcastle upon Tyne, 1933–4.

12 Paul Lawrence, *The Founders of Roedean*, privately printed by Farncombe's, Brighton, 1935.

13 L. Cope Cornford and F. R. Yerbury, *Roedean School*, Ernest Benn, London, 1927.

14 Kathleen E. McCrone, *Playing the Game: Sport and the Physical Emancipation of English Women, 1870–1914*, University Press of Kentucky, USA, 1988.

15 Lawrence, *The Founders of Roedean*.

16 Ibid.

17 Ibid.

18 *Roedean School Magazine* 1901–3.

19 Information about the Keary sisters provided by Jo Stanley.

20 Letter of 1903 from Charles Parsons to George Johnstone Stoney, Tyne & Wear Archives.

21 *The Age*, Melbourne, Australia, 17 January 1934.

22 Carroll Pursell, 'Am I a Lady or an Engineer?, The Origins of the Women's Engineering Society in Britain, 1918–1940'. Essay published in Annie Canel, Ruth Oldenziel and Karin Zachmann (eds), *Crossing Boundaries, Building Bridges, Comparing the History of Women Engineers 1870s–1990s*, Harwood, Ontario, 2000.

23 Information from Jo Stanley.

24 Archives of Newnham College, Cambridge.

25 Onora O'Neill, Baroness O'Neill of Bengarve, principal of Newnham College 1992–2006, in a private letter dated 1 May 2001.

26 Flora Johnston (ed.), *War Classics, the Remarkable Memoir of Scottish Scholar Christina Keith on the Western Front*, History Press, Stroud, 2014.

27 E. M. (Eliza Marian) Butler, *Paper Boats*, Collins, London, 1959.

28 Leonard Woolf, *Beginning Again: An Autobiography of the Years 1911 to 1918*, Hogarth Press, London, 1964.

29 F. G. H. Bedford, *Sixty Years with C. A. Parsons & Co., 1901–1961* (unpublished), Tyne & Wear Archives.

30 *Daily Express*, London, 4 July 1956.

31 Obituary of Alexander Law, *Journal of the Institution of Electrical Engineers*, 1956.

32 Bedford, *Sixty Years with C. A. Parsons*.

33 Accident reported in *The Times*, London, 19 February 1910.

34 Bedford, *Sixty Years with C. A. Parsons*.

Chapter 4: A New Dawn (pages 55–69)

1 Rosalind Messenger, *The Doors of Opportunity, A Biography of Dame Caroline Haslett*, Femina Books, London, 1967.
2 Essay by Caroline Haslett in Margot Asquith (ed.), *Myself When Young by Famous Women of Today*, Frederick Muller, London, 1938.
3 BBC radio broadcast, 1943, transcript at IET Archives.
4 Haslett, *Myself When Young*.
5 Messenger, *The Doors of Opportunity*.
6 Ibid.
7 Haslett, *Myself When Young*.
8 Gertrude Entwisle, 'Engineering as a Career for Girls', a talk given at Portsmouth College of Technology, May 1955, transcript at IET Archives.
9 All details of HM Factory Gretna come from the Devil's Porridge Museum, Eastriggs, Dumfries and Galloway.
10 This and other details of the social impact of women's munitions work comes from L. K. Yates, *The Woman's Part, A Record of Munitions Work*, Hodder & Stoughton, London, 1918.
11 Obituary of Margaret Moir by Caroline Haslett, *The Times*, London, 19 October 1942.
12 *Oxford Dictionary of National Biography*, online edition, entry on Ernest Moir by Henrietta Heald, and information from Nick Moir.
13 Charles Parsons' role in the Ministry of Munitions, not widely known, is recorded in the National Collections Centre of the Science Museum, Wroughton, Wiltshire.
14 *Oxford Dictionary of National Biography*, online edition, entry on Margaret Rowbotham by Nina Baker.
15 Mary Smith, article in *DGB Life* (a magazine covering Dumfries and Galloway and the Scottish Borders), 2006.

16 *Oxford Dictionary of National Biography*, online edition, entry on Dorothée Pullinger by Georgine Clarsen.

17 Smith, *DGB Life*.

18 Ibid.

19 *Oxford Dictionary of National Biography*, entry on Dorothée Pullinger.

20 'A New Profession for Women', *The Lady*, 8 November 1917.

21 'A Feminist Munition Factory – Automobile Engineering as a Permanent Career for Women', *The Autocar*, 10 November 1917.

Chapter 5: Seeds of Revolution (pages 71–89)

1 Millicent Garrett Fawcett, *The Women's Victory – And After: Personal Reminiscences*, Sidgwick & Jackson, London, 1920.

2 Quoted in Deborah Thom, *Nice Girls and Rude Girls, Women Workers in World War I*, I. B. Tauris, London, 1998.

3 *Daily Mail*, London, 7 February 1919.

4 This letter and others in the chapter, including those between Caroline Haslett and Katharine Parsons, are held at the archives of the Women's Engineering Society, which are on permanent loan to IET Archives.

5 Rosalind Messenger, *The Doors of Opportunity, A Biography of Dame Caroline Haslett*, Femina Books, London, 1967.

6 Rachel Parsons, 'Women in Engineering', *The Queen*, 15 March 1919.

7 Archives of the Women's Engineering Society, IET Archives.

8 Viscountess Rhondda, *This Was My World*, Macmillan, London, 1933.

9 Angela V. John, *Turning the Tide, A Life of Lady Rhondda*, Parthian, Cardigan, 2013.

10 Ibid.

11 Ibid.

12 Ibid.

13 Rhondda, *This Was My World*.

14 Held on 19 May 1920. Minutes of the meetings of the Women's Engineering Society, IET Archives.

15 Blanche Wiesen Cook (ed.), *Crystal Eastman on Women and Revolution*, Oxford University Press, New York, 1978.

16 *Time and Tide,* vol. 1: 14 May–31 December 1920.

17 Cheryl Law, *Women, A Modern Political Dictionary*, I. B. Tauris, London, 2000.

18 Archives of the Women's Engineering Society, IET Archives.

Chapter 6: Virgin Huntresses (pages 91–106)

1 Claudia Parsons, *Century Story*, with a foreword by Anthony Parsons, The Book Guild, 1995.

2 Ibid.

3 Ibid.

4 L. K. Yates, *The Woman's Part, A Record of Munitions Work*, Hodder & Stoughton, London, 1918.

5 Claudia Parsons, *Century Story*.

6 Ibid.

7 Obituary of Claudia Parsons by Emma Parsons, *Independent*, London, 26 June 1998.

8 Mary Smith, from an article in *DGB Life* (a magazine covering Dumfries and Galloway and the Scottish Borders), 2006.

9 *Oxford Dictionary of National Biography*, online edition, article on Cleone de Heveningham Benest by Nina Baker.

10 Smith, *DGB Life*.

11 *Motor World* 1922, archives of Stewartry Museum, Kirkcudbright.

12 *Oxford Dictionary of National Biography*, online edition, article on Dorothée Pullinger by Georgine Clarsen.

13 *Oxford Dictionary of National Biography*, online edition, article on Verena Holmes by Autumn Stanley.

14 *The Times*, London, 23 February 1921.

15 This letter and others quoted in the chapter are held at the archives of the Women's Engineering Society, which are on permanent loan to IET Archives.

16 Caroline Haslett, 'A Brief History of Atalanta Ltd', notes written for Dr Lillian Gilbreth, 10 July 1924, IET Library and Archives, London.

17 Shirley Stewart, article on Loughborough History and Heritage Network website, 5 April 2018.

18 *Woman Engineer*, September 1920, IET Archives.

19 *Woman Engineer*, December 1921, IET Archives.

20 *Oxford Dictionary of National Biography*, online edition, article on Victoria Drummond by Cherry Drummond.

Chapter 7: Political Longings (pages 107–121)

1 Anne Parsons, Countess of Rosse, obituaries column of *The Times*, London, 18 July 1956.

2 Ibid.

3 Minutes of the meetings of the Women's Engineering Society, IET Archives.

4 F. G. H. Bedford, *Sixty Years with C. A. Parsons & Co., 1901–1961* (unpublished), Tyne & Wear Archives.

5 Law family private letters.

6 Information about the character and behaviour of Tommy Parsons was provided by Deborah Martin and based on an unpublished memoir by her father, Norman Parsons, managing director at NEI Parsons in Heaton, Newcastle, during the 1980s.

7 Sheila Jeffreys, *The Spinster and Her Enemies, Feminism and Sexuality 1880–1930*, Pandora, London, 1985.

8 Patricia Hollis, *Women Elect, Women in English Local Government 1865–1914*, Oxford University Press, 1987.

9 Ibid.

10 *Exeter and Plymouth Gazette*, Devon, 25 February 1922.

11 *Woman Engineer*, June 1922, IET Archives.

12 Martin Pugh, *Women and the Women's Movement in Britain*, Palgrave, London, 2015.

13 Ray Strachey, *The Cause*, Kennikat Press, New York, 1928.

14 Ibid.

15 Pugh, *Women and the Women's Movement.*

16 Her campaign was covered by, among others, the *Wigan Examiner*, *Wigan Observer* and *Manchester Evening Chronicle*.

17 This speech was reported in detail in the *Wigan Examiner*, 1 December 1923.

18 Hollis, *Women Elect.*

19 Archives of the Women's Engineering Society, IET Archives.

20 *Sunderland Daily Echo and Shipping Gazette*, 19 September 1935.

Chapter 8: Good Times and Bad Times (pages 123–138)

1 BBC radio broadcast, 1943, transcript at IET Archives.

2 Rosalind Messenger, *The Doors of Opportunity, A Biography of Dame Caroline Haslett*, Femina Books, London, 1967.

3 Report of the Wembley conference in *Woman Engineer*, September 1925, IET Archives.

4 Ibid.

5 The society's financial crisis and the controversy surrounding the creation of an electrical association are covered in the minutes of meetings of the Women's Engineering Society 1924 and in *Woman Engineer*, IET Archives.

6 Messenger, *The Doors of Opportunity.*

7 From an essay by Caroline Haslett in Margot Asquith (ed.), *Myself When Young by Famous Women of Today*, Frederick Muller, London, 1938.

8 Letters between Margaret Partridge and Caroline Haslett and minutes of meetings concerning the resignation of Katharine Parsons are held at the archives of the Women's Engineering Society, IET Archives.

9 *Woman Engineer*, September 1925, special conference edition.

10 Ibid.

11 Jill Liddington, *Rebel Girls, Their Fight for the Vote*, Virago, London, 2006.

12 Ibid.

13 Information from John Pickles. Calderdale Industrial Museum Association, West Yorkshire.

14 Information from Joanna Stoddart.

15 Information from John Pickles. Calderdale Industrial Museum Association, West Yorkshire.

16 *Woman Engineer*, September 1927, IET Archives.

17 Ibid.

18 *Woman Engineer*, September–October 1928, IET Archives.

19 Vera Brittain, *Women's Work in Modern England*, Noel Douglas, London, 1928.

Chapter 9: The All-Electric Home (pages 139–152)

1 BBC radio broadcast, 1943, transcript at IET Archives.

2 Rosalind Messenger, *The Doors of Opportunity, A Biography of Dame Caroline Haslett*, Femina Books, London, 1967.

3 From an essay by Caroline Haslett in Margot Asquith (ed.), *Myself When Young by Famous Women of Today*, Frederick Muller, London, 1938.

4 Graeme Gooday, 'The Authoritative Hertha Ayrton' in *Viewpoint 109*, newsletter of the British Society for the History of Science, February 2016.

5 Haslett, *Myself When Young*.

6 Ibid.

7 *Electrical Age*, October 1926, IET Archives.

8 Messenger, *The Doors of Opportunity*.

9 Ibid.

10 Ibid.

11 Letter from the archives of the Women's Engineering Society, IET Archives.

12 *Oxford Dictionary of National Biography* online edition, entry on Margaret Partridge by Anne Locker.

13 *Oxford Dictionary of National Biography* online edition, entry on Dorothy Buchanan by Mike Chrimes.

14 Eleri Kyffin, 'Electricity and Women – the EAW in the inter-war years', University of Westminster blog, 22 August 2011.

15 Margaret Moir, 'A Vision of the Home of the Future', *Morning Post*, London, 11 July 1931.

16 Ibid.

17 Ibid.

18 'The All-Electric Home', *Electrical Age*, December 1935, IET Archives.

19 Ibid.

Chapter 10: Conquest of the Air (pages 153–168)

1 H. F. Morriss, *Two Brave Brothers*, privately published by Richard J. James, 1919.

2 *Flight* magazine, 6 November 1909.

3 Matthew Freudenberg, *Negative Gravity, a life of Beatrice Shilling*, Charlton Publications, Taunton, 2003.

4 Ibid.

5 This and other information about female engineers at RAE Farnborough comes from 'Wind Tunnels and Slide Rules', an unpublished essay by Nina Baker, made available to the author.

6 Freudenberg, *Negative Gravity*.

7 Ibid.

8 Ibid.

9 Ibid.

10 Pauline Gower, *Women with Wings*, with a prologue and epilogue by Dorothy Spicer, John Long, London, 1938.

11 Ibid.

12 Lettice Curtis, *The Forgotten Pilots, A Story of the Air Transport Auxiliary 1939–45*, privately published.

13 Ibid.

14 Amy Johnson, 'A Day's Work in the ATA', *Woman Engineer*, March 1941, IET Archives.

15 Curtis, *The Forgotten Pilots*.

16 Reported in *Woman Engineer*, March 1931, IET Archives.

17 Caroline Haslett on the BBC radio programme *Woman's Hour*, speaking about Amy Johnson in the series 'I Knew Her', 17 November 1952.

18 Amy Johnson, a speech of March 1932, reprinted in *Woman Engineer*, 5 January 1981, IET Archives.

19 Midge Gillies, *Amy Johnson, Queen of the Air*, Weidenfeld and Nicolson, London, 2003.

20 David Luff, *Amy Johnson, Enigma in the Sky*, Airlife, Shrewsbury, 2002.

21 Claudia Parsons, *Century Story*, The Book Guild, 1995.

22 Haslett on *Woman's Hour*.

23 Luff, *Amy Johnson*.

24 Gillies, *Amy Johnson*.

25 Ibid.

26 Haslett on *Woman's Hour*.

Chapter 11: Conflicts and Dreams (pages 169–184)

1 *Observer*, London, 28 April 1938.

2 E. L. Raphael, 'Rachel Mary Parsons' www.rachelparsons.co.uk.

3 Ibid.

4 Anne Parsons, Countess of Rosse, obituaries column of *The Times*, London, 18 July 1956.

5 Raphael, 'Rachel Mary Parsons'.

6 Ibid.

7 Queen Elizabeth the Queen Consort, formerly Duchess of York, the wife of King George VI.

8 Sent from Buckingham Palace, signed by Helen Graham, a lady-in-waiting, 19 February 1940, IET Archives.

9 *Woman Engineer*, autumn 1940, IET Archives.

10 Rosalind Messenger, *The Doors of Opportunity, A Biography of Dame Caroline Haslett*, Femina Books, London, 1967.

11 Claudia Parsons, *Century Story*, with a foreword by Anthony Parsons, The Book Guild, 1995.

12 Ibid.

13 Ibid.

14 Ibid.

15 Carroll Pursell, 'Am I a Lady or an Engineer? The Origins of the Women's Engineering Society in Britain, 1918–1940'. Essay published in Annie Canel, Ruth Oldenziel and Karin Zachmann (eds), *Crossing Boundaries, Building Bridges, Comparing the History of Women Engineers 1870s–1990s*, Harwood, Ontario, 2000.

16 From an essay by Caroline Haslett in Margot Asquith (ed.), *Myself When Young by Famous Women of Today*, Frederick Muller, London, 1938.

17 Messenger, *The Doors of Opportunity*.

18 Haslett, *Myself When Young*.

19 *Crystal Eastman on Women and Revolution*, edited by Blanche Wiesen Cook, Oxford University Press, New York, 1978.

20 Messenger, *The Doors of Opportunity*.

21 Ibid.

22 *Electrical Age*, autumn 1945, IET Archives.

23 *Woman Engineer*, spring 1957, carried a series of tributes to Caroline Haslett following her death in January, IET Archives.

24 Messenger, *The Doors of Opportunity*.

25 Ibid.

26 Walter Citrine, in an appendix to Messenger, *The Doors of Opportunity*.

27 Henry Self in an appendix to Messenger, *The Doors of Opportunity*.

28 *The Times*, London, 5 January 1957.

29 *Woman Engineer*, spring 1957.

30 Haslett, *Myself When Young*.

Chapter 12: Jagged Abnormalities (pages 185–200)

1 Details of events leading up to and following the killing of Rachel Parsons have been reconstructed from police reports, witness statements and newspaper stories relating to the trial of Dennis Pratt on 12 and 13 November 1956. National Archives, Kew: *R. v. Dennis James Pratt*.

2 E. L. Raphael, 'Rachel Mary Parsons' www.rachelparsons.co.uk.

3 Birr Castle Archives, Birr, Ireland.

4 Obituary of Alexander Law, *Journal of the Institution of Electrical Engineers*, 1956.

5 *The Age*, Melbourne, 28 February 1960.

6 Birr Castle Archives.

7 Correspondence between the cousins and between John Randal Parsons and Barclays Bank is held at Birr Castle Archives.

8 Not until 1966 were women permitted to hold training licences; from 1972 they were allowed to be jockeys. In 1993 governance of the sport was taken over by the British Horse Racing Board, with the Jockey Club retaining the role of regulator.

9 From the 'Tattenham Corner' column in the *Observer*, London, 2 December 2001.

10 *Newmarket Journal*, 5 July 1956.

11 *News of the World*, London, 18 November 1956.

12 Birr Castle Archives.

13 Anne Parsons, Countess of Rosse, obituaries column of *The Times*, London, 18 July 1956.

14 National Archives, Kew: *R. v. Dennis James Pratt*.

15 Ibid.

16 Ibid.

Chapter 13: A Defence of Provocation (pages 201–214)

1 Details of the judgement in the case against Dennis Pratt come from the National Archives, Kew: *R. v. Dennis James Pratt*, and newspaper reports.

2 E. L. Raphael, 'Rachel Mary Parsons' www.rachelparsons.co.uk.

3 Obituary of Caroline Haslett in *The Times*, London, 5 January 1957.

4 Dora Russell, *Hypatia, or Woman and Knowledge*, Kegan Paul, London, 1925.

5   Ibid.

6   Angela V. John, *Turning the Tide, A Life of Lady Rhondda*, Parthian, Cardigan, 2013.

7   *Oxford Dictionary of National Biography*, online edition, entry on Margaret Rowbotham by Nina Baker.

8   Sheila Jeffreys, *The Spinster and her Enemies, Feminism and Sexuality 1880–1930*, Pandora, London, 1985.

9   Ibid.

10 Gertrude Entwisle, 'Engineering as a Career for Girls', a talk given at Portsmouth College of Technology, May 1955. IET Archives.

Acknowledgements

Charles Parsons' beguiling little ship *Turbinia* takes pride of place in Newcastle's Discovery Museum, where the idea for this book emerged. At Discovery, I learned that Charles – long revered as an inventor of genius – came from a family of outstanding engineers, some of them women. His wife and daughter, Katharine and Rachel, played leading roles in C. A. Parsons and Company at nearby Heaton before going on to found the Women's Engineering Society.

The repository of the Heaton Works history is Tyne & Wear Archives, which is integrated with Discovery Museum. I should like to thank all the staff of the museums and archives service who assisted me in my research, in particular John Clayson, Iain Watson and Alan Hayward. The archives include a full set of the *Heaton Work Journal* and *Sixty Years with C. A. Parsons*, an unpublished memoir by F. G. H. Bedford, both of which contain many interesting details about the firm and the characters involved in it. The Science Museum Archives at Wroughton in Wiltshire hold records of the activities of C. A. Parsons during the First World War. For supplying additional information on the firm's history, thanks are due to Richard Maudslay, formerly managing director of NEI Parsons Turbine Generators, and to Geoff Horseman and Ruth Baldasera at Siemens, which acquired the Heaton business in 1997.

Acknowledgements

Brendan and Alison Parsons, the Earl and Countess of Rosse, are the custodians of the Parsons family history in Ireland and the current occupants of Birr Castle, Co. Offaly, where they have established Ireland's Historic Science Centre. They kindly granted me permission to use material from the Birr Castle Archives and enhanced my understanding with personal reminiscences. I am also grateful for the information provided by Sir John Parsons and Deborah Martin (née Parsons). Hugh and Sarah Bethell welcomed me to Rise, near Beverley, in the East Riding of Yorkshire, the home of the Bethells, Katharine Parsons' family, for more than 470 years. The archives of Newnham College, Cambridge, and Roedean School, Brighton, yielded useful information about Rachel Parsons' academic career.

Among the descendants of the magnificent women who have given valuable assistance are Joanna Stoddart, the granddaughter of Laura Annie Willson, and Nick Moir, the great-grandson of Margaret, Lady Moir. Jill Liddington supplied information about Laura Annie Willson's involvement in the suffragette campaign. Edmund Raphael Beldowski was kind enough to share his research into the personal and professional life of Rachel Parsons, much of which is available on the website www.rachelparsons.co.uk. Rosemary McCray spoke to me about her grandfather, Alexander Henry Law.

Jon Cable, the archivist of the Institution of Engineering and Technology (IET) at Savoy Place in central London, has been unstinting in his help and encouragement. The archives of the Women's Engineering Society (WES) are on permanent loan to the IET, and the archives of the Electrical Association for Women (EAW), which include an abundance of material on Caroline Haslett, are also held at the IET. All the correspondence from and between the women engineers featured in this book, the transcripts of their speeches and radio broadcasts, and the minutes of their meetings derive from the IET. I am grateful to Jon Cable for permission to quote from this material and to reproduce (by approval) photographs from the WES and EAW archives. Anne Locker, the IET librarian and archives manager, generously shared her knowledge of individual engineers, particularly Margaret Partridge, and helped in other ways. A complete digitised set of *Woman Engineer* journal 1919–2014 is available on the IET website.

In bringing this project to fruition, I owe a great debt to Dawn Bonfield, a former president and chief executive officer of WES, who now works independently to promote diversity and inclusivity in engineering. Dawn believed in the book from the start and championed it at every stage. The engineering historian Nina Baker, who has compiled a unique database of women engineers, has been generous in sharing her knowledge and wisdom, especially concerning the Royal Aircraft Establishment at Farnborough. Jo Stanley, a writer with a particular interest in women engineers and the sea, provided details about the Keary sisters. Many other members of WES have contributed to the project in various ways, and I should like to thank in particular Benita Mehra, Sarah Peers, Shiva Dowlatshi, Jess Wade, Elizabeth Donnelly and Dawn Childs, the society's current president, who wrote the Afterword.

Thanks for encouragement and support are also due to Peter Stark, Liz Mayes and Emily Tench of the Mining Institute in Newcastle; Kay Easson of the Lit & Phil; Robert Allison and Steve Rothberg of Loughborough University; Graeme Gooday of Leeds University; Sally Horrocks of Leicester University; Elizabeth Bruton of the Science Museum in London; Jane Hamlett and Katie Broomfield of Royal Holloway; Alice White of the Wellcome Institute and Wikipedia; Mark Curthoys of Oxford University Press; Antony Firth of Fjordr Ltd; and David Sproxton of Aardman Animations.

For information about houses connected with the Parsons family, I am grateful to Terence Kearley, Viscount Devonport (Ray Demesne), Alastair Balls, Ian Murdoch and Ann Brough (Holeyn Hall), and Christina Robson and Melissa Turner (Branches Park).

Laura Thompson, who has written a history of Newmarket, helped to enlighten me about Rachel Parsons' experience of the racing world.

The Stewartry Museum in Kirkcudbright holds press cuttings about the Tongland factory and the exploits of Margaret Rowbotham and Dorothée Pullinger, designer of the Galloway car. Devil's Porridge Museum near Annan, Dumfries and Galloway, offers a fascinating exposition of HM Factory Gretna, the largest munitions factory in the world during the First World War.

Among the few published memoirs by and about the women featured in this book, the following have proved particularly helpful in retelling their stories: *The Doors of Opportunity, A Biography of Dame Caroline Haslett* (Rosalind Messenger), *Myself When Young* (essay by Caroline Haslett), *This Was My World* (Viscountess Rhondda), *Turning the Tide, A Life of Lady Rhondda* (Angela V. John), *Century Story* (Claudia Parsons), *Amy Johnson, Queen of the Air* (Midge Gillies), *Negative Gravity, a Life of Beatrice Shilling* (Matthew Freudenberg).

It has been fun and illuminating to work for the first time with the crowdfunding publisher Unbound, who are pioneering a new style of publishing in which, among other things, the author feels more valued. My deep appreciation goes to all at Unbound who have worked so diligently to produce and market this lovely book, in particular Imogen Denny (editor), Phil Connor (commissioning editor), Georgia Odd (crowdfunding campaigns) and Amy Winchester (publicity). And many thanks, as always, to my stalwart literary agent, Broo Doherty. Peter Dillon and Ciarán Charles of Sweethope Films have started work on a film version of the Rachel Parsons story.

Adam Curtis, my husband of thirty-seven years, was seriously ill during much of the period in which *Magnificent Women* was written, and he died in December 2017. As a highly respected editor at the BBC World Service and, later, at BBC News Online, Adam was always fiercely critical of my work, and the book has no doubt suffered from the absence of his keen editorial eye, but he would have been proud and thrilled to know that it has finally seen the light of day. I shall always be grateful to him for his love and support, and for that of my talented children, Sophie and Jamie Curtis. I'd also like to take this opportunity to thank the many family members, friends and colleagues – too numerous to mention by name – who, wittingly and unwittingly, have contributed to the creation of this book.

A Note on the Author

Henrietta Heald is the author of *William Armstrong: Magician of the North*, which was shortlisted for the H. W. Fisher Best First Biography Prize and the Portico Prize for non-fiction. She was chief editor of *Chronicle of Britain and Ireland* and the Reader's Digest *Illustrated Guide to Britain's Coast*. Her other books include *Coastal Living, La Vie est Belle, Amazing and Extraordinary Facts about Jane Austen* and a National Trust guide to Cragside, Northumberland.

Index

Index

Institution of Naval Architects, 48, 72, 87, 244

Institution of Production Engineers, 228

Institution of Structural Engineers, 237

International Balloon Race, 153

International Federation of Business and Professional Women, 14, 181, 227, 230

International Women's Service Groups, 179

Irish famine, 21–2

Iron and Steel Institute, 96

Jackson, Mary, 237

James, Henry, 207

Jayne, Ethel, 103, 223

Jeffreys, Sheila, 112, 207–8

Jellis, C. H. 'Harry', 186

Jockey Club, 195, 232–3

Johnson, Amy, 159, 161–8, 206, 212, 215, 227

Johnson, John, 164

Johnson, Katherine, 237

Johnston, W. M., 53

Jordan, Carole, 235

Joynson-Hicks, William, 120

Jukes, Martin, 199

Kazan, Elia, 185

Keary, Eily, 46, 48–9, 71, 222–4

Keary, Elsie, 46, 48, 222

Keith, Christina, 49

Kennedy, Elizabeth, 141, 166, 228

Kenney, Annie, 7, 83–4

Key-Jones, Miss, 81

King, David, 167

King, J. G., 29

King George V Bridge (Tyne Bridge), 147–8, 226

King's College of Household and Social Science, 181

King's County Chronicle, 29

Knight, Margaret, 220

Knott-ter Meer, Ilse, 226

Kubaszewska, Marie, 228

Labour Party, 104, 113–14, 116, 119, 124

Ladies' Automobile Club, 221

Lady, The, 67

Lalitha, Ayyalasomayajula, 229

Law, Alexander Henry, 51–3, 108–9, 192

Lawrence, D. H., 87

Lawrence, Dorothy, 44

Lawrence, Millicent, 44, 46

Lawrence, Penelope, 44–5, 48

Lawrence, Susan, 74

Lawrence, Theresa, 45

Lawson, Susan, 22

League of Nations, 108, 144

lesbianism, 113, 207–8

Leverhulme, Lord, 77

Leyland, Christopher, 38

Leyland, Joan, 39

Liberal Party, 115, 118

Life Peerages Act, 86, 230

Little Laundries network, 103

Liversidge, Pamela, 235

Llewelyn Davies, Harry, 57

Llewelyn Davies, Moya, 57

Lloyd George, David, 5–7, 74, 83, 223

London Aeroplane Club, 159, 164

London County Council (LCC), 113–15, 166

London Mathematical Society, 231

London Society for Women's Service, 82

London Underground, 148

Lonsdale, Kathleen, 229

Loughnan, Naomi, 7

Lovelace, Ada, 219

Lyon, Hilda, 156

MacArthur, Ellen, 236

Macarthur, Mary, 74, 221

MacDonald, Ramsay, 118, 120

Mackworth, Humphrey, 83, 207

McSally, Martha, 236

Maguire family, 203

Maloney, John, 190

Manchester Evening Chronicle, 116

Manchester United plane crash, 159

Mansell-Moulin, Edith, 7

Margaret, Princess, Countess of Snowdon, 198

Marina, Princess, Duchess of Kent, 171

Index

Index

Unbound is the world's first crowdfunding publisher, established in 2011.

We believe that wonderful things can happen when you clear a path for people who share a passion. That's why we've built a platform that brings together readers and authors to crowdfund books they believe in – and give fresh ideas that don't fit the traditional mould the chance they deserve.

This book is in your hands because readers made it possible. Everyone who pledged their support is listed below. Join them by visiting unbound.com and supporting a book today.

Simon Agate

Deborah Agulnik

Susan Aldworth

Alec Anderson

Gunilla Andersson

Katrin Andersson

Igor Andronov

Phoebe Annett

Helen Arney

Christine Arrowsmith

Arup Connect Women network

Paul Askew

Anna Baker

Nina Baker

Paula Baker

Ruth Baldasera

Jenifer Ball

Andrew Ballantyne

Lizzie Ballantyne

Jason Ballinger

Ariane Bankes

Lydia Bauman

Andrew Beale

Kerry Becker

Katherine Beckett-Suter

Adrian Belcher

Emily Bell

Francis Bennett

Claudia Berg

Tim Berry

Hugh Bethell

Julian Birkett

Sarah Blenkinsop

Margaret Bluman

Dawn Bonfield

Charles Boot

Chris Bowen

Michael Bowen

Rachel Bower

Faye Bowser

Lorna Boyd

Catherine Breslin

Rhea Brooke

Katie Broomfield

Cath Brown

Robyn Brown

Elizabeth Bruton

Christine Burns

Michael Bussell

Hannah Butlin

Jon Cable

Sandra Cairncross

Catherine Campbell

Jessica Campbell

Mary Carter

Susan Catley

Jane Chalaby

Becky Chantry

Julia Charles

Mark Chichester-Clark

Dawn Childs

Suzy Clack

Sabrina Clarke

Liz Clasen

Garrett Coakley

Laraine Cobbing

Clive Coen

Nick Collin

Christopher Collingridge

Ciaran O Conghaile

Allan Cook

Jacqueline Cook

John Cooper

Caspar Corrick and Kizzy
    Makinde Corrick

Gillian Cottray

Robert Cox

Rachel Coxcoon

Peter Crouch

Heather Culpin

Adam Curtis

Christopher Curtis

Jamie Curtis

Jonathan Curtis

Julie Curtis

Martin Curtis

Miranda Curtis

Vivien Cutler

Anna Dale-Harris

Alice Darby

Gillian Darley

Geoffrey Darnton

Steph Davies

Jonathan Davis

Michael Davison

Maria Dawson

Eilín de Paor

Althea de Souza

Imar de Vries

Roseni Dearden

Dale DeBakcsy

Peter Dillon

Lorna Dixon

Broo Doherty

Sally Doherty

David Dow Smith

Shiva Dowlatshahi

Ann Dowling

Lawrence T Doyle

Barb Drummond

Christopher Dudman

Dan Duffek

Lindsay Duguid

Suzie Dummett

Peg Duthie

Carole Edmond

Rebecca Edwards

Jane Egginton

Max Eilenberg and
    Caroline Royds

Alyson Elliman (nee Dembovitz)

Tricia Emlyn-Williams

Engineering & Innovation,
    The Open University

Liz Faber

Mary Jane Fahy

Louise Farquharson

Jane Fenn

Dawn Fitt

Sue and Paddy Foley

Nicole J Ford

Sally Fowler

Jackie Fox

Bernard Gabony

Sarah Gale

Kati Gastrow

Carol Gazzard

Ben Gerrish

Rosa Gindele

Edward Girardot

Jenny Goldie-Scot

The Gooda family

Graeme Gooday

Joanna Goodwin

Pippa Gough

David Gould

Petra Gratton

Tessa Green

James Gregory-Monk

Sharon Griffiths

John Paul Haden

Dani Hall

Russ Hancock

Irene Hannah

Georgina Harding

Caroline Hargrove

Philippa Harrison

Lara Hassan

Lucinda Hawksley

Louise Hayman

Rob Heald

Annabel Healdsmith

Nicky Hellier

John Henderson

Vera Herrmann

Carol Hicks

Julian Hicks

Eleanor Hill

Emily Hodder

Jane Hodgson

Helen Holmes

Jennifer Holmes

Allegra Hopkinson

Violet Hopkinson

Stephen Hoppe

Katherine Howard

John Howkins

Val Hudson

Lawrance Hurst

Michael Hush

Sara Hyde

Roxanne Inglis

David Ingram

Richard Innes

Laura James

Angela John

Richard Johnson

Al Johnston

Dorothy Jones

Shelley Joyce

Stephen Kamlish

Jonathan Keates

Dan Kieran

Noel Kilby

Helen Kirby

Tim and Anne Kirker

Doreen Knight

Jen Kreysa Essig

Mit Lahiri

Elizabeth Lane

Valerie Langfield

Piers Larcombe

Sue Laurence

Andrew Law

Deborah Lazarus

Alison Levey

Marina Lewycka

Clarissa Lodge

Carol Long

Karl Ludvigsen

Charles MacCarthy

Kate Macdonald

Susan Macdougall

Linda MacFadyen

Judith Mackrell

Brigid Macleod

Donald Macleod

Richard Macrory

Catherine Makin

Audrey Mandela

Jonathan Marcus

Peter Marsh

Susan Matoff

Richard Maudslay

Tim May

Clare McCaldin

Sarah McCartney

Grace McCombie

Rosemary McCray

John A C McGowan

Fiona McGowran

Derrik Mercer

Jenny Milligan and
    Tim Ewington

John Mitchell

John Mitchinson

Nick Moir

Mary Monro

Chris Moore

Jonathan Moore

Jessie Moorhouse

Chloe Moran

Mark Mordey

Annabel Morgan

Hannah Morley

Eleanor Morrison

Joerg Mueller-Kindt

Geoffrey Mulligan

Jude Murphy

Stu Nathan

Carlo Navato

Nigel Newbery

Susie Nicoll

Kim Norris

Giles O'Bryen

Sara O'Connor

John O'Hagan

Mark O'Neill

Dominic Ockenden

Elena Oliva

Phil and Pat Orr

Sophie Orr

Tom Orr

Julia Palca

Gillian Palmer

Petros E. Panagopoulos

Lev Parikian

Oliver and Amanda Parker

Alison and Brendan Parsons

Mark Parsons

Michael Parsons

Sir John Parsons

Richard Paterson

Sarah Peers

Susannah Penrose

Jan Peters

Charles Phillips

Sue Phipps

Philip Podmore

Justin Pollard

Isobel Pollock-Hulf

Leanne Potter

Anna Poulton

David Poulton

Gavin Poulton

Jane Priston

Oli Pritchard

Sean Raffey

David Randall

JP Rangaswami

Sheila Ravenscroft

Janet Reibstein

Roxana Reid

Barbara Rickwood

Andrew Ritchie

Elizabeth Roberts

Juliet Roberts

Michael Robertshaw

Cheryl Robson

David Roche

Jane Rolo

Andrew Saint

Richard Salmon Hon.FBKS

Christoph Sander

Jenny Sands

Marcus Saul

Carol Sayles

Anne-Marie Scott

David Seager

Asha Senapati

Andrew Shead

Fiona Shelton

Hannah Simpson

Jane Simpson

Olivia Simpson

Deborah Sims

Catherine Skowron

Claire Smith

Drew Smith

Ella Smith

Ken Smith

MTA Smith

Claire Snodgrass

The Society of Model and
    Experimental Engineers

Lili Soh

David Sproxton

Germaine Stanger

Pete Stanton

Peter Stark

Murray Steele

Joanna Stoddart

Sharon Strahand

Matthew Studdert-Kennedy

Beth Syme

Karen Taube

Andrew Taylor

Hal Tepfer

David Thomas

Laura Thompson

Jim Todd

Peter Towner

Dawn Townsend

Christopher Trent

Richard Truscott

Melissa Turner

Jessica Twentyman

Nicholas Underhill

Matilda Vaughan

Christopher Walker

Jeni Walwin

Rachel Warren Chadd

Caroline Watson

Iain Watson

Colin Watts

Lucy Way and Rachel Way

Rebecca Weaver

Tanya Weaver

Robynn Weldon

Alexandra Welsby

Katie Weston

Paul Whelan

Alice White

Hilary White

Margaret White

Andrew Whitehouse

Annalise Whittaker

Alison and Paul Wilenius

Lucy Wilkins

Paul Willcox

Helen Williams

Sean Williams

Daniel Wood

Peter Wood

Daphne Wright

Rachel and Colin Wright

Thomas Yellowley

Claire Zammit